CHILDREN'S BOOKS
on the BIG SCREEN

D1424016

Children's Literature Association Series

CHILDREN'S BOOKS on the BIG SCREEN

Meghann Meeusen

University Press of Mississippi / Jackson

The University Press of Mississippi is the scholarly publishing agency of
the Mississippi Institutions of Higher Learning: Alcorn State University,
Delta State University, Jackson State University, Mississippi State University,
Mississippi University for Women, Mississippi Valley State University,
University of Mississippi, and University of Southern Mississippi.

www.upress.state.ms.us

The University Press of Mississippi is a member
of the Association of University Presses.

Portions of chapter 4 are reprinted with permission from Springer Press and were previously published in *Children's Literature in Education*, under the title "'Unless Someone Like You' Buys a Ticket to This Movie: Dual Audience and Aetonormativity in Picturebook to Film Adaptations," Volume 49, no. 4, 2018, pages 485–98.

Portions of chapter 5 first appeared in *Children's Literature Association Quarterly*, Volume 22, Issue 2, Summer, 2017, pages 185–204. Copyright © 2017 Children's Literature Association.

First printing 2020
∞

Library of Congress Cataloging-in-Publication Data

Names: Meeusen, Meghann, author.
Title: Children's books on the big screen / Meghann Meeusen.
Other titles: Children's Literature Association series.
Description: Jackson : University Press of Mississippi, 2020. | Series:
Children's Literature Association series | Includes bibliographical
references and index.
Identifiers: LCCN 2020006514 (print) | LCCN 2020006515 (ebook) | ISBN
9781496828644 (hardback) | ISBN 9781496828651 (trade paperback) | ISBN
9781496828668 (epub) | ISBN 9781496828675 (epub) | ISBN 9781496828682
(pdf) | ISBN 9781496828699 (pdf)
Subjects: LCSH: Children's literature—Film adaptations. | Film
adaptations—History and criticism. | BISAC: LITERARY CRITICISM /
Children's & Young Adult Literature
Classification: LCC PN1009.5.A33 M44 2020 (print) | LCC PN1009.5.A33
(ebook) | DDC 809/.89282—dc23
LC record available at https://lccn.loc.gov/2020006514
LC ebook record available at https://lccn.loc.gov/2020006515

British Library Cataloging-in-Publication Data available

I dedicate this book to my parents, whose encouragement of my love of children's literature and support in my academic endeavors has made my work possible. Thank you, Mom and Dad, for helping me believe that there are always new adventures waiting second star to the right and straight on until morning.

CONTENTS

CHILDREN'S BOOKS
on the BIG SCREEN

CHAPTER ONE

The Need for a Theory of Children's and YA Adaptation

Reader, do you know the definition of the word "chiaroscuro"? If you look in your dictionary, you will find that it means the arrangement of light and dark, darkness and light together. Rats do not care for light. Roscuro's parents were having a bit of fun when they named their son. Rats have a sense of humor. Rats, in fact, think that life is very funny. And they are right, reader. They are right.

In the case of Chiaroscuro, however, the joke had a hint of prophecy to it . . .

— *The Tale of Despereaux*, Kate DiCamillo

In directing readers to consider the complex interplay of light and dark in the character of Roscuro, Kate DiCamillo does more than enrich vocabulary or have her own bit of fun in the Newbery Award–winning *The Tale of Despereaux*. Her commentary on Roscuro's name as speaking to "darkness and light together" harkens a key component not only of her tale, but also of children's literature itself. As Perry Nodelman explains, one of the defining characteristics of children's literature is inclusion of "clearly established binary oppositions . . . [wherein] because there seem to be clear winners and losers, these texts remain inherently and unceasingly bipolar" (*Hidden* 80). Still, like the term "chiaroscuro" implies, DiCamillo's story seems to blur these polarized extremes . . . at least in the novelized version. In contrast, the film adaptation of *The Tale of Despereaux* offers very little chiaroscuro at all, reworking the character who bears this name to align far more closely to Nodelman's observation of the "inherent opposition" that characterizes books for young people.

This polarization of binaries in the film adaptation of DiCamillo's work offers more than a key distinction between her novel and its movie—it also represents a striking example of a consistent binary polarization in children's and adolescent film more broadly, wherein film adaptations almost always adhere to the inherent opposition Nodelman describes more than their source text predecessors. In fact, films adapted from books for young readers so often polarize the binaries of the source text that I would build from Nodelman to call this binary polarization a defining characteristic of children's and young adult (YA) film adaptation.

Binaries in children's literature are important for many reasons. For example, DiCamillo uses the metaphor of dark and light to illuminate other binaries in her text, exploring the inherent oppositions of good/evil, conformity/individually, and adult/child through four principle characters—Despereaux, Roscuro, Miggery Sow, and the Princess Pea. Exploration of these binaries affects the messages the text sends, for while each character possesses a heart that is "complicated, shaded with dark and dappled with light" (197), all four also come to learn that finding peace through a unification of these oppositions is only possible if they are willing to forgive those who have wronged them. In the film, this notion of the value of forgiveness is not only intensified, but characters also more strongly illustrate either darkness or light, creating a wider binary of good versus evil wherein characters move from good to evil and back, rather than possessing both simultaneously. This changes the message of the film in meaningful ways.

Additionally, the film fits the idea of forgiveness, and especially that a child must forgive an adult, to a binary system that more fully emphasizes the conceptual differences between adults and children, linking these to a clearer conformity/rebellion binary. This shift results in an alteration of a dominant theme of the text; instead of suggesting that children all possess darkness and light within them, the film posits that individuals must ask for forgiveness in order to choose light over darkness within themselves. Rather than allowing for an intermingling of two seemingly oppositional concepts, the film polarizes them, and as a result, the story changes, presenting a new set of ideologies related to the power dynamics the binaries represent.

The Tale of Despereaux offers a strong example of this polarization, but such polarization of binaries also represents a trend that can be witnessed across children's and young adult film adaptation. In studying adaptations through this theoretical lens, I have observed that every time a book for young readers is adapted to film—whether beginning as a fantasy like *The Tale of Despereaux*, or as a young adult text, a picturebook, or a repeatedly adapted classic—the same consistent pattern emerges. Moreover, the ideological results of a repeated binary polarization can be profound. Considering this trend, as well as its ideological repercussions, offers a new way of thinking about children's adapted texts: one that delves into more than the adaptations themselves, but the very essence of what happens when a children's book hits the big screen.

So often, the only consistency critics seem to recognize in children's adapted film is that books are better than movies. Now I cannot deny that most of the time, I find this to be true; as much as I enjoy watching a movie, reading frequently seems the more rewarding and meaningful experience of a story. Still, adaptation studies scholars have recognized that this sentiment is only productive to a point. As such, instead of simply comparing books and their filmic counterparts, I am interested in what happens when a book for young people is transformed into an entirely new medium through the process of adaptation. To explain this process and its consistent results, one useful approach can be to trace patterns in book to film adaptations, seeking connections across the great variance in children's and adolescent books that are adapted. The pattern I see again and again in studying film adaptation is a widening of binaries.

In addition, when readers examine the effect of this trend on the way adaptations change a story, it becomes clear that polarized binaries yield important ideological results— key power dynamics and textual messages change when concepts like adult and child or good and evil are positioned in starker contrast from one another. This is certainly the case in the film adaptation of *The Tale of Despereaux*, in which Roscuro's final cathartic act of asking the Princess Pea for forgiveness does not emerge from an intermingling of darkness and light together, but his linear progression from light to darkness and a return to light. This new approach to the story suggests that individuals can, and even must, move between binary oppositions in order to find happiness, rather than struggle to continually navigate the internalization of two contradictory concepts simultaneously.

Still, while binary polarization consistently causes ideological shifts in children's and YA films, there are also consistencies in both the binaries most frequently polarized and the kinds of ideologies most often affected by this polarization. To track these patterns, and in doing so, posit a theory of adapted children's film, I build from the work adaptation studies scholars have done to rethink the problematic hierarchies critics and viewers often impose upon especially children's adapted film. Thus, before delving more deeply into individual movies, in this chapter I will examine why scholars might benefit from thinking about children's adapted film in a new way, ending the chapter by explaining how a focus on binary polarization, as well as its causes and its effects on ideology, offers a possible means of tackling this challenge. By exploring the trend of binary polarization and its ideological implications, I believe we might more effectively consider films adapted from children's and adolescent literature in all of their complexity, coming to understand the very nature of the adaptive process.

Critical Challenges and Violent Hierarchies

If there is one term that comes up again and again in the study of adapted texts, both within and outside of the realm of children's film, it is the concept of fidelity. Adaptation studies scholars consistently problematize study of a text's fidelity to its source, and yet, the impetus of this as a scholarly premise seems as instinctual as it is foundational. As Julie Sanders notes, there is great "pleasure to be had in tracing the relationships and overlaps between two texts" (27), and consistently, the pleasure of this comparative study results in a single reaction, whether coming from the most casual viewer or the most renowned critic: the book is better than the movie.

Nevertheless, as critical study of adaptation has developed over time, most scholars have come to a definite conclusion regarding fidelity-based studies that judge film adaptations against their source texts. Scholars agree that this approach can only ever do limited work because no matter how interesting it may be for a critic to pick apart consistency with and departure from a source, and no matter how much viewers might enjoy comparing a film to its novel counterpart, books and movies are two very different mediums. Acknowledging this premise has become the foundation of contemporary adaptation studies, and since George Bluestone's 1966 landmark attempts to problematize a strictly hierarchical or fidelity-based approach to novel to film adaptation, the idea that a "good" adaptation is a faithful adaptation has been largely dismissed as unproductive. Bluestone makes clear the obvious: that because novels and films are different mediums, "the filmed novel, in spite of certain resemblances, will inevitably become a different artistic entity from the novel on which it is based" (64). As a result, contemporary adaptation scholars often position themselves in reaction to the idea of fidelity, pointing out that although a comparative hierarchical study may be a viewer's instinct, scholars must pave new paths to truly understand and comment meaning-fully on adapted work.

Despite this drive to acknowledge Bluestone's contention that "what happens, therefore, when a filmist undertakes the adaptation of a novel, given the inevitable mutation, is that he does not convert the novel at all. What he adapts is a kind of paraphrase of the novel" (62), a true departure from a study of fidelity has proved difficult for adaptation studies scholars, especially in the study of children's adapted film. This too make sense, for especially when it comes to literature for the young, source texts hold significant weight in our cultural understanding, often fostering an emotional resonance distinctive from other texts. The inherent nostalgia associated with children's literature makes a departure from the "essence" of these texts feel troubling, thus encouraging viewers to judge a film against its source. If we remember with fondness, for example, the nostalgic domesticity of Maurice Sendek's powerful pastel crosshatching and playful foray into the imaginative world of the Wild Things, how does one respond to the melancholy, dark, and strikingly violent quality of Spike Jonze's *Where the Wild Things Are*? While all adaptation faces this kind of drive to compare, in children's film, there seems more at stake, at least from an emotive perspective.

From a critical standpoint, children's literature scholars have spent decades proving the value of their field of study, often against significant odds. Beverly Lyon Clark perhaps best exemplified this in her discussion of *kiddie lit*, a term she suggests "captures our culture's ambivalence toward children and children's literature" by reflecting "dismissive," "self-mocking," "pejorative," and "ironical" attitudes about study of such works (2). Clark, like many others, seeks to "revalue what has been dismissed as kiddie lit . . . [to] reveal the complexity of changing attitudes toward children and children's literature" (15). Within this scholarly context, however, the notion of needing to defend the literary merit of children's texts may create a particularly strong underlying hesitation when it comes to departing from fidelity studies. In a system wherein high and low culture seem forever at odds, critics may find the study of adaptations as separate and valuable textual entities concerning, because it might challenge the hard-fought canonical positions of source texts. It is understandable that from this point of view, it may seem difficult to reconcile the literary significance of a text like *Alice's Adventures in Wonderland, Peter Pan,* or *The Wonderful Wizard of Oz* with a study of these works' many, and often quite problematic, filmic versions.

Critical scholarship of adapted children's film reflects this perspective, especially in some of the foundational studies of this corpus. Most of the individual essays in Douglas Street's *Children's Novels and the Movies,* for example, detail why the film adaptation misses the main point, the most important meaning, the nuance, or the essence of the original text. Even positive readings such as Nodelman's chapter regarding *Treasure Island* are hierarchical. Nodelman goes further than others by suggesting that Disney's *Treasure Island* "did indeed strike exactly the right note—and struck it so profoundly that I never forgot it, and recalled reading a book I'd never opened," but even this reading ends with an evaluative caveat, suggesting although the film is "amazingly good . . . Nobody was trying to make a great picture" ("Treasure Island" 68).

Even though critics have established that fidelity offers a problematic standard against which adaptations might be judged, this concept still acts as the foundation for discussions of adapted texts, especially in critical work related to children's film. While an exact conversion of a novel into a film is impossible, abandonment of comparative study of adaptations is also far from feasible. The very nature of adaptation—the notion that the source text is the basis of the new text—invites comparison. Yet comparison, even when resisting an emphasis on fidelity, often results in hierarchical models based on how closely the film adheres to its novel counterpart. This is the case for scholars like Dudley Andrew, Geoffrey Wagner, and Kamilla Elliott, who seek categories of adaptation as a way to complicate textual interaction, but face criticism in terms of the hierarchical nature of their approaches. Deborah Cartmell and Imelda Whelehan, for example, suggest that "hidden in these taxonomies are value judgments and a consequent ranking of types, normally covertly governed by a literary rather than cinematic perspective" ("Introduction" 2).

If not through a system of fidelity-based categorization, how might scholars approach and consider adapted texts in terms of their merit and unique qualities? Linda Costanzo Cahir attempts to answer this question by putting forth a theoretical framework for understanding and evaluating literature-based film. One key criteria, she suggests, is that a film must "communicate definite ideas concerning the *integral* meaning and value of the literary text, as the filmmakers interpret" (99, emphasis in the original). She posits that when viewers are disappointed with a film, it may be because they disagree with the filmmaker's interpretation of this integral meaning and value of the text. This concept of essence, of a key element that is transferable to film, also poses problems, for as Christa Albrecht-Crane and Dennis Cutchins write, such integral meaning is "neither knowable nor directly representable. A novel's imagined essence remains elusive and ambiguous" (17). Moreover, focus on essence typically deemphasizes the significance of divergences between adaptation and source text, failing to situate the purpose of comparison as more than identification or evaluation, but a study of what differences reflect about message and culture.

This is why I believe focus on a trend, and in particular, the commonality with which binaries are polarized, makes a crucial contribution to adaptation studies. I do not seek to abandon comparative study, nor do I wish to cease in evaluating texts for their merit, and more importantly, the weight and meanings of their ideological underpinnings. However, as adaptation studies critics have done for over fifty years, I suggest that how closely a film matches its source text—whether its exact details or integral meaning—should not be the focus of such a study. Instead, I believe in focusing on what is happening within the adaptive process, and I thus seek patterns in the kinds of changes filmmakers make when rewriting, or as Bluestone describes, "paraphrasing" a book and presenting it in a new medium.

Again and again, I see one key consistency in adaptations of children's and YA texts that seems to account for so many of the changes from book to film, and especially, those changes in the nature of ideologies presented in the movie version. In each case, the binary oppositions of the source text—whether self/other, male/female, adult/child, or others—are set in more stark contrast to one another once adapted into the new medium of film. Binaries are a part of all texts, because, as theorists such as Jacques Derrida have established, language itself is built on the idea of meaning created through opposition. When describing how binaries act as a key element of children's literature, Nodelman explains, "the characteristic of implying that which is different and other is an inherent quality of all uses of language, which operates by allowing us to understand things and concepts exactly in terms of how they differ from what they are not and that, consequently, always carry within themselves the very meanings they exclude" (*Hidden* 265). Binaries place concepts in opposition in order to understand and define them, but my contention is that the divide between these concepts is starker—more polarized—when a children's story is adapted to film.

Although the concept of binaries has an extensive theoretical framework, Derrida's work to consider problematic hierarchical relationships within binary systems is especially relevant here, building on Ferdinand de Saussure's concept of terms defined in relation to each other. Derrida's definition of a binary as "a violent hierarchy" wherein "one of the two terms governs the other" (41) describes exactly what I mean when I speak to more polarized binary systems in children's and young adult film. Yet it also explains, to some degree, why hierarchical models of adaptation studies are so difficult to overcome. If binaries are not neutral, but "violent" in the ways they place one concept in a power position over another, then a widening or polarization of these concepts would, in many cases, be negative. As such, it can be very difficult to escape comparative discussions of texts that hold that books are "better" than movies. Nonetheless, critics find evaluation based simply on comparison unproductive, or at the very least, a limiting critical stance. Similarly, while I do not believe it possible to completely abandon comparative studies, I do wish to take such studies further by also tracing patterns. In examining changes in binaries in order to understand why consistent polarization occurs and what effects it has on ideology, I see potential to move from evaluation into greater understanding of adaptation itself.

Adaptations as Textual Productions in Context

Going beyond not only fidelity, but also a focus on essence or integral meaning, requires acknowledging a key element of adaptation that contemporary critics have sought to illuminate: that in order to understand how texts are transformed, critics must consider adaptations as part of complex textual webs. Albrecht-Crane and Cutchins engage such work by pulling from Mikhail Bakhtin and Derrida to clarify that a text is not one entity, but a textual production affected by the perspectives of the creator and reader/viewer, both situated within a distinctive cultural context. Bakhtin refers to this as dialogism, which describes both individual expression and cultural expression like film as always already in response and presupposing a future response, so that an adaptation (or any text) is part of a complex contextual network of other texts or utterances. As Robert Stam explains, a source novel "can be seen as a situated utterance, produced in one medium and in one historical and social context, and later transformed into another, equally situated utterance, produced in a different context and relayed through a different medium. The source text forms a dense informational network, a series of verbal cues which the adapting film text can then selectively take up, amplify, ignore, subvert, or transform" (Introduction 46).

This network has been acknowledged as crucial to children's film as well, especially in Ian Wojcik-Andrews's *Children's Films: History, Ideology, Pedagogy, Theory,* which serves to position adaptations within historical context, and in doing so, reflects willingness to put aside fidelity studies and accept the notion of studying, as noted adaptation theorist Linda Hutcheon describes, "adaptations as adaptations" (*Theory* 4). Yet because Wojcik-Andrews's text focuses on a wide range of filmic elements rather than specific processes of adaptation, it cannot draw the kinds of connections that are necessary to advance a consideration of adaptation itself. Furthermore, when children's literature critics do use what Sarah Cardwell calls a "pluralist" approach to adaptation, or "a more explicit awareness of film and television conventions, and cultural and historical contexts" (70), they often do so only to return to hierarchical patterns that reproduce fidelity-based studies that favor source texts over adapted versions.

This approach only goes so far, often seeming in service of critiquing a text as a poor imitation of the source, rather than understanding why it is different. For example, Lindsay Myers's "Whose Fear Is It Anyway? Moral Panics and 'Stranger Danger' in Henry Selick's *Coraline*" presents a sophisticated reading of how the film adaptation reflects conventions of classic horror films and contemporary fears about childhood safety, but her comparison is built on evaluation. She notes, "far from challenging dominant stereotypes and conventions, as does Gaiman's literary masterpiece, Selick's *Coraline* presents a fundamentally unprogressive vision of childhood, trading off the novel's underlying theme" (247) to "distort the message of Gaiman's original" (250). I think this kind of evaluation diminishes the otherwise meaningful observations Myers makes about *Coraline,* several of which I will discuss more fully in the next chapter. Instead of focusing on the book as superior, I suggest examining changes in binaries as a way to take this evaluation further. This approach shifts critical

focus so that instead of seeing the *Coraline* film as a failure, ideological problems can be more fully explained. Looking at the ways binaries are polarized
in the adaptation helps critics think about why negative messages emerge in
this, as well as so many other adaptations.

Film adaptations are here to stay, and viewers—including me—both love
and love to hate them. Seeing this as a delightful reality, I want to be more
pragmatic in my critical approach, taking films for what they are and examining what is happening to make them this way. Whether or not critics or
children enjoy or value a book more than its film adaptation, and whether or
not critics believe children *should* enjoy or value a book more, children's film
adaptations are not going away, nor should they. Thus, I would suggest that we
might look at these movies through a more productive lens, one that theorizes
what adaptations do when they offer us a children's story in a new medium,
and what effect this shift might have in terms of the kinds of messages and, in
particular, the kind of ideologies these films offer.

Overall, I think it important to articulate what happens when texts are
adapted, considering some of the ideological implications of consistent patterns
that result from the process of adaptation itself. I suggest, as Albrecht-Crane
and Cutchins do, "not only that sameness is impossible, but that difference, in
fact, makes art possible" (16–17). Still, I also believe critics can to do more than
identify individual differences of note, instead considering a wider-reaching
paradigm that can help us to understand adaptation itself. Binaries lie at the
heart of this paradigm.

More Than Individual Studies, We Need a Theory

My approach poses a challenge identified as both critical to and missing from
adaptation studies, identified perhaps most succinctly in Thomas Leitch's discussion "Twelve Fallacies in Contemporary Adaptation Theory." Leitch suggests that
the "flood of study of individual adaptations proceeds on the whole without the
support of any more general theoretical account of what actually happens, or
what ought to happen, when a group of filmmakers set out to adapt a literary
text" ("Fallacies" 149). The idea of developing a theory of adaptation is certainly
a wide-reaching goal and one that several critics have made strides toward
achieving. Brian McFarlane, for example, moves away from fidelity criticism by
building from scholars such as Christian Metz and Roland Barthes to focus on
narrativity, believing that narrative is "not only the chief factor novels and the
films based on them have in common but is the chief transferable element" (12).
Hutcheon similarly seeks theoretical underpinnings of adaptation by titling her

text on this very premise—*A Theory of Adaptation*—and identifying the what, who, why, how, where, and when of adaptation in ways that take medium into account. I emulate this kind of work but also consider the elements of children's and adolescent film, as well as the ways that this corpus might yield particularly meaningful forays into the ideological implications of adaptation itself.

Such study of trends and patterns in children's film is sparse, however, and in fact, children's film itself is, as Bettina Kümmerling-Meibauer observes, still "somewhat marginal in academia, with no international journals or regular conferences devoted to the subject . . . we do not yet have a fully developed theory of children's films to draw upon in our research" (40). Still, as Hutcheon describes in her article "Harry Potter and the Novice's Confession," this venture is potentially very fruitful. Hutcheon confesses that she "deeply regret[s] that it has taken me this long to realize that I could have studied (and taught) all of the things I did study (and teach) in my entire career using the vast and rich corpus of children's literature" (170). By acknowledging the unique perspectives children's texts might offer her work with adaptation, Hutcheon identifies this kind of study as something valuable she has previously overlooked (exclaiming "mea culpa" for doing so). Furthermore, she describes how the popularity and unique dual audience of children's adapted texts might be worthy of further study, especially in considering whether there are different stakes associated with fidelity in children's film. It is from this launching point that I move the critical discussion forward, suggesting that a focused consideration of the consistent patterns in children's adapted film would meaningfully continue the work that critics like Hutcheon and McFarlane have begun.

While Hutcheon focuses on the process of adaptation and McFarlane traces the role of narrativity in these processes, my observations engage another key element that might contribute to a kind of "more general theoretical account" that Leitch describes, especially within the context of children's film. I believe more attention needs to be paid to the ideological elements of adaptation and, in particular, the role that binaries play in how children's films repeatedly shift the content of their source texts with consistent kinds of ideological results. Cartmell and Whelehan draw particular attention toward this kind of study in *Adaptations: From Text to Screen, Screen to Text*, noting that the collected essays they present can aid in "looking beyond issues of success or failure" to consider, in part, "whether the ideological perspectives offered seem to echo those of the literary narratorial perspective," an approach that emphasizes textual relationships and "the possibility of identifying trends in adaptation practices" (17).

Cartmell and Whelehan's collection, while valuable in illuminating specific ideological and other elements worth noting in a variety of adapted texts, nonetheless participates in what Leitch calls the "flood of study of individual adaptations" because, while most contributors certainly consider ideology to some degree, the very nature of an edited collection emphasizes the inclusion of various approaches that examine individual or small groups of adaptations. The edited collections of Robert Stam and Alessandra Raengo; Christa Albrecht-Crane and Dennis Cutchins; and Dennis Cutchins, Laurence Raw, and James Michael Welsh (who also consider pedagogy) similarly represent examples of this trend: groups of scholars offering individual analyses that point out interesting or important elements of various adapted works, but are unable within this context to delve into connections that characterize adaptations overall.

Such work has even been taken up in children's literature by Benjamin Lefebvre's *Textual Transformations in Children's Literature: Adaptations, Translations, Reconsiderations* (2013). The chapters of this collection offer a wide variety of individual studies of adapted texts, frequently commenting on or alluding to what Lefebvre calls "the ideological underpinnings that drive both the process and product" of adaptation (2). Yet just as in earlier compilations of the same nature, such as Lucy Rollin's *Antic Art: Enhancing Children's Literary Experiences through Films and Video* (1993) and Fiona Collins and Jeremy Ridgman's *Turning the Page: Children's Literature in Performance and the Media* (2006), the nature of an edited collection seems to limit the conclusions that can be drawn about adaptation itself or trends in the ways ideologies are shifted across large groups of children's adapted texts. These individual studies allude to concepts within an individual adaptation or small group of texts that might have the potential to be considered more broadly, but development of a more wide-reaching theory of adaptation means taking this connection making a step further. I believe an ideologically driven focus on binary polarization as a critical consistency across all children's and YA adapted film is the beginning of this kind of connection making, and thus can have resonance as a more comprehensive theory.

A focus on binary polarization achieves what Katharine Capshaw describes in her introduction to the Summer 2013 issue of *Children's Literature Association Quarterly*: that critics should "consider further intervention in wider discussions about adaptation . . . in order to make clear the particular dimensions and stakes of children's texts in relationship to source materials" (134). By illuminating trends and consistencies across adapted texts, critics can explore, as Margaret Mackey describes, "the tri-fold nature of literary materials, interpretive responses, and institutional enablements and constraints, preferably as they all relate to each other" (505). For there *are* patterns in adaptations, trends that go beyond evaluative judgments that suggest that a novel is simply better—more enjoyable, more meaningful, more complex, or more profound.

There are also a few scholars who have begun to identify some of these patterns. Deborah Ross, for example, takes up a discussion of ideologies of gender in noting how several Disney movies shift notions of the female imagination in their alteration of their source material. This conclusion about an ideological pattern is useful, but I believe critics also need to think about the reason for this kind of ideological shift. What is happening in an adapted text that yields this result? If we can find a consistent kind of causation, a patterned way that ideas are altered when moved from book to film, perhaps we can do more productive work to not only point out the problematics, but also consider ways that films might more positively engage their source texts to avoid such serious missteps. Binary polarization is the essence of this causation, and by exploring the ways that binaries are reshaped to create a starker opposition between them, critics can understand the kinds of ideological shifts that Ross describes.

Joel Chaston comes perhaps the closest to identifying a binary-based trend in children's film, using the term "ozification" to highlight *The Wizard of Oz* film as establishing a precedence that other filmic adaptations follow. Chaston presents the idea that female heroes in a variety of films, not only *Oz*, traverse fantastical adventures only as they seek to return to the domestic sphere, a notion he suggests is not the driving force of these adaptations' source texts, but is emphasized in the films. This is exactly the kind of connection lacking from most other scholarship on adapted children's works, for although Chaston does not go on to theorize adaptation itself, he touches on the kind of work that such study might do—identifying trends in adapted texts and especially trends in these works' treatment of ideologies. Moreover, he hints at a binary—home versus away—and posits this as a crucial component of the ozification he describes. This is the precedent I follow in my study of patterns in films adapted for young people, making clear that binaries lie at the heart of the trends that emerge across a large number of films made from children's books and young adult texts.

Working Against (and Within) Problematic Hierarchical Models

Like Chaston does in identifying the consistency of ozification, I too suggest that there are patterns that can be traced across adapted films for young people, and moreover, I would identify these on a broader scale than Chaston does, including adapted films made from contemporary fantasy, young adult novels, picturebooks, and canonical texts with many adapted versions. Chaston begins this work in identifying some of the structures inspired by *The Wizard of Oz*,

and building from this premise, as well as the individual studies of particular adaptations conducted by various film and children's literature critics, I note consistencies in the ways messages and ideologies are shifted every time a children's or young adult text is adapted to film. More importantly, I suggest that again and again, these shifts can be attributed to binaries that are more polarized in the adaptation than in the source text.

My study of adaptations is comparative, for I do examine the ways that content, messages, and themes shift when transferred into film adaptations. However, like many contemporary adaptation scholars, I see the dangers of hierarchical comparison as well and thus wish to stress that while looking comparatively at adaptations and their source texts can be a necessary component of adaptation studies, the two texts must be viewed as unique entities and not evaluated in ways that suggest one is inherently better than the other. Nonetheless, for the reasons I have described, complete escape from hierarchical discussion of a film and its source text is likely impossible. Even when evaluating ideological moves of books/films separately, there is always some element of identifying the success and/or failure of one or the other. Studying ideology means looking at positives and negatives—what textual messages foster a more positive worldview and which messages reinforce destructive or harmful beliefs and value systems.

The work of critics to examine and critique ideology offers a different kind of hierarchy than we often see in adaptation criticism. On the one hand, comparison of texts is an integral part of the study of adaptations, and such comparison can often lead to pointing out flaws of one text that do not exist in another. Engaging in this work from a perspective that focuses on ideology, however, allows critics to also acknowledge that film is, as a medium, not inherently better or worse than written prose.

This is especially evident in the range of examples I have chosen to consider when tracking the trend of binary polarization across a wide corpus. For example, in some cases, my study focuses on remarkable films made from excellent books (as in *Coraline*), whereas other times, I use examples of fantastic films made from less than stellar books (arguably the case with most Oz adaptations). Yet by the same note, some of the problematic films I have chosen for my study are made from wonderful books (*The Tale of Despereaux* comes immediately to mind), while others are made from ideologically troubling source texts (as is especially the case in my study of films adapted from the works of John Green). There are even times when there is far more complexity, as in the example of *How to Train Your Dragon*, which I would call a great film with some concerning elements, made from a mediocre book with some shining qualities. Movies and books are different, and neither is categorically "better."

I see film as an equally or perhaps even more complex medium when compared to the alphabetic narratives upon which adaptations are so often based. Film adaptations do different work than books, but that work is no less powerful a craft, and the nature of a visual form means that filmmakers must engage in an array of creative choices, making the medium rich for analysis and complex in its intricacy. Part of such study involves considering what ideologies appear most commonly in film, while also exploring how the polarization of binaries impacts the consistency with which these ideologies are presented.

The focus of my work is thus not on fidelity or even hierarchy, but on ideology, for I believe film must always be evaluated in terms of the messages it presents to viewers. Ideology is crucially important in children's film, for as Louis Althusser's use of the term "obviousness" reflects, the messages texts send can be exceptionally pervasive, forming the basis of society. My use of the term ideology echoes this perspective, acknowledging that when messages are presented as "obvious" or "true," they profoundly impact the way children see the world, enculturating and indoctrinating young people into often problematic hegemonic systems. As Catherine Belsey suggests, "ideology resides in common-places and truisms, as well as in philosophical and religious systems. . . . If it is true, however, it is not the whole truth" (53). Moreover, as Peter Hollindale describes, implicit ideologies can be just as powerful as those that are explicit, for "even if beliefs are passive and unexamined, and no part of any conscious proselytizing, the texture of language and story will reveal them and communicate them" (12).

As these critics suggest, ideology is pervasive and powerful; Hollindale goes so far as to describe it as a "climate of belief" (19). Ideology, however, is also a complex term with a rich history. In thinking about how ideologies shift when binaries are polarized, I build on work of critics like Hollindale as well as Robyn McCallum and John Stephens to view the term ideology through the lens of Althusser. Althusser brings to a Marxian perspective the concept of the "Ideological State Apparatuses," distinguishing this from Marx's State apparatus, which creates a dominant belief system that favors the ruling class by means of violence and repression (e.g., government, army, police, courts, prison). While Marxian theory includes the concept of ideology, Althusser uses the term "Ideological State Apparatus" to emphasize the impact of forces such as religion, education, family, the legal system, the political system, and culture. These aspects of the Ideological State Apparatus are pivotal in reproducing social structures, but also serve to constitute individuals into being; people are, in Althusser's view, the products of ideology.

By examining how ideologies shift when a children's book is adapted into film, critics and viewers can come to understand how children's adaptations act as part of the Ideological State Apparatus to, as Elizabeth Parsons describes, sometimes uphold "the values of the culture in which it is produced and consumed as part of an inherently didactic agenda" (114), and sometimes, as Stephens and McCallum describe, provide opportunity for transgression by making "ideologies apparent and seek[ing] to redefine or even overthrow them" (367). A study of children's texts as part of the Ideological State Apparatus is important because, as Nodelman and Reimer point out, far too often "people simply take their ideological assumptions for granted as the only whole, and unquestionable truth" (*Pleasures* 80). Similarly, Roberta Seelinger Trites writes, "We believe some ideologies so deeply that we consider them Truth: such ideologies . . . can be difficult for people brought up in capitalist societies to recognize as arguable positions" (*Disturbing* 24). Examining how adaptation causes a binary polarization that shifts ideologies in children's adapted film can help bring to light the ideologies within texts as just that—arguable positions—and in doing this work, viewers can be critical of the belief systems these texts present as, in Althusser's term, "obvious."

More than contending that polarization of binaries in film has meaningful ideological effects, however, I also suggest that such greater conceptual opposition often also reinforces problematic power hierarchies—the kinds of "violent hierarchies" Derrida describes. As such, binary polarization often has ideologically negative results; it reinforces socially constructed paradigms that are destructive, especially in forming beliefs and value systems surrounding certain groups of people. The messages in these film adaptations are therefore often more than different; they are more problematic than their source text. This is particularly true when binaries relate to selfhood, and in most of the examples I study, these are the binaries that have the most profound effect on ideology. For example, shifts in ideologies are especially problematic when the polarized binary is self v. other (as in *How to Train Your Dragon*), male v. female (as in most YA adaptations) or having to do with race (as in several Oz adaptations).

While the nature of binary polarization may mean that abandoning hierarchical analysis of film adaptation is potentially impossible, I wish to distinguish this kind of hierarchy from fidelity studies. I may judge films comparatively, but my criteria has nothing to do with how closely the film adaptation matches the details or essence of its source; this, I would suggest is the biggest concern emphasized by contemporary film critics. My ideological critique, and any subsequent suggestion that the adaptation may be more problematic than its source, is unrelated to fidelity, but rather a comparative study of the ideologies presented by each text.

Additionally, this question of a film's ideology is not a question of the merits of the medium itself, and certainly, not a question of film's complexity. I agree with critics that film as a medium should be considered separately from alphabetic texts and evaluated in nonhierarchical ways. Yet I also contend that part of the reason critics of children's and YA films often find themselves reinforcing film/book hierarchies is because of binary polarization. I see this trend as a defining element of the adaptive process in films made for young viewers, and because it often has negative ideological ramifications, it is difficult to escape hierarchies within which critics have so long found themselves entrenched.

More than just a theory of adaptation, an exploration of binary polarization also explains why scholars have long struggled to break free of hierarchical models. I contend that critics have faced difficulty evading hierarchical comparisons in the study of children's and YA film adaptations because binaries are consistently polarized in these films. This is the trend I wish to explore, but I also see it as the reason why scholars in children's literature have had such difficulty embracing a theoretical framework that positions films and books without hierarchy, even as this is approach is encouraged by contemporary adaptation studies criticism. While I do not suggest that I can break this paradigm or abandon hierarchy altogether, I do think that looking at binaries can help critics understand why this hierarchy, despite its problematics, is difficult to break.

A Function of Form?

While I suggest that polarization of binaries in adapted film may lead to hierarchical evaluation because presenting more violent divergences between concepts often creates problematic representation of power dynamics, I nonetheless believe that adaptations offer a distinctively complex and nuanced representation of ideas. Adaptation studies critics comment on these complexities in discussing the differences between books and film, as Stam does by writing, "the shift from a single-track, uniquely verbal medium such as the novel, which 'only has words to play with,' to a multitrack medium such as film, which can play not only with words (written and spoken), but also with theatrical performance, music, sound effect, and moving photographic images, explains the unlikelihood—and I would suggest even the undesirability—of literal fidelity" ("Beyond" 56). In fact, most contemporary adaptation critics emphasize that film offers a great deal to consider and explore, and in some ways, even more complexity as a creative process than alphabetic written mediums.

Nonetheless, when the ideologies presented in adaptations of children's and YA film are lined up side by side with those of the source texts, polarization of binaries does often yield negative results. This is, to some degree, influenced by the nature of film as a medium. For example, when readers are presented with a description in a novel, they are necessarily only offered certain details. If an author were to write every single detail to describe a character's appearance or the nuances of every element of setting, this would quickly overwhelm the story. In film, however, this is exactly the case— viewers see everything and filmmakers must decide all of those details.

Filmmakers, however, are also often trying to grab the attention of their viewers with exciting, striking, or beautiful imagery and other film elements to match. As such, contrasts can appear stronger. For example, Toothless's transformation from fearsome to lovable in *How to Train Your Dragon* highlights the self/other binaries that act as the basis for the conflict between Vikings and dragons, a plot structure added to the story in the film. Similarly, the teen zombie protagonist in *Warm Bodies* seems far more dead than his female paramour when donning pasty makeup and stuffing his face with brains, as opposed to when we are reading his deep and existential thoughts. And of course, Oz and Kansas emphasize the differences between home and away far more clearly when Dorothy steps into stunning Technicolor. While visual imagery does not necessarily have to highlight contrasts that lead to conceptual divides, it often does in films made for children and young adults.

Additionally, film and alphabetic texts (especially novels) differ significantly when it comes to their use of time. Typically, children and teens tend to read books over several sittings, perhaps even stopping to contemplate or respond in some way to what they have read before continuing further. This allows for a much slower development of ideas over a greater span of time, especially because it is typical to take breaks between reading sessions. In contrast, film must achieve exposition and character development more quickly so as to move with expediency toward a climax and eventual resolution, and very little time is allowed for contemplation until the movie has ended. As such, viewers are not only encouraged to arrive at an understanding of the film's meaning with far less opportunity to consider its nuance, but they also must get to know characters over a shorter period, gathering all relevant details to understand the film's message very quickly. A novel, on the other hand, can include varying episodes to more slowly build character development, which is perhaps why the most episodic novels (such as *Alice's Adventures in Wonderland* or, as I describe in the next chapter, *How to Train Your Dragon*) are either especially criticized when adapted or changed significantly in the film version.

Expediency, however, can contribute to binary polarization because the easiest way to quickly posit an idea is to show its opposite. For example, while readers of Gaiman's *Coraline* ponder the other mother's power and position over many pages as Coraline thinks through these elements, it is much faster in film to simply show this villain as first visually and deceptively benign and then as a startlingly horrific monster. In doing so, this choice polarizes perceptions of good/evil, independence/dependence, and adult/child. It seems important to note, however, that this expediency does not diminish the film in terms of either complexity or quality. In fact, while offering a different way of thinking about Coraline's process of maturing, the exciting visual spectacle presented in the film also adds to the story in ways that further delve into some of its nuance and symbolism, which I will discuss further in chapter 2.

Similarly, another element differing from books to film that affects binary polarization is how character thoughts are made evident, which is, like pacing, an essential part of characterization. A character in a novel can contemplate elements of the text's theme internally, thus giving the reader the chance to similarly ponder this textual message. Form necessitates a shift in how these emotions are portrayed, which is especially crucial in adaptations of novels for teens because they so frequently rely heavily on character thoughts. I will discuss the effects of this shift further in chapter 3. Furthermore, the difference between telling and showing character thoughts also emphasizes the auditory elements of film. Sound plays a significant role in expressing emotion, for as Hutcheon describes, "visual and gestural representation are rich in complex associations; music offers aural 'equivalents' to the audience; sound, in general, can enhance, reinforce, or even contradict the visual and verbal aspects" (*Theory* 23). I would take this even further, suggesting that music is uniquely powerful in the kinds of emotions it can represent and stir. Showing emotions tied to theme visually, and especially presenting these emotions aurally through music, is often a stronger or more explicit form of representation, a concept I will explore more in considering *How to Train Your Dragon* in chapter 2.

In addition to the qualities inherent to film as a form, the material factors of its reception and viewing experience are also significant, and the differing ways that audiences interact with and physically experience a film can affect binary polarization. This is perhaps most evident in the adaptation of books for very young readers, who often experience a book when it is read to them, but conversely watch a film with their parent or other supervising adult (especially in a movie theater). While this aspect of film likely contributes to filmmakers' decisions when they adapt a book into a movie, it is also less an element of production and more an aspect of the reception of the text. In chapter 4, I discuss how this dynamic affects representation of adults and adult/child binaries in more polarized ways.

In considering reception, audience is also paramount, and as Bakhtin and those adaptation studies critics who utilize his work suggest, the dialogism of all language and cultural expression means we must take this side of the adaptive process into account as well. Audience expectation and reception of a text are related to production choices, for filmmakers make decisions based on what they suppose audiences want (and will pay to see) and, over time, such production choices create a foundation from which audiences build expectations. This is a chicken and egg situation: do we expect fairy tales to end with a couple blissfully in love because we have seen it a hundred times or do filmmakers continue to produce films with this ending because they believe it is what audiences expect? Whichever the case, even the most progressive fairy-tale films typically end with this sort of happily ever after. Moreover, decisions about what an audience wants is a weighty issue because expectation, and the funds that are attached to it, drives the film industry, which is above all a commercial enterprise. If widened binaries are the norm, and as a result, filmmakers believe a starker conceptual divide between concepts will sell, the cycle will continue, making industry-driven expectations of audience an important part of why the trend is perpetuated.

Still, there is another factor that I believe is crucial to consider in thinking about how and why binaries are polarized in film: a quality that seems both part of the form of film, but also tied to what audiences expect and filmmakers believe audiences desire. In every example I have studied, binaries are polarized, at least in part, because a key theme or lesson from the source text has been amplified. Books often contain a wide range of themes, but when they are adapted, filmmakers often choose a central idea around which to focalize their story. Yet such a theme is not simply the focus; because filmmakers make it so central, they also amplify the theme, making it far more pronounced and explicit. This, I suggest is a major cause of polarized binaries in children's and YA adapted film, and a concept I will explore further in the next chapter.

Cause and Effect: A Theory of Children's and YA Adaptation

In thinking about possible reasons for binary polarization and noting an amplification of theme as a consistent cause for this more stark opposition between concepts, I find that the easiest way to understand this trend is a model of cause and effect. Thus, in studying children's and YA adapted film, I ask three questions:

1. Why are binaries more polarized in a film adaptation than in the source text?
2. What effect does this polarization have on ideologies?
3. What kinds of ideologies are most often affected, and how?

To answer these questions, each chapter that follows tackles one aspect of this cause and effect model. Chapter 2 focuses on causes of binary polarization in children's adapted film, delving specifically into thematic amplification as a crucial reason for this pattern to occur so regularly. Then, chapters 3, 4, and 5 consider patterns in the ideological effects of binary polarization. In particular, chapters 3 and 4 tackle groups of texts wherein a particular binary seems especially central: male/female binaries in YA films and adult/child binaries in picturebook adaptation. Chapter 5 concludes this consideration of the effects of binary polarization by looking at cases wherein multiple different films are adapted from a single source. Before digging into these specifics, however, it seems important to first frame this discussion by laying out the theory of binary polarization as having two parts: cause and effect.

Thematic Amplification as the Cause of Binary Polarization

A reading of adaptations as consistently amplifying theme, and thus often intensifying ideologies and textual messages, can be seen to run in contrast with many dominant views of adapted texts, wherein critics characterize shifts from book to film as a failure of the adaptor to understand a text's theme. I do not see adaptations this way. Instead, in all cases I have studied, an adaptor seems to have taken what he or she believes to be a key theme or message of the source text, using this one element as a focal point of the new text. This process of identifying a major explicit ideology of the source text and making it the narrative touchstone of the film does not simply focalize, however, but consistently amplifies: the theme or message is stronger in the adapted film. As a result, rather than diminished, I believe ideologies (or at least, whatever ideology the filmmaker deems as central) are often intensified in adaptations.

In some instances, this intensification means a shift from an implied theme to a more concrete or explicit message, a concept that some critics have alluded to in their more hierarchical studies. Leonard J. Deutsch, for example, alludes to the amplification I describe in suggesting that the film version of *Sounder* "makes explicit what had remained implicit in the novel" (222). Still, Deutsch maintains a hierarchy of book over film, for while he acknowledges that "audiences have been deeply moved" by the adaptation, he also identifies amplification as a problem, noting "the novel, so spare and spartan in its telling . . . is perhaps even more moving" (226). Critics referencing the idea of amplification of message typically do so to judge the film as less than the novel, suggesting that a subtler presentation of message is inherently better.

While I can name several instances in which I feel this is the case (*The Tale of Despereaux* being the best example, in my mind), my reading of this element is simply that—a feeling. While I sometimes have a more profound emotional response to a text with subtler themes, this seems a question of taste, or perhaps more importantly, a question of context. In a book, which I can read over several days, quietly sipping tea while seeping myself into the story, a slowly building message and a theme thoughtfully articulated over time resonates with me. In a movie theater, I expect something different. For better or worse, I have been trained by the mode of contemporary feature-length children's films to expect a clearer problem-solution model, wherein tension and conflict simmer for less than two hours before building to a poignant climax in which the meaning of the text is made clear.

As a result, to meet the expectation established throughout decades of children's film productions, a movie's blockbuster status typically hinges on imparting a lesson within a traditional narrative structure, one that Wojcik-Andrews identifies by using Annette Kuhn's term of "disruption-resolution." Wojcik-Andrews describes this as a defining textual characteristic of children's film, noting how "beginning disruption or conflict forces the hero or heroine on a physical or psychological journey. Upon completion of the journey, said conflict is resolved" (7). This is the typical form of children's film—what is more, it is what viewers expect from movies for young people. Thus, an adaptation must adapt its source material to this model, and as a result, messages and/or ideologies regularly become more explicit, amplified to take on greater weight or be more obvious and clear.

When adaptors engage in this amplification and shape explicit ideologies, themes, and conflict into an abbreviated and more highly linear structure based on a model of disruption-resolution, the result is a greater polarization of binary systems and, in particular, representation of binary systems that are more polarized than in the novel counterparts. For example, in a children's book, there might be overlap and/or muddling between such concepts as good/evil, adult/child, or male/female. In a film, these concepts are presented in ways that make them appear more diametrically opposed, wherein one concept serves to represent a lack of the other. Often, this is the result of a greater amount of conflict in the text, wherein characters representing these concepts are situated with a greater degree of physical or emotional opposition, thus resulting in the concepts themselves becoming a more polarized binary. In these cases, notions of good versus evil, hero versus villain, adult versus child, male versus female, etc. do not present evidence of a tension between ideas, but represent binary oppositions.

As I described in the opening of this chapter, Nodelman and others suggest these binaries are a key part of how critics define children's literature. In explaining how "childhood inevitably implies its opposite," Nodelman describes

Derrida's argument, suggesting, "this is how language in general and human thought in general operate" (265). David Rudd uses Derrida's *différance* toward similar means, describing the binary relationship between childhood and adulthood as foundational because "without a recognition of what it is different from, differences cannot be sustained. Hence difference is always tainted by 'the other,' and must always be dependent upon it" (14). Rudd also acknowledges Michel Foucault's "'power/knowledge' coupling" as an important contribution in how the power dynamics of a child/adult binary might be envisioned, noting that "in connection with children this means that, as a conceptual category, they have become increasingly inscribed in a variety of discourses . . . [and] this has given authorities greater power over them" (14–15). It is this way of thinking about binary oppositions that I find most useful in describing the patterns I have noticed in children's adapted film.

Nodelman takes the concept of binaries one step further than Rudd, however, including in his extensive list of the qualities that define children's literature that a crucial ambivalence "emerges from the interplay of clearly established binary oppositions: home and away, safety and danger, desire and knowledge, adult and child," and further noting that "even when one opposite triumphs, it tends to do so by negating its other entirely, thus still insisting on the inherent opposition" (80). While Nodelman explores the ways that "children's literature is binary in structure and in theme," I would extend this idea to suggest that it becomes more so in adaptations of children's literature into film. Herein lies the cause and effect relationship in my theory of children's adapted film: not only are messages and ideologies amplified, but as a result, binaries are also intensified. This intensification creates a polarization, wherein the opposing concepts that make up the binary system move further away conceptually from one another.

The Tale of Despereaux demonstrates this polarization, but also its theoretical weight when it comes to the "violent hierarchy" Derrida describes. In addition to complicating the binary between light/dark and good/evil, DiCamillo pens characters for whom internal intermingling of these elements results from the conflicts they have with adults in their lives. These adult/child oppositions offer commentary on binaries between conformity and rebellion, but also autonomy/dependence, which is linked very closely to adult/child. All of DiCamillo's main characters internalize both light and dark, hope and despair, and love and hatred primarily because of the profoundly negative influences of adults in their lives, which creates an emphasis not just on thematic elements, but also on key power dynamics between adults and children.

When the film version of DiCamillo's story polarizes these binaries, shifting light/dark and good/evil to systems with far greater opposition and lack of intermingling, it also affects the ways that adult/child relationships are depicted. I explore this element more in chapter 2, relating it to two other children's fantasy adaptations that similarly polarize binaries: *Coraline* and *How to Train Your Dragon*. In each of these cases, adult/child binaries interact with other kinds of binary systems that are similarly polarized as a result of thematic amplification. Furthermore, binary polarization leads to key ideological differences in all three of these adaptations, as well as all of the other texts I have studied.

Effects of Binary Polarization on Ideology

As I notice more and more films that fit into the trend of binary polarization, I am struck by the consistency of this pattern. Still, this observation alone does not seem to be enough to develop a theory of adaptation. Binary polarization is part of "what happens" when children's and young adult texts are made into movies, but when I share this idea with people, whether casual film viewers or scholarly colleagues, they frequently want to know if this is something good or something bad. "It doesn't matter!" I want to yell (and sometimes have), for I wish to think about films in nonhierarchical ways. Adaptation has a consistent effect on a story, but I want to believe it is not necessarily a negative effect; thinking so slips back into approaches adaptation studies scholars seek to avoid. Still, my reaction that "it doesn't matter" is just as flawed as making evaluation the focus, for it *does* matter what effect binary polarization has on a film. In fact, if taken in tandem with an understanding of the role that ideology plays in children's literature—indoctrinating young people into belief systems they may hold their entire lives—then the effect of consistently polarized binaries in film matters a great deal.

The exact nature of the ideological changes that result from binary polarization depends on the source; different pieces of children's and young adult literature present different kinds of viewpoints, and thus the ideological changes that result from binary polarization are case specific. Nonetheless, there are also some striking consistencies across certain groups of adapted texts. Thus, in subsequent chapters, I examine some of these patterns, seeking to illuminate exactly what kinds of ideologies are at stake as a result of binary polarization.

After more fully examining binary polarization and its causes in chapter 2's study of films made from fantasy children's novels, chapter 3 considers how polarization shifts ideologies in adolescent texts. In young adult film adaptations, ideologies related to gender seem most commonly affected by polarization of especially the male/female binaries of their source texts. Thus, not only does thematic amplification lead to binary polarization in adolescent filmic adaptations, but this also repeatedly shifts depictions of female characters in ways that position them as the emotional and spiritual savior of their male counterparts. By focalizing on the romance of the story and fitting female characters to established motifs, a striking number of contemporary young adult film adaptations engage a problematic paradigm wherein men are saved by the women they love. While these films seem to reverse more traditional male/female dynamics, binary polarization results in a recreation of unequal power structures, simply via new means.

Chapter 4 similarly tackles a subset of children's adapted film that presents some consistent ideological implications of binary polarization: picturebook adaptations. In these films, the need to add substantial content affects the kinds of ideological changes that result from polarization of especially the adult/child binary systems of the source text. I want to point out, however, that although I have collected films in various chapters based on similarities in their source text counterparts, I do not see these as "categories" of adaptations. Instead, I think of these subsets from a view based more on materiality. In filmic adaptations of picturebooks, for example, one key material element is that content must be contributed to the story in order to fill the expected length requirements of a feature-length film. Thus, while the consistency of binary polarization remains in this text, it manifests uniquely because of this material constraint, thus making the additional content element worthy of particular attention. This is the case with each chapter of my study: rather than categorizing adaptations, I trace a single pattern across them by examining how ideological implications change given various material factors.

Focusing this approach in chapter 4 on films created from iconic texts like those produced by Dr. Seuss, Sendak's *Where the Wild Things Are*, and works by Chris Van Allsburg, I argue that amplification/polarization trends consistently shape added content so that it highlights adult roles and presence within the story more than the source. By interrogating adult-centered filmic representations, this chapter considers how such alterations reveal a great deal about the unique qualities of dual audience in children's film.

While chapters 3 and 4 focus on one-to-one adaptation (wherein only one film has been made from a source text), chapter 5 uses film adaptations of a canonical children's text, *The Wonderful Wizard of Oz*, to explore instances in which many films have been made based on one children's novel. In this chapter, I trace multiple adaptations across many decades, wherein each adaptation interacts not just with the source text, but also with other adaptations. This chapter builds from the others to further examine ideological implications of consistently polarized binaries, suggesting that in the case of multiple adaptations of a single source, one ideological ramification is what I term *adaptive dissonance*, or an increased ideological conflict *within* the adaptation as compared to the source. This chapter considers the implications of such adaptive dissonance, especially when it comes to depictions of race and gender in contemporary Oz retellings.

By exploring the causes and ideological implications of binary polarization across a range of film adaptations for young people, I offer more than the recognition of a trend, but also a new way of thinking about adaptation itself. By resisting the pull of a focus on fidelity that seems so strong in children's adapted movies, I believe critics can do new work to think about the nature of children's film and the process of adapting a book into a movie meant for young viewers. It is with this goal in mind that I posit a theory of children's and adolescent film adaptation, one that uses an exploration of trends to begin to explain what happens—and what is at stake—when children's and young adult books are made to movies.

I end my study with a particularly pragmatic application of this theory by discussing specifically how it might be useful in a classroom setting and implemented as a foundation for the teaching of film. In this final chapter, I tackle a text set that I believe is especially relevant (and beloved) by teachers who wish to help their students consider ideology in film: movies created by the Walt Disney Corporation. Perhaps more than any other group of films, Disney movies have been repeatedly criticized for their ideological underpinnings. I believe that teachers can build from this criticism, but also pair it with a consideration of the trend of binary polarization in order to help students delve more deeply into children's film studies, adaptation studies, and analytical thinking and writing. My final chapter offers specific suggestions of how to approach this work in the classroom, thus closing my study by not only recapping key tenants of my theory, but also examining how to apply them.

CHAPTER TWO

Choosing a Theme and Sticking to It

When tracking a trend, repetition is key, for if film adaptations shift their source texts in consistent ways, then this can reveal something about adaptation itself. As I have discussed in chapter 1, this kind of study can offer a valuable contribution to scholarly work because it alters the discussion surrounding adaptations, moving away from comparative evaluation (aka, why the book is better than the movie) to a question of what happens—a theorization that can help viewers to understand adaptations as unique, complex, and meaningful textual entities.

Exploring this concept allows for a reworking of the common critical attitude that adaptations are inferior to their source texts, setting aside, as David Buchbinder describes, discussions focused on whether adaptations are "accurate re-representations of the original or are always-already inferior reworkings" (127). In surveying adaptation studies, Buchbinder notes that a "more generalized theorization of adaptation *as a practice* is comparatively recent" (127), and I would suggest that this kind of study reflects a valuable move, and one which allows for more productive work than using comparison to judge texts, whether by fidelity or some other means. In particular, I believe that one way of theorizing adaptation as a practice hinges on recognition of repetition, so that instead of looking at fidelity or lack thereof, we might track trends and consistencies in order to delve into the actual process of adaptation and, more importantly, the repeated effects of that process.

To really understand a theory or how something that happens again and again works, it is important to first understand what causes it. Consistency is key, but to simply offer example after example as proof that binaries are polarized consistently across children and young adult film adaptations does not get at the heart of the issue; instead, I want to explore why this happens and what is the result. This chapter examines a factor that I see as a foundational element causing binary polarization in children's film. Every time I watch a movie based on a children's or young adult novel or picturebook, I notice something from the source text that seems to have particular weight or importance in the film, something that filmmakers seem to want to focus the movie around. Whether a key theme or important message, this component becomes a touchstone for the adaptation, and creative decisions seem to revolve around it. As filmmakers select and focus on a theme or explicit ideology of the source text, they do more than highlight it, but consistently, the adaptation presents this textual message in a stronger way, amplifying it. I call this strengthening of a single message *thematic amplification*.

Now, to be clear, there are often a lot of important messages or themes of the source text that are not amplified in the film adaptation, and this is often where viewer disappointment comes into play. When I think about the times that I was most upset or frustrated by an adaptation, it is those times when my response has been "they completely missed the point." Often, this idea refers to what adaptation studies scholars call the "essence" of the source text, and that is sometimes what these critics look for when analyzing the new version. Such critics decide what they believe to be the book's essence, and then determine whether the film presents this idea effectively.

Contemporary critics challenge this, noting the problematics of, as Whelehan describes, a critical approach wherein "the main purpose of comparison becomes the measurement of the success of the film in its capacity to realize what are held to be the core meanings and values of the originary text . . . the degree to which the film is 'successful' in extracting the 'essence' of the fictional text" (3). Like Whelehan, I do not want to focus on how well a film retains a book's essence, for first of all, determination of essence is quite subjective. Who am I to say whether the religious aspects of Hans Christian Anderson's "Little Mermaid" are the most important, or if it is a story about independence and defying expectation, or even if Disney's focus on romance captures the key theme? Furthermore, I, as a critic, can be open to all of these elements being equally crucial parts of the story's essence. A filmmaker cannot.

Herein lies the key factor I posit as a cause of binary polarization in children's and adolescent adapted film: filmmakers choose a central theme or idea around which to tell the tale of their adaptation. Moreover, one might make a case that they must do so, that children's film itself is predicated on a centralized theme in a way that other mediums are not. Critics (and even viewers) may prefer a subtle exploration of one or more themes, but for filmmakers, this is often not an option, and not simply because of their preferences. Instead, the structure of children's film, honed over decades, is predicated on the film's ability to impart a lesson within a traditional narrative structure of disruption-resolution. Furthermore, reader expectation plays a huge role in filmmakers' decisions to focus on a centralized theme and weave the film around this element. When a filmmaker must adapt source material to this model, messages and/or ideologies regularly become more explicit, amplified to take on greater weight and highlighted in ways that make the theme more obvious and clear.

Audience expectation and history are certainly important elements of thematic amplification as a frequent cause for binary polarization. Still, when it really comes down to it, the ways that filmmakers choose a theme to focus their adaptation around has to do with the medium of film and the nature of children's film in particular. As critics such as Stam, Albrecht-Crane, and Cutchins have suggested, drawing especially on Bakhtin, language is always situated and contextual, and children's movies are no exception. Part of considering the patterns of children's and adolescent adapted texts is thinking about the mediums and material factors that play a role in the adaptive process—the ways that decisions (like amplifying a theme) are not arbitrary or related to preference, but built out of an established understanding of how film for young viewers works. If adaptors stray too far from established structures or viewer expectations, they risk losing their audience, which means losing money as well. Because the children's film industry is, above all, a commercial enterprise, this is not a risk many filmmakers are willing to take.

Still, I would go even further to link the nature of film to thematic amplification, for factors like time and pacing represent a crucial difference between a reader's experience of a text and a viewer's experience of a film. A quicker pace or more limited amount of time spent with a story often translates into a greater emphasis on theme, wherein a particular textual message becomes the focus of a film, instead of one of many concepts explored bit by bit over a longer period spent reading a book. Because of the limited time to tell their story, filmmakers must often choose a theme and stick to it.

Furthermore, as Hutcheon describes, "being shown a story is not the same as being told it" (*Theory* 13). Authors are able to tell a story in ways that allow readers access to elements that are often inaccessible to film viewers, "unconstrained by the limits of the visual or aural" (*Theory* 23). For example, filmmakers must use a wide range of tools to establish setting differently than print narrative. While a novelist may include a little description to set the scene or choose to craft abundant details, either approach can be effective, as readers are capable of filling in gaps. In film, mise-en-scène, which translates to "staging in action," attests to the complexity of setting, as it includes both design elements (such as props, set design, lighting, costuming, and makeup) and composition (blocking, camerawork, etc.). Each minute detail of setting must be decided in film, and often, copious amount of time and resources must be used to create the effect. More than simply complex, though, this part of the form of film contributes to thematic amplification. Each of the choices a filmmaker makes to build a set and compose a scene adds together toward a common goal. If a central theme is acting as the cornerstone of the film, such mise-en-scène choices can be crafted around it, thus offering a stronger focus and representation of that theme: aka, thematic amplification.

For example, in the first text I explore in this chapter, Neil Gaiman does not, and need not, tell us every detail of Coraline's kitchen or its distinction from the kitchen in the home of the other mother—readers will fill in the gaps when they picture the setting in their minds. When Henry Selick adapts Gaiman's work, however, he must make decisions as to every detail of the kitchen, including how much of Gaiman's description to use, and Selick draws on a wide range of tools to craft these decisions into existence. How might a director make such a wide range of choices, and moreover, craft them together cohesively? The easiest answer seems to be that all filmmaking choices connect back to a central theme. When all filmic choices relate back to such a theme, it is no wonder that it is amplified.

I posit that this amplified theme leads to binary polarization, and to make this case, I use three middle-grade fantasy adaptations that demonstrate particularly strong evidence of this link: *Coraline, The Tale of Despereaux,* and *How to Train Your Dragon.* In each case, a theme of the novel becomes the cornerstone of the film, leading to concepts being drawn further apart until there is no middle ground between the key ideas of these children's texts. Binaries—such as good/evil, independence/dependence, real/imaginary, conformity/individuality, adult/child, and self/other—are polarized because adaptors have chosen a single theme around which to base their adaptation.

I have also chosen these three texts to explore thematic amplification as a cause of binary polarization because they are films I regularly teach in my classroom. All three work well in this regard because they offer an opportunity to consider some of the key ideologies of children's fantasy, while also allowing for discussion about how filmmaker's decisions to focus on a particular message reflects the nature of children's film.

Additionally, these three fantasy texts each offer something different to a broader study of children's adapted film. For example, Selick's stop-action animated adaptation of Gaiman's *Coraline* (a novel that has received much critical attention) highlights ways that refocusing questions of adaptive merit might yield productive results. I suggest that looking at the material factors of filmmaking can allow for a reinterpretation of the ways critics have thus far characterized the film, seeing Selick's interpretation not as a distortion, but an amplification of certain elements at the expense of others.

Frequently, in order to focus a film around a single theme, adaptors will also weave together various parts of the story, linking them together so that they overlap. In doing so, thematic amplification also ties together various binaries of the story, interlocking such concepts as adult/child with independence/dependence, and independence/dependence with rebellion and conformity. I use *Despereaux* to look at how amplifying themes affects such interwoven or overlapping binaries, considering, in particular, how they refigure adult/child power dynamics to alter the messages presented.

Finally, the film version of Cressida Cowell's *How to Train Your Dragon* employs a far more drastic departure in content and storyline than *Coraline* or *Despereaux*, but it nonetheless bases these changes on thematic amplification, which results in an even stronger polarization, using the same kind of binary systems overlap as *Despereaux* within a culturally and historically situated space and time. As a result, *How to Train Your Dragon* suggests that the more changes are made, and as a result, the more binaries are polarized, the more ideologies shift as well . . . and not always in positive or even neutral ways. This is what sets *How to Train Your Dragon* apart, for while binary polarization in the adaptations of *Coraline* or *Despereaux* yield notable ideological implications, the result of the same trend has far more concerning consequences in terms of the messages presented by the film version of *How to Train Your Dragon*.

Amplification versus Distortion: *Coraline* Reinterpreted

While many critics describe adaptations in ways that suggest that filmmakers have missed the point of the source text, I contend quite the opposite: that filmmakers often choose a key theme and attempt to make it the driving point of their adapted film. As such, I begin my discussion of thematic amplification as a cause of binary polarization by distinguishing between these two ideas: distortion versus amplification of a theme or textual message. While I would not say that these concepts are mutually exclusive, by and large, what I notice many critics call a distorting of an author's key message or main idea is actually a reworking of a story to fit a central guiding objective, and with very few exceptions, this objective is textually founded. As such, rather than diminished, I believe ideologies are typically intensified in adaptations. This is certainly the case with Selick's film version of *Coraline*.

Adapted to the screen in 2009, Gaiman's *Coraline* portrays a conflict between an eleven-year-old and her parents, which critics have suggested reflects her internal conflict between autonomy and dependence. Scholars such as Karen Coats; Richard Gooding; and Elizabeth Parsons, Naarah Sawers, and Kate McInally interpret this concept through a psychoanalytical lens, analyzing how Coraline's struggle to navigate her burgeoning desires allows her to develop a self apart from her mother. Gaiman's protagonist is, as Coats describes, "caught in that liminal moment when she finds herself cut off from her parent's desire, and not yet sure of her own" ("Horror" 87), and Coraline explores this moment in her childhood by way of an adventure that pits her against a devious version of her mother, a controlling and manipulative "other mother."

All of these elements are reproduced in the film adaptation, which might be considered, as Wagner would describe, a transposition of the novel, in that it is "directly given on screen, with the minimum of apparent interference" (222). However, despite the similarities between the movie and its source, there are also key differences, and these act as the focus of Myers's study "Whose Fear Is It Anyway? Moral Panics and 'Stranger Danger' in Henry Selick's *Coraline*." Myers's analysis focuses on the ways the film adaptation pits adults of the text against the child positioned as savior, and in addition to critiquing the ways the film "limits Coraline's agency" (248), Myers considers how Selick's other mother is a more manipulative villain than in Gaiman's text, especially by including a new character, Wybie, and luring Coraline with a look-alike doll. Calling the film "alarmingly disturbing" (255), Myers worries that "Selick's moral message may ultimately supplant Gaiman's original intent in the public mind" (255).

What I wish to call attention to in this interpretation is the emphasis Myers places on using comparative analysis to suggest that Selick's film distorts or diminishes Gaiman's work, thus implying that a stronger film would be one that does the opposite, maintaining fidelity to what Myers calls Gaiman's "literary masterpiece" (247). This characterization aligns with many children's literature critics' view of adapted films, wherein the seeming purpose of the adaptation, or at the very least, the marker of a successful adaptation, hinges on fidelity, and departure from the text not only produces a substandard result, but somehow takes away from the source text itself.

What interests me even more about Myers's analysis is that each change or difference between the film and source that she describes seems, in my characterization, not a distortion, but actually an amplification of the textual components Gaiman puts forth in his novel. I suggest that these changes and additions are not diminishing the content of source text, but actually doing the opposite—they emphasize, and even more forcefully present elements of Gaiman's novel, and thus might best be described as amplification.

I agree with Myers's contention that the film features more focus on the other mother's abduction of Coraline, shifting the power dynamics between adults and children and emphasizing the differences between the real and other world, all while shifting Coraline's mission away from an experiment in identity toward a clearer fight against the villainous other mother. Yet I see all of these elements as working together toward one key goal: an emphasis of the conflict between the other mother and Coraline that posits this as the primary thematic take away of the book. Thus, the changes and differences that Myers describes, and indeed, I suggest nearly all of the significant changes in the text when it is transposed to the screen, work together to dramatize the conflict Gaiman has already put in place. Furthermore, while critics focus primarily on the internal conflicts that Coraline traverses in her struggle, they also suggest that this is represented through the external conflict between her and the other mother, who may even be a metaphorical figure created in Coraline's own mind (although this is certainly debatable). As Gooding describes, "although Coraline imagines the game as a struggle against a hostile antagonist, it is more fundamentally a struggle against her own desire for dependency and identification" (397–98).

The film certainly seems more focused on this conflict, and especially in representing the external conflict between Coraline and her other mother in more obvious ways. To consider this, I would again call upon Wojcik-Andrews's work to define the nature of children's film, which hinges on the term conflict. When Wojcik-Andrews describes the Aristotelian narrative pattern of beginning, middle, and end, he characterizes each of these steps as connected to the "conflict" of the text: "beginning disruption or *conflict* forces the hero or heroine on a physical or psychological journey. Upon completion of the journey, said *conflict* is resolved" (7, emphasis added). Furthermore, a key element of the pattern that Wojcik-Andrews focuses on is the way "character development is subordinated to the requirements of the narrative," a requirement that also seem related to the idea of conflict. I return to Wojcik-Andrews's words to suggest a crucial distinction—that film, as Bluestone so famously characterized, is "medium specific." The medium here, as Wojcik-Andrews describes, preferences narrative at the expense of character development, building this narrative primarily on representation and resolution of conflict.

Of course, while conflict may take on a more important role in film, it is also an important part of many novels and other alphabetic texts as well. In fact, Gaiman's text is actually very much about conflict. Gooding describes this in a physical sense, writing that "the act of closing the door on the other mother confirms the resolution of Coraline's conflicts with her parents and her successful integration into a web of social relationships" (398). Coats and others similarly characterize key plot elements as representative of a more internalized conflict, suggesting that Coraline's battle with the other mother serves to reflect her negotiation "between that which we control and that which controls us" (Coats, *Looking* 5). It is through this conflict that Coraline develops, growing as a protagonist to be more self-reflexive and thoughtful, and eventually coming to balance her own needs and desires with those of the adults in her life, while also negotiating a space between autonomy and dependence. In the book, readers come to understand this in part because they are privy to many of Coraline's musing and thought processes, but the film, a medium in which thoughts are very difficult to represent, focuses more fully on the physical, tangible, and external conflict between Coraline and her other mother.

My argument here is twofold. First, the emphasis the film places on the other mother abducting Coraline, which sets up a greater focus on the battle between them, is textually founded. Secondly, and more to my overall point, if we might read Coraline's battle with her other mother as representative of her difficult internal development, Selick's film focalizes on this element. The adaptation amplifies the external dichotomy between mother and daughter, thus emphasizing the conflicting desires of both Coraline and her mother (real and other) as a more tangible and visually dramatic battle between the child and adult forces of the text. This is the kind of thematic amplification I believe is as a key element of all children's and adolescent film adaptations.

Moreover, thematic amplification here is not simply a coincidence, but is entrenched in the form of film itself. While the novel uses subtle, but often sparse description, Selick must decide on how to bring to life every detail of Gaiman's world. The choices he makes to do so and, in particular, his choices related to the visually stunning quality of the other world as contrasting Coraline's home all serve to enhance the focus on the conflict between a problematically controlling other mother and a protagonist exploring her own ability to assert control over her own life. As way of an example, I would point to one particular aspect of the other mother's manipulation that filmmakers focus upon and enhance in their crafting of the mise-en-scène of the other world. While this filmic element might seem like a departure or addition, and perhaps to some, even a distortion, it actually falls far more under the category of amplification.

The film version of *Coraline* features a focus on gardening largely absent from the source text. In the movie, Coraline's parents do not simply work on a computer, but create gardening catalogs, and Coraline describes the irony of this by expressing disdain that although her parents "get paid to write about plants," her mother hates dirt. Later, gardening takes on an even more prominent role in film, for in Coraline's first visit to the other world, her father shows her around a magical and magnificent garden that the other mother has created just for her, fashioning the remarkable plants into the shape of her head.

This section, and the gardening motif in general, is an addition to the film that departs from Gaiman's novel. Still, I would suggest that this inclusion actually amplifies the themes surrounding the conflict between Coraline and the other mother. Gardening is an activity defined very much by control, for gardeners typically tame the natural world to fit into very exacting parameters.

This makes for a very useful and compelling motif in the film, for the other mother's gardening is a tangible example of the more metaphoric control that she wishes to exert upon Coraline. Furthermore, while Coraline is at first enamored by the other mother's garden, it later becomes a frightening place, and yet one that she is able to use to her advantage, first finding the soul of one of the ghost children there, and later, in the real world, hosting a party for the adults in her life.

By exploring the question of control by way of a gardening motif, the film aligns with Coats's description of the conflict between autonomy/dependence as being defined as a struggle "between that which we control and that which controls us" (*Looking* 5). Thus, the negotiation of control implied by the use of gardening as a new textual motif seems to fit thematically with Gaiman's text, amplifying an element that Coats describes as a crucial component of Coraline's development. Furthermore, the gardening motif draws from historical uses of gardening in children's literature such as *Alice in Wonderland* or *The Secret Garden*, wherein young women learn to navigate their power in the face of systems and forces that control or frighten them.

The implementation of motif is a storytelling element that exists in both print narratives and film, but what makes this example especially distinctive is the ways that the film's uniquely form-driven and filmic qualities also reinforce much of what Gaiman's novel puts forth. This motif is not simply enhanced, but put forward in a far more visually stunning way. By creating a Coraline-inspired garden, the other mother takes this level of control to a magnificent, yet ultimately horrible degree, a point enhanced by the use of lighting, color, visual effects, and sweeping camera movements that take readers on an enticing visual tour of the space painstakingly created in miniature by stop-motion animators. Furthermore, the danger here is also alluded to visually, especially when Coraline and the other father ride a praying mantis—an insect that eats its mate after copulation—to gain an aerial view of the stunning garden in the shape of Coraline's face. Then, later in the film, mise-en-scène choices shift the tone, so that decaying garden becomes a frightening space Coraline must traverse to find the first of the ghosts' souls. It seems also interesting to note that in the film, Coraline's parents' more casual relationship with gardening (writing catalogues, yet disliking the activity; refusing to plant with Coraline only to do so in the end for a special occasion) perhaps indicates a more tempered relationship with issues of control and more balance between desires to control or be controlled.

Then, at the end of the film, Coraline's parents somewhat grudgingly participate in Coraline's garden party, a scene in which Coraline appears more changed than they do, for she has decided to take on the project of the garden herself and use it as a way of entertaining the adults, rather than desiring to be entertained by them. The camera angles of this scene are shot primarily as if shown though Coraline's eyes, highlighted by seeing her hands lift a tray in the lower portion of the frame and moving around the scene as if walking (a shot likely produced by a dolly or similar technique). Even this shot style seems to show Coraline now assuming a role of tempered control, reinforcing the narrative elements. Coraline facilitates the activity, demonstrating her independence, and although she still desires to share this with her mother, her planning and seeming nonchalance over her mother's negativity reflects a relationship that balances autonomy and dependence. In each of these instances, the motif of gardening enhances messages already present in the text. These elements act as a shorthand for some of the thematic elements, amplifying them, but also creating a greater sense of cohesion and focus around this element of the conflict between the other mother and Coraline, a conflict that hinges on control.

Selick's film version of *Coraline* not only amplifies theme, however, but also does so in a way that emphasizes the binaries of the text, and in reinforcing these more strongly, it polarizes them. The most obvious of these binaries is the one I have already mentioned: autonomy and dependence. By placing the other mother at greater odds with Coraline and characterizing Coraline's real parents as more actively creating boundaries and separation (so much so that they appear frustrated with her neediness), the film offers little subtlety when it comes to the question of independence versus dependence, and there seems little overlap between the two. In order to defeat the other mother, a goal that becomes absolutely essential as Coraline realizes that other children have been abducted in the past and thus this villain poses a great and continuing threat, Coraline must embrace a striking independence, rather than exploring a possible movement along a continuum of relying upon adults to varying degrees. This stems from the amplification; the other mother's villainy and the conflict between her and Coraline are treated with greater emphasis in the movie, especially in the ways the other mother reaches out into the other world using dolls as lures and spies. By amplifying this threat and the ensuing battle, the movie leaves very little room for prolonged consideration of a middle-ground between these conceptual states of being. Coraline must be independent, rejecting adult authority and dependence in order to rise to the more high-stakes challenges fostered by the amplified conflict and theme.

Moreover, there are other binaries at play in the text similarly polarized because of these thematic amplifications. For example, Gaiman explores the complex nature of adult/child binaries in terms of independent subjectivity, but Selick takes this same binary and intensifies it, associating it with other more obvious binaries of the text—good versus evil and the real versus other worlds. The other world is more fully other and more obviously evil *because* it is seemingly representative of adult forces of control, linking these elements together and depicting them all in stark opposition to their counterparts. The film's other world differs more from the real world than the book's more understated distinctions between these two spaces, but the key here is that it is an amplification of theme that polarizes this real/other binary.

To clarify, when I describe the text's binaries, I do not simply mean conflicts; adult/child binaries, for example, are different than conflicts between adult and child characters. While I would suggest that such conflicts are amplified in most adaptations as well, I also refer to the dichotomy between concepts of adult and child. This certainly has to do with power relationships, as Derrida's characterization of the "violent hierarchy" between binary oppositions suggests, but a concept of binary opposition that draws from both Derrida and other poststructuralism theorists focuses on the ways in which we define and understand the world around us through language and, in particular, through sets of words and ideas that exist only in their pairing, wherein one concept/word reflects the absence of its opposite. When the binary between adult and child is polarized, the emphasis is placed on the very notion of what it means to be adult as inherently oppositional to being a child—that the very definition of adult is "not child."

If we dive further into this concept of especially the adult/child binary, inherent in the binary are also the ideologies associated with adults and children that stem from it. This is the content, or meaning, behind the binary. Children are innocent and naïve but also have a sense of hope and wonderment lost to adulthood. They are also in transition, moving from dependence to autonomy in ways that require rebelling and asserting themselves against forces of conformity. These are, of course, qualities that reflect an essentialized view of childhood, but this is what binaries are predicated upon—that "adult" and "child" each have definable and more importantly, oppositional, qualities.

My contention is that film adaptations polarize the two ends of such binaries by placing the qualities as more strongly oppositional and more conceptually separate. Sometimes, as in the case of *Coraline*, they do so by creating greater textual conflict, wherein adult/child conflicts might offer commentary on the binary between what it means to be adult/child or independent/dependent. For *Coraline*, this is certainly the case, for in facing adult opposition, Coraline is also working through what it means to be child versus adult and the challenge of traversing the binary of autonomy/dependence. Still, it is also the concepts of adult and child themselves that are polarized and represented in more concretely oppositional ways, wherein autonomy is a lack of dependence, and children are inherently not adult.

What seems particularly interesting about the film version of *Coraline* is the way that filmmakers very purposefully use techniques unique to the medium of film in order to demonstrate the polarization of the binaries of the text, and most especially, the difference between the real and other world. For example, filmmakers used special techniques like ranking or angling of the scene backdrops in the real world to create the appearance of flatness, while the scenes in the other world use 3D technology, appearing to extend beyond the screen. Additionally, producers use dull coloration when Coraline is at home, which acts in sharp contrast to the other world's brilliant coloring. These were not mistakes that the filmmakers made or a failure to correctly interpret Gaiman's text, but a conscious decision to create a more significant contrast between what is real and other, whereby one seems to reflect an absence of the characteristics of the other. They chose to polarize the real/other binary.

Furthermore, these decisions are set within a context of the history of filmmaking, wherein the distinction between a real and fantasy world is often characterized by a striking opposition, accentuated through coloration and other material elements. The most famous example of this is surely the 1939 film *The Wizard of Oz*; when Dorothy steps out of her sepia Kansas home into the amazing Technicolor of Oz, the visual contrast similarly highlights a polarization of the home/away or real/other binaries of the text. In both of these cases, changes in the adapted film are made possible or even facilitated by the material difference between a novel, which asks readers to create a visualization of real and fantasy spaces themselves, and a visual text, which does this work for (or at least *with*) the viewer. In this case, the difference is a matter of technique, and different techniques are available in each media depending upon the tools chosen and utilized to achieve unique goals and purposes.

The use of such tools has specific results that affect what each text offers the reader. In the film, the visually stunning other world not only emphasizes a contrast to the real world, but this portrayal also creates another binary more polarized in the film than in the novel. Not only is the other world strikingly different and far more magical than the real world, but it also undergoes a significant change throughout the course of the film. Whereas Gaiman's other mother appears strange and different from her real mother even at the very beginning, the movie initially portrays the other mother as a near replica of Coraline's mother, except for her button eyes. The visual imagery of the other mother changes dramatically throughout the film, moving from only small changes in dress at first to an eventual distinctive spiderlike appearance, and ending with a metallic creature that does not even seem human.

Coraline's initial interactions with the other mother represent what she thinks she wants, but the sharper contrast with the horror that follows serves to underscore Coraline's negotiation of how much attention, and consequently control, she wishes to receive from her parents, and especially her mother. The doll spy the other mother creates initially reports Coraline's desire for the complete attention of her parents, but it also reflects a desire the other mother shares. Coats observes that Lacanian theory "posits desire as the organizing feature of the modern subject . . . desire as an opening in the surface of the Other, that which allows, indeed compels, the traversing of distances between oneself and other, between oneself and Otherness" (*Looking* 78–79). For both the other mother and Coraline, this is what Selick's doll facilitates. Thus, it is no surprise that Coraline views the marvels fashioned out of her desires with wide-eyed wonderment, a reaction that the stunning visuals of the film also elicit from the audience. Yet the desire elicited in these portrayals becomes particularly suspect when she (and viewers) then see the distortion of this world and how it visually disintegrates as Coraline develops more autonomy and triumphs over the other mother's increasingly desperate attempts to hold onto her. The majesty of the other world in the film sets up this contrast more than the book, but seemingly to send the same message to a greater degree.

Again, this seems not an error or misrepresentation of the novel, but a conscious choice to focus on an amplified conflict and, specifically, one which places the story in a greater binary system of good versus evil with more obvious division between heroes and villains. This increased opposition emphasizes the text's messages about how Coraline must traverse these spaces; Coraline comes to see the value in the real world, where she can and must experience greater autonomy and move toward an adult independence. The film uses techniques specific to its form to enhance and explore this theme in a meaningful way and, in my assessment, in a way that is just as complex and nuanced as Gaiman's text. The result is a very different text, but one that seems not a distortion; Selick's work is complex and meaningful, as is Gaiman's.

Adaptation critics might ask, if filmmakers are only seeking to reinforce messages presented in Gaiman's novel, why make these changes at all? If the book effectively sends these messages, why try to amplify them or polarize the binaries presented? The movement away from emphasis on fidelity in adaptation studies begins to answer these questions, for even as early as 1982, J. D. Stahl writes that more important than being faithful, an adaptation should "employ the artistic character and potential of its medium as fully as possible" (6). Hutcheon extends this, suggesting critics "expand the traditional focus of adaptation studies on medium-specificity and individual comparative case studies in order to consider as well relations among the major modes of engagement" (*Theory* 22). Even Myers alludes to this factor in describing Selick's use of classic horror movies tropes and how these choices appeal to the dual movie-going audience of children and adults. While Myers criticizes this influence, I believe we can see it in a more productive way. Selick does not simply place horror motifs in his adaptation, but also demonstrates an important element of both horror movies and children's film—the dramatic conflict and extreme polarization of good/evil binaries. These shifts are not arbitrary choices of the adaptors or a failure to understand the merits of Gaiman's text, but rather reflect expectations associated with two key genres: Hollywood horror films that can capture Gaiman's creepy, gothic approach and the children's family film, which can draw young viewers and their parents to the theater. The features of genre, like the elements of form and technique, are a reflection of the medium, and as such, the adaptation does different work—work that fits this new context and the material limitations and expectations inherent to it.

The Ideological Implications of Forgiving Despereaux

I began chapter 1 with the example of Kate DiCamillo's *The Tale of Despereaux* and its 2004 computer-animated adaptation directed by Sam Fell and Robert Stevenhagen in great part because DiCamillo's work seems so very obviously focused on the concept of binaries; not only is the dichotomy of light and dark a clearly important part of the thematic exploration of the book, but this binary also acts as a stand in for a rather in-depth consideration of other oppositions. The text uses light and dark to question notions of good and evil, but like *Coraline*, even this binary suggests other kinds of dichotomies, including binaries of conformity/individuality as well as adult/child.

The film version of *The Tale of Despereaux*, adapted only four years after the text was published, does more than offer a strong example of filmic binary polarization. Additionally, it highlights the ways that focalization on a central theme leads to this phenomenon in a consistent way. What I believe sets *Despereaux* apart, thus making it a strong example to really dig into thematic amplification as a cause of this trend, is how DiCamillo herself uses the binaries of the text in ways that present several key ideologies related to questions of conformity as they relate to power dynamics between adults and children. More than other examples I have studied, the source text in this case is self-reflexive and referential when it comes to its use of binaries, seeming to intentionally toy with and explore ideologies by asking readers to consider the binaries that facilitate them. Thus, when the binaries are polarized in the film adaptation, the result is especially interesting. While one might think that ideological representations would simply be amplified as a result of this consistent element of the adaptive practice, changes in ideological representation are actually far more dramatic.

More importantly, this is something that I have noticed across all of the examples of children's and young adult adaptation I have studied. Not only are binaries polarized in consistent ways, but ideological ramifications of this polarization are always weighty. Of course, how such messages and power dynamics are changed is at least in part dependent on what ideologies are present in the source text, so that in children's texts, for example, adult/child binaries often play a more significant role than in adolescent texts, wherein male/female binaries take center stage. Yet I believe *The Tale of Despereaux* offers a particularly strong example to begin to describe what I mean by ideological implications, primarily because the source text so closely ties binaries and ideology, and as a result, when themes are amplified, the link between amplification and polarization seems especially obvious.

As I briefly mentioned in my introduction, DiCamillo's tale centers on questions of conformity and forgiveness and explores these concepts through the interwoven stories of four key characters. Despereaux, Roscuro, Miggery Sow, and the Princess Pea each make difficult decisions about whether they will conform to the expectations set upon them or seek another path, but the story complicates these choices by demonstrating that even those brave enough to desire a different perspective are not always able to achieve it. DiCamillo's characters are troubled, but they also make troubling choices in their quests against conformity, revealing that perhaps everyone possesses elements of both good and evil. The text's narrator frequently addresses the reader to highlight this message explicitly, describing hearts as "complicated, shaded with dark and dappled with light" (197).

Nodelman, as I have suggested, highlights such binaries as a crucial element of children's literature as a genre, but he also notes that while he once believed children's texts sought to bring these binaries "into balance, so that both can be included in a vision of what life is" ("Sameness" 19), he now sees attempts at balance in children's texts as reflecting "an uneasy and complex ambivalence about the constituent pairs" (*Hidden* 228). I agree that contemporary texts seem frequently to delve deeply into questions of power and representation by incorporating such "uneasy and complex ambivalence" surrounding binary oppositions, and in fact, I would suggest this is something that distinguishes those pieces of children's literature that do especially intriguing and nuanced work from those that take a simpler road, presenting a more concretely didactic view in which binaries are polarized. To me, the more interesting piece of children's literature is the one in which such concepts are somewhat muddled.

This is how I would characterize DiCamillo's text, which uses light and dark to comment on this kind of ambivalence in very direct ways. Good and evil, light and dark, conformity and rebellion, and even adult/child hierarchies are not so simple in this text, and even more interestingly, DiCamillo uses these oppositions to present the idea that unification of binary oppositions may be desirable, but is often impossible. Just as in *Coraline*, an exploration of the complex intermingling of binary oppositions is in part explored by presenting a push and pull between opposite forces, and especially between adults and children. In DiCamillo's story, this is especially true, as child characters seek lives different from those adults expect from them, and adults represent the harsh, even violent forces of conformity.

For example, Despereaux's father betrays him because Despereaux does not conform to the ways of mice, and Botticelli similarly forces Roscuro to take up the dark doctrines of the rat community, despite Roscuro's fascination with and yearning for light. Finally, Mig endures abandonment by her father and physical abuse so consistent that it disables her sense of hearing, and adults consistently tell her that "no one cared what she wanted. No one had ever cared. And perhaps, worst of all, no one ever would care" (253). In each of these instances, not only do the characters find themselves trying to balance a complicated intermingling of love/hatred, hope/despair, and light/dark, but they are also placed in a position in which they need to do so because the adults in their lives have such negative impacts on their experiences.

This is most evident in the novel's representation of Roscuro and Miggery Sow, both of whom are at times sympathetic characters and yet also engage in acts of disturbing villainy. Still, even the Princess Pea faces this same dichotomy, becoming aware of "how fragile her heart was, how much darkness was inside it, fighting, always, with the light" (264). Pea discovers, though, that she can "save her own heart" by forgiving Roscuro, an important theme of the text. Despereaux has a similar experience, forgiving his father's betrayal "because he sensed that it was the only way to save his own heart, to stop it from breaking in two," a point the narrator emphasizes via direct address, commenting that "Despereaux, reader, spoke those words to save himself" (208). Unlike Despereaux and Pea, who find peace in forgiving, Roscuro must seek forgiveness instead of giving it, and thus ends the story torn: "he was allowed to go back and forth from the darkness of the dungeon to the light of the upstairs. But, alas, he never really belonged in either place, the sad fate, I am afraid, of those whose hearts break and then mend in crooked ways" (266). This is a central message of the book; although all individuals possess darkness and light, forgiveness given and received can lessen their burden. Moreover, Roscuro complicates this, demonstrating that even those who are forgiven may never truly find peace.

I take the time to explicate the notions of binaries and the primary themes about forgiveness that DiCamillo constructs in her novel because these elements, although present in the 2008 adaptation, are substantially reordered, repositioned, and recontextualized because of the polarization of binaries in the film. The story's major themes regarding darkness, light, and forgiveness are the driving force of the film—thematic amplification at its finest. Yet this focus also intensifies binaries of the text, so that characters do not explore or represent internal intermingling of binary oppositions, but instead possess just one or the other, especially in the ways they move from good to evil and back again.

In addition to offering another example of the link between thematic amplification and binary polarization, *Despereaux* also offers a unique example of overlapping and intermingling binaries. For in polarizing binaries of good/evil, the film also creates a greater polarization between binaries of conformity/rebellion and adult/child, resulting in key overall ideological differences, especially in how the film represents the concept of forgiveness, as well as how adult/child power dynamics work when it comes to forgiving and being forgiven.

Viewers can see this most strongly in the film's depiction of Roscuro, who is positioned as the movie's central character, and for whom darkness and light do not internally coexist, but act as binary forces between which he moves. Herein, viewers can see how an amplified emphasis on forgiveness in the film not only affects representation of adult/child binaries, but also affects the overall take-away messages of the movie and the ideologies that go along with this reworking of power structures. Rather than positing that good and evil exist within each of us, the film suggests the asking for or giving of forgiveness is crucial in a choice between darkness and light. This is an important distinction because it emphasizes the idea that an act of choice—the choice to ask for or grant forgiveness—determines an individual's relative darkness or light. No longer are these binaries intermingled within all people (or mice and rats); instead, individuals must decide between good and evil, and they do so by either asking for forgiveness (if they are adults) or granting such requests (if they are children). This substantially reworks power dynamics in ways stemming directly from the polarization of good/evil and adult/child binaries in the text.

Roscuro demonstrates this idea most clearly. Instead of being initially introduced by the definition of his name, "the arrangement of light and dark, darkness and light together" (85), Roscuro arrives on the scene bathed in light and eager to experience the magical soup of Dor. Although he mistakenly scares the queen to death as in the novel, Roscuro remains an endearing character, consistently resisting Botticelli's villainous influence and even saving Despereaux from him, then teaming with the mouse as brothers in arms. This relationship, which is absent from the novel, reinforces the book's messages about individuality over conformity, for not only do Roscuro and Despereaux both resist separate oppressive adult forces, but they are supported by each other in these endeavors.

In addition to amplifying themes related to conformity, shifts in Roscuro's characterization reposition him as a hero forced into darkness, instead of having internalized both darkness and light. As in the novel, Roscuro is pushed to hatred by Princess Pea's withering stare, but this does not occur immediately after her mother's death in the film. Instead, Roscuro dramatically flees the scene to live in despair and shame until, at Despereaux's suggestion, he seeks forgiveness from the Princess Pea. It is only in asking for forgiveness and failing to receive it that he embraces the dark, and he only does so momentarily, eventually returning to hero status by saving Pea from the dangerous rat underground community. In this, Roscuro does not represent the concept of darkness and light together, but a linear progression from light to darkness and a return to light. As in the *Coraline* adaptation, this harkens back to Wojcik-Andrews use of Kuhn's term of "disruption-resolution" (258)—changes in plot and characterization shift novel elements to fit the typical structure of children's film. By molding Roscuro's character into this narrative structure, the film does not stress an overlapping between light and dark or good and evil, but rather polarizes these binaries and suggests that characters can move between them, rather than struggling to continually navigate the internalization of both simultaneously. The binaries in the film are not overlapping or intermingling, but diametrically opposed or defined as the absence of the other.

This binary polarization affects the themes, messages, and ideologies presented in the text. First, rather than highlighting Roscuro's ongoing struggle, the film posits Roscuro as a savior, for upon seeing the evil ways of the rat community (a concept amplified in the film by the somewhat horrific arena scenes), he literally wields the light through a refraction of mirrors, saving Pea and killing Botticelli. In doing so, he becomes truly good again, while also overturning the oppressive social structure of the rat community. DiCamillo's textual Roscuro similarly has a change of heart when he smells the soup and is reminded that all he ever wanted was "some beauty . . . some light of my own" (263), but the film's Roscuro does not simply have a crisis of conscience. Instead, he becomes the hero, asking for forgiveness a second time instead of pleading for death as an end to his miserable turmoil (as in the book). DiCamillo's Roscuro never actually asks for forgiveness or forgives Pea for her part in his heartbreak, but is simply overcome by his intense despair. Pea forgives him, offering that if he turns from the darkness and leads them to freedom, she will give him a place in the light, where he can even eat soup in the banquet hall. Forgiveness is thus important in the novel, but not an all-powerful agent of change, for Roscuro still ends the story with a "sad fate."

In contrast, the film amplifies this message, especially in its climax. Again, like in the *Coraline* film, this is a scene added to enhance a key theme, and filmmakers make dozens, even hundreds, of specific mise-en-scène choices to craft it. These choices are not arbitrary, but intentional, working together to reinforce the theme. In what is perhaps the most pivotal moment of the movie, Roscuro watches the princess tied in the arena, and Botticelli tells him it is his responsibly to facilitate her death. Camera shots make clear the power dynamic between them, alternating between shots of the restrained princess taken from above to shots from below looking up at Roscuro. Sound editing also plays a role, with a building score melded with the chanting of the rats. Then suddenly, filmmakers backlight Roscuro (or simulate a backlight effect, since the film is animated), and the action of the story pauses.

The narrator interjects, "Ok, remember when we said that grief was the strongest thing a person could feel?" As she speaks these words, the camera focuses on Roscuro, holding a weapon-like bone in the foreground of the shot. Then the camera focus shifts, and the previously fuzzy image of the princess behind Roscuro comes into sharp focus as the narrator continues, "Well, it isn't. It's forgiveness. Because a single act of forgiveness can change everything." Here, filmmakers are mimicking the second-person narration style of the novel, but to interrupt the action of a climax in film makes this choice particularly distinctive. Camerawork reinforces this, as the camera then zooms to Roscuro's eyes, which soften, then become determined, and he utters simply "no." This is a conversion moment for him, and one which puts forth even more strongly the novel's notion that to forgive is, as DiCamillo similarly uses her narrator to point out, "a powerful, wonderful thing" (207). In this way, the movie presents a message from the book, but in a more obvious, dramatic way, and within the more polarized binary system that posits Roscuro as hero made villain and redeemed.

While this is a memorable moment, the details are what matter; camerawork, lighting, sound, and mise-en-scène elements work together to focus on a theme. As such, viewers can see two concepts at play here: an amplification of the importance of forgiveness and a widened binary between good and evil. More importantly, these elements change the message and ideologies presented by the text. For the novel versions of both Despereaux and Pea, the act of forgiving saves their hearts from being overcome with darkness, even though the darkness may still remain. The same is suggested by the narrator of the film, but the emphasis is shifted from forgiving to asking for forgiveness, for after heroically saving her, Roscuro tells Pea "I'm sorry"—the second time he has said these words to her. Pea responds to his asking for forgiveness not by saying she grants it, but admitting blame, saying "I'm the one who should be sorry." Here Pea (a clear child character) is reestablishing the adult-child hierarchy between her and Roscuro by admitting to her own culpability in the situation.

This scene demonstrates that the polarization of binaries surely affects the messages of the film, in this case altering the commentary on forgiveness. Still, this change also bears greater significance because the result of this polarization of good/evil, conformity/independence, and adult/child binaries also affects the power dynamics of the text, wherein implicit ideologies about adults and children also shift. In the novel, action focuses on adults asking children for forgiveness, as when DiCamillo's version of Despereaux's father, Lester, goes against the mouse community in a singular act of rebellion, ignoring the head mouse and begging Despereaux's forgiveness. This scene is cut from the film, but in the book, it demonstrates an adult rebelling, suggesting that this kind of resistance to conformity is not regulated simply to the young. In the film, adults are more consistently aligned with conformity.

Moreover, the book focuses on Despereaux's choice to forgive, while in the movie, the value of forgiving is secondary to the asking of forgiveness. The filmmakers use techniques specific to film to highlight this point in two ways. First, resolution in children's film is often visually depicted through montage, and *Tale of Despereaux* is no exception. After Roscuro and Pea exchange the sentiment "I'm sorry," the viewer is taken on a journey throughout the kingdom, hearing "I'm sorry" again spoken by two other adult characters, Mig's father and the King. Then, animators simulate a specific lighting choice, wherein sunlight literally returns to the kingdom just as these adult characters ask for forgiveness from those over whom they hold power, just as Roscuro says he is sorry in the moment of his greatest power, when he holds the bone with which to strike the gong that would begin the attack on Pea, who is physically bound in the rat arena. This not only stresses asking for forgiveness over granting it, but it also suggests the need for the powerful to seek forgiveness from those they oppress in order for light to overcome darkness. This is a theme that emerges in the film but is largely absent from the text, which instead suggests that it is forgiving, not asking for forgiveness, that brings peace.

This change is not necessarily negative, for an emphasis on the importance of forgiving others seems a thoughtful and powerful sentiment. Still, I think it is worthy of particular note that this new or shifted ideology is born out of the greater binary system of the film, which changes Roscuro's role in the story and alters the level to which dark/light and good/evil can overlap and intermingle. What is more, this shift happens not through a distortion of the primary messages of DiCamillo's work, but in an attempt to reinforce them. Still, in this case, the result is not just a stronger message, but one that refigures power dynamics in critical ways by upsetting hierarchies and systems in conflict between the powerful and the powerless.

Again, this concept exists in DiCamillo's novel, but by connecting the characters through the "I'm sorry" montage wherein those in power ask for forgiveness, this message is made more explicit in the film. The distinction between the powerful and the powerless amplifies what the text is saying about forgiveness, but in doing so, it changes the text's message. The final "I'm sorry" scene stresses not only powerful, but also adult characters who ask for forgiveness. This is true of the book as well, for Despereaux's father asks Despereaux to forgive him. However, by expanding this notion to emphasize other adult characters not simply being forgiven, but also asking for forgiveness, the film's emphasis suggests a slightly different way of thinking about the roles of adults and children and how these intersect with the binary of conformity versus rebellion.

The binaries of powerful/powerless, conformity/rebellion, and even adult/child are not only widened, but the film's more explicit ideology that adults must sometimes ask forgiveness from their children also results in further implicit ideological implications. For although this new structure might seem to reverse the adult/child hierarchy, it actually results in a reestablishment of adult power in the text, for after asking for forgiveness, both Mig's father and the king return to a clearer place in the adult/child hierarchy. In the movie, child characters disagree with adult decisions and, in doing so, help to overturn the detrimental systems of the kingdom, including the soup ban, Mig's oppressed position, and the gladiator-style underground arena of the rat world. Thus, the film not only amplifies adults asking for forgiveness, a concept that only Despereaux's father exemplifies in the novel, but it also creates an ideology that the youth of a society can and should attempt to fix the adult world.

Readers could discern this emphasis on child rebellion followed by a return to adult/child power constructs in DiCamillo's novel as well, for there is certainly a positive reinforcement of Despereaux and Roscuro's attempts to resist conformity, and indeed, positive change exists in the book. Mig similarly reunites with her father, who "to atone for what he had done, treated her like one [a Princess] for the rest of his days" (267). The soup ban is apparently lifted, as the narrator asks the reader to imagine all of the characters eating soup together in the final scene, including both sets of parents (the King/Queen and Lester/Antoinette), who either maintain or reassert adult/child hierarchies. But the film's polarized binary between good/evil and adult/child climactically demonstrated by a heroic Roscuro defeating the evil of the rat community (which he essentially dismantles in killing the aged Botticelli) seems to take this idea of rebelling against conformity further. Furthermore, it is this kind of ideological implication that I suggest is a key result of the binary polarization that exists in nearly all children's and YA film adaptations.

Shifts and alterations in the ideologies presented by the film version of *Despereaux* are not arbitrary decisions, but a result from more polarized binaries in the adaptation than in its source. Seen through this lens, the reasons for the changes that moviemakers employed make sense—they not only fit the structure and context of typical children's film, but they also frequently result from an amplification of theme. Moreover, if we see changes in this light—as a result rather than a distortion, I do not think that we can fault the film as "less than" the book. Certainly, I could go on to critique animation style or dialogue choice, but as an adaptation—a separate entity that is nonetheless inextricably linked to its predecessor—the text does not fail, and it does not distort. It is simply different, and while those differences, especially in their ideological implications related to power dynamics between adults and children, are exceptionally interesting, we can look at them from a viewpoint that does not evaluate comparatively, but compares to understand the ways binary polarization impacts the kinds of messages a text can send.

I reiterate this idea not only because it is why I think it valuable to consider trends based in binaries and ideologies when theorizing adapted children's and YA film, but also because it offers a certain kind of analysis—one which illuminates differences without a hierarchy between book and film. In the next example I explore, however, I consider another kind of analysis and critique, wherein I analyze ideological implications of thematic amplification and binary polarization for their potential problematics.

How to Train Your Text and What Happens When You Do

The 2010 adaptation of *How to Train Your Dragon* certainly provides further evidence to support that thematic amplification leading to binary polarization is more than just an isolated occurrence in these films, but is consistent across a huge number of children's and YA film adaptations. Yet this popular movie, produced by DreamWorks Animation and directed by Chris Sanders and Dean DeBlois, also offers additional insight into this trend. First, part of the way that binaries are polarized in this and other children's film is through overlap—like the other two examples I have explicated thus far, adult/child binaries are linked in the film version with good and evil, as well as conformity/rebellion or autonomy/dependence. In *How to Train Your Dragon*, however, an especially interesting new binary is also connected to these other concepts: self/other. By meshing these binaries together and polarizing them collectively, ideological implications take on even greater weight, for while a good/evil or autonomy/dependence binary might offer representation that can be interpreted in a variety of ways, when the binary of self/other is polarized, the resulting changes in power dynamics is likely to be negative.

This leads to the second reason why it is important to further consider the emphasis on adult/child binaries as frequently the most polarized in children's adapted film. Examining *How to Train Your Dragon* opens a discussion of the potential problematics of polarization. In general, it is my supposition that, as I describe in the *Tale of Despereaux*, muddling of binary opposition makes for a more interesting story. But on the flip side of this, I believe it important to consider whether polarization of some binaries, such as self/other, is going to result in a problematic depiction more often than not. In fact, I would go so far as to say that it seems worth considering whether in certain cases, such polarization is inherently negative.

Taking this approach treads dangerously close to an evaluative or hierarchical stance, however, which is why I first describe polarization in two texts wherein the ideological ramifications of this polarization are not necessarily negative. I do not think that all binary polarization in film adaptations necessarily equates to problematic ideological implications. Still, I also think that it is necessary to take a critical eye to the results of this trend. As I have described, the hierarchies inherent to binary systems often reflect an unequal distribution of power, and consequently, polarization of this inequality can have concerning results. When power differentials are reflected in self/other (or, as I will discuss more in the next chapter, male/female) binaries, the results have the strong potential to be problematic.

This is what I will explore in the example of *How to Train Your Dragon*, which not only follows the same pattern in thematic amplification causing binary polarization as in *The Tale of Despereaux* and *Coraline*, but also reflects a similarly consistent focus on adult/child dynamics and an overlay of binary systems. What most distinguishes this film is that it cannot be considered a transposition. Unlike the film versions of DiCamillo's or Gaiman's texts, which hold to major plot and character developments of the novel, *How to Train Your Dragon* eliminates main plot points, adds new ones, and dramatically changes both events and relationships to create a story with a far greater degree of divergence from its source text. Yet even though the movie version seems a very different text than its novel counterpart, all significant changes still have a basis (albeit a loose one) in the book's primary messages and themes.

This leads to one further reason for why *How to Train Your Dragon* offers an important film to consider when theorizing children's adapted film. In addition to its usefulness in providing further evidence of a trend and exploring the potential problematics of polarization, this example seems to suggest that when dramatic changes are made and substantial additional content is added to reinforce or make more explicit the messages of a source text, binary polarization is also greater. Furthermore, because new content is necessarily going to engage with contemporary cultural context, there is potential for a more significant polarization to also further reinforce the potentially negative ideological implications associated with that polarization. The film adaptation of *How to Train Your Dragon* offers a strong example of this phenomenon.

Cressida Cowell's books are humorous middle-grade series texts, each recounting an adventure of Hiccup Horrendous Haddock III and his dragon, Toothless. Hiccup catches Toothless in the initial volume as part of the Dragon Initiation Test, and his successful ability to train him is the first of many rites of initiation as a Viking. Herein lies the most significant difference between *How to Train Your Dragon* and its movie adaptation: whereas it is part of Viking culture to capture and train dragons in Cowell's novel, the film version begins by describing dragons as the enemy of the Vikings, and what defines their community is the perpetual battle raging between them. Hiccup recounts in the opening film sequence that he wishes to "make his mark" by killing a dragon, because it would make his life "infinitely better" and he "might even get a date." In the film, Hiccup only seeks to train Toothless when he discovers he cannot kill him as he has intended. This act of compassion spawns a friendship that ultimately allows Hiccup to not only save the Viking community, but also to turn their opinion of dragons from "pests" to "pets."

Especially in a movie made from a children's novel, where it is infrequently necessary to add substantial content in order for a plot to fill the length requirements of a feature film, critics might wonder what purpose is served in such substantial changes. Again, it is worth mentioning that these changes are not coincidental or even simply choices made by the production team; rather, shifts in the story are driven by the context and materiality of children's film, which exists in contrast to a novel, and especially a novel like Cowell's series. In this case, part of the reason for such a substantial change might be explained in the ways the episodic humor of Cowell's series does not fit with the climactic plotline viewers expect from children's animated film. This divergence in part results from the producers' desire to meet with audience expectation, but there are factors based on the timetable and structure of film as well. The rise and fall of action in the book is difficult to achieve over the shortened time of film, and humor is achieved very differently in vocal and visual medias than in written text, both elements influenced by the simple fact that film and novels do different work—produced with differing contextual expectation and engaged with in very different physical and temporal spaces.

Regardless of reason, this choice also fits exactly with a trend in polarization of binary systems. While catching and training the dragon in the novel is interesting and humorous, these acts do not hold the same intensity as the film's conflict between Vikings and dragons at war. Certainly, there is animosity between Hiccup and Toothless, but in pitting the dragon and Viking communities as enemies, this binary reflects not just conflict, but an exploration of self versus other whereby the two are diametrically opposed. Nonetheless, the underlying drive of the film is one based on the book—Hiccup's curiosity and desire to understand Toothless. In the movie, however, the conflict of dragon versus Viking leads Hiccup to examine how different the two really are and if they can indeed be defined in a hierarchical opposition.

Additionally, Hiccup finds that his attempt to interact differently with Toothless puts him at odds with traditional models of Viking, thus identifying him as an outsider in his community. Although alluded to in the novel, when this idea is placed in the polarized system of dragon versus Viking, a new ideology emerges. Hiccup feels "different," which contributes to his ability to identify with Toothless, thus presenting the very basic message that different is not bad, a concept made far more explicit in the movie. The increased emphasis on this message results in a significant ideological divergence; in the film, curiosity and a unique perspective does not just lead to connection, but a connection that is socially and culturally charged.

The film achieves this amplification and new ideology by using a technique similar to *The Tale of Despereaux*. Just as the montage scene of "I'm sorry" suggests an overlap and connection of various elements of the story to move toward a cohesive thematic framework, *How to Train Your Dragon* does the same. In this case, there are three conflicts at play, each of which reinforces the idea that overcoming difference can be done through learning about the other, suggesting that increased knowledge can result in greater understanding and subsequently, peace. The film connects Hiccup with his Father, Hiccup with Toothless, and the Vikings with the dragons to achieve this idea, for each pair begins at odds, but learns to understand and appreciate the other, ultimately leading to peace and contentment at the level of both family and community.

First, Hiccup begins the story in conflict with his father, perhaps best summarized when Hiccup gives a sarcastic impression of him, saying "Excuse me, barmaid? I'm afraid you brought me the wrong offspring. I ordered an extra-large boy with beefy arms, extra guts and glory on the side. This here, this is a talking fish-bone," to which his mentor Gobber responds, "Now you're thinkin' about this all wrong. It's not so much what you look like, it's what inside that he can't stand." Similarly, as Hiccup begins to chronicle what he learns about Toothless, he discovers "everything we know about you guys is wrong," including the idea that they are entirely different and natural enemies. But at the heart of the story is the conflict between Viking and dragon, which Hiccup learns exists because the dragons must bring food to a terrifyingly massive dragon overlord or else be eaten themselves. It is this imperative that drives them to torment the Vikings, and without this domineering force, the Vikings need only to attempt to reach out to the dragons to become not only allies, but also companions mimicking contemporary human/pet relationships.

Again, viewers see two factors at work—an increase in conflict and a widening of binaries. Just as in *Coraline* and *The Tale of Despereaux*, conflict between the adult and child characters of the text is increased, and again, this reflects a greater binary between concepts of adult and child, thus making it more difficult for the young protagonist and his parental figure to navigate what it means to be adult versus child. As before, this conflict is textually founded, for in the novel, Hiccup's father even exiles him and the other boys when chaos at the Thor'sday Thursday celebrations causes them to fail the Viking initiation test. Stoick the Vast laments this decision, worrying "what kind of father *did* put his precious Laws before the life of his son? But then what kind of son would fail the precious Laws that his father had looked up to and believed in all his life?" (129). Here, though, readers can note another muddling between the concepts of adult and child, with Stoick's uncertainty complicating any clear hierarchy between the two.

In the film, the conflict between father and son is increased, thus reflecting a greater conceptual difference between notions of adult versus child. Stoick as father more clearly represents the traditional, problematic worldview in sharp contrast to Hiccup's progressive, productive way of thinking, so that even as Hiccup initially seeks to be more adult, the story eventually demonstrates his youthful viewpoint as the better of the two. Once again, even this temporary reversal of power between adult and child is exactly that—temporary. Not only does the story end with a return to traditional adult/child power structures when Stoick realizes his mistake, but Hiccup also matures significantly in the story, eventually being recognized as an adult or mature Viking. Although Hiccup ends the story with greater power and agency than he began his journey with, he does so only by developing in a way that brings him closer to being an adult member of his community.

Furthermore, in the film, Stoick seemingly does not attempt to learn about his son or understand their difference; instead he simply wishes to make Hiccup more like him. This lies at the heart of their difficult relationship, and because this message is so obviously layered over Hiccup's growing understanding and thus respect for his supposed enemy, Toothless, it reinforces the adult/child binary, but it also strengthens the self/other binary. This makes for an even stronger explicit message in the end of the film, when being different and seeking to understand or learn about someone who is different is not just positive, but instrumental in saving their community.

This concept that children can or must save their communities is common in much of children's literature. Yet I think it takes on a much greater role in children's film, a point I will explore further in the examples of picturebook to film adaptation, wherein this element seems especially weighty. This concept is certainly reinforced in the film adaptation of *How to Train Your Dragon*, where despite being indoctrinated to believe in killing dragons, Hiccup is incapable of doing so because he, also feeling as an outsider in his community, sees that Toothless is "just as scared as I was," a realization that provokes both compassion for his enemy and a desire to know him better. Again, this derives from the action of the book; Hiccup similarly tries to learn about Toothless in order to train him because the direction given to him—"yell at it! (the louder the better)" (57)—is unsuccessful. Hiccup in the novel has a natural curiosity about dragons, having attempted to learn their language before even meeting Toothless. Still, the film takes this curiosity to a dramatic new level, for the desire to learn about Toothless is not for the purpose of more effective training in an attempt to be a better Viking. Instead, doing so goes against the beliefs of his community. This mimics the *Tale of Despereaux* film in its favoring individuality over conformity and similarly leads to a change in culture. In this way, both films offer an amplification of explicit messages, but also shift implicit messages.

Additionally, and as I have described in both *Coraline* and *Tale of Despereaux*, the specific form of film exists at the heart of this polarization, and amplification of this message is driven by specific filmmaking technique. Music and sound, for example, play a significant role in this film, especially in showing Toothless's transformation from feared other to trusted friend. When Hiccup first returns to the valley because he has begun to suspect what he has been taught about dragons is false, he emerges slowly, set to music that intensifies this suspense and paints Toothless as frightening and suspicious. This music ends as Hiccup approaches the fearsome dragon, and his caution is intensified as Toothless growls and snorts, sounds created by a sound mixing and editing team. When Toothless grabs the fish, the music again begins quietly and after he swallows it, he advances on Hiccup. The music here is very different, with a staccato alternating tone creating a light, bouncy rhythm of curiosity and expectation. As the two observe each other and Hiccup realizes that Toothless wishes him to share the food, new notes are added to the music to shift this again, creating a buoyancy to the sound that represents a growing connection.

The addition of tones and new instruments continues as the scene develops and Hiccup cautiously learns more about his new friend, connecting with him.

The music becomes increasingly complex in structure as this happens, building and swelling until a pivotal part of this connection, at which point, the music pauses and voices simulating awe are added to emphasize the significance of the movement. Hiccup, with great attempts at deference and respect, touches Toothless, with music and lighting both seeming to glow around him. The music and sound choices of this scene, which takes place over nearly five minutes but has very little dialogue, create a profound sense of emotion and suggest that Hiccup's willingness, even eagerness, to learn about his enemy transforms that enemy into a friend. The self/other binary is established in the film, new from the book, only to be broken down as a way of amplifying a key theme.

The greater self/other binary derived from the positioning of dragons as enemy builds to a far more dramatic climax in the film than in the novel, for although the movie mirrors the novel in featuring a final showdown between the Vikings and a terrible giant dragon, this scene in the film sends a very different message. In both texts, Hiccup and his young friends work with the dragons to defeat the dragon monster, but in the film, this represents a paradigm shift; after that point, the dragons are no longer seen as enemy, but more as domestic animals—somewhere between a pet and a beast of burden like a horse. To make this change and suggest that learning about individuals of another culture can eliminate them as an enemy, however, the film must depict the giant dragon monster in some way that differentiates him from the other dragons, making him (but not them) the true villain. The movie facilitates this by explaining that all the other dragons are subservient to this ancient beast, bringing him food and other offerings they catch by attacking the Vikings in order to save being eaten themselves.

This refigures the clever, riddle-loving but independent giant dragon of Cowell's novel as a nameless dictatorial dragon ruler who controls the kinder, though misunderstood other dragons like Toothless. Attempting to learn about the dragons helps Hiccup to see this distinction between the dragon dictator and other dragons in the film, an insight that allows him to draw a clear division between good/evil, as is frequently a part of children's film. Critics have commented on this element most frequently in criticized Disney retellings. A. Waller Hastings, for example, suggests that Disney perpetuates conservative ideologies by simplifying moral complexities in films such as *The Little Mermaid*, which "encourages a pervasive world view that sees malignant evil, not human fallibility, as the chief source of conflict . . . [for] in a Manichean world, one party to any conflict must always be 'bad,' and the other 'good'" (90). The *How to Train Your Dragon* film presents just such a Manichean worldview, wherein combining messages of the novel with this polarized good/evil distinction offers an interesting ideology not present in its source text.

The film positively depicts Hiccup's desire and efforts to learn more about dragon culture, which eventually leads to an end to the Viking/dragon conflict. This suggests the same underlying ideology of the novel (the usefulness of learning about those who seem different than us), but amplifies it by positioning self/other and good/evil as more polar opposites. In the climate of contemporary world politics, however, the way this ideology is amplified also suggests it as somewhat of a metaphor. It seems no accident that the ancient, powerful, evil dragon of the film rules and defines the dragon culture through fear, and it is in following this leader that the other dragons take on the perception of similarly violent, frightening enemies. This depiction plays into the ideologies Hastings describes as part of the Disney hegemony built out of a specific political climate, one he identifies in chronicling the "transformation of the Gulf War from a geopolitical conflict into a crusade against the person of Saddam Hussein" (90). To a certain extent, contemporary American politics continue to reinforce this ideology, and individuals like Osama bin Laden seem to play a similar role. It seems not a great leap to see this ideology reflected in the figuring of the dragon dictator, because of whom the misunderstood dragon community commits violent acts. Yet the film takes this ideology one step further, suggesting that an overthrow of this evil individual begins when two cultures seek to learn about and understand one another more fully.

By engaging with this ideology from contemporary culture, the film uses the value the novel places on learning as a means to cooperation, but amplifies this message and combines it with additional content. This shifts the text's implicit ideologies. By engaging with ideas related to contemporary international conflict, the film presents a changed, even new commentary on the danger of preconceived perceptions versus the positives that come from learning, even study of another culture (as Hiccup chronicles what he learns about the dragons in a journal). What is more, Hiccup is the only Viking able to see past what he is told to believe about dragons and look for something more, suggesting the role of the youth of a community to do this work.

This ideological framework represents not a distortion of the source text, but the result of using contemporary cultural beliefs and values to mold the novel's messages into a system of greater binaries and amplified explicit ideologies. The book, although certainly touching on notions of knowledge-building and even ideas about difference, does not emphasize this in a way that alludes to *cultural* differences because the dragons are not the Vikings' enemy—they are animals, either domesticated or dangerous, but not standing in for an enemy culture. In the film, ideologies change because of the polarization of self/other binaries reflected in increased conflict, whereby dragons start as both enemy and other, and become like a pet (perhaps friend, but not an equal).

It nonetheless seems worth noting the additional and perhaps unintended result of fashioning a new ideology about overcoming cultural differences while still holding to the basic premise of the novel. Toothless, although powerful and independent, fulfills the role of friend in the way of a pet. How does the idea that we might overcome differences through knowledge and compassion and thus end a war with an enemy change when that enemy also becomes a domesticated animal in the community? I am not sure I can offer a firm answer to this question, but it certainly seems troubling. Toothless is one of the most endearing creatures animated in recent years, but if we are meant to see him as representative of another culture as the film seems to suggest, it seems problematic that after a dramatic cultural paradigm shift, he goes from being an enemy to a domesticated, albeit powerful, pet.

This is just one reading, however, and one based within a particular line of critical interpretive practice that explores a possible metaphor put forth by animal characters to problematize the ideologies that might result from such an interpretation. Taken another way, the dictatorial dragon might actually represent fear itself, which enslaves both the dragons and Vikings. In this case, we might see the dragon community not as culturally divergent, but representing a difference in species. If Toothless is only an animal (after all, he lacks many human characteristics and social structures we associate with human communities), then this changes the message as well, for if he is simply a pet, then he instead offers an example of actual human/pet relationships that can teach us a great deal about caring for others, identifying unspoken needs, and offering respect and compassion to those different from ourselves.

Still, I would suggest the media of film allows for producers to create Toothless as "more" than a pet, even if this is all he is truly meant to represent. While Toothless in the book clearly takes on this role despite his ability to communicate with Hiccup, the movie version of Toothless engages in movements and articulations that seem more human than animal. Again, this is a product of the nature of film, not only because it is common in children's film for animals to be anthropomorphized in this way (aka, in nearly every Disney movie ever made), but also because film allows and even necessitates this kind of animated depiction. When authors write a story about a dragon, you can easily make clear its status as pet, but when animators bring it to life within the context of a substantial antecedent precedence of animal animation, it is difficult to do anything else but make it appear human, thus opening the film up to questions of animal as human metaphor.

In either case, the film offers a meshing of novel elements with new elements added in the film to amplify conflict and messages. If the film suggests that learning about someone who is different (either in terms of culture or species) and believed to be an enemy can foster a more positive relationship, this lesson only seems productive if the power dynamic between these two individuals is equal. In a pet relationship, the power dynamic is inherently unequal because of the relationship between human beings and animals. But when learning results in one culture holding power over the other, whether enemy or not, increased knowledge and understanding loses its value. Thus, this message works well in the book when the dragons are always animals, never really standing in for a divergent culture. When this ideology is amplified in a way that connects the dragon to notions of cultural difference, the messages sent about relationships between self and other become far more complex and even problematic.

Once again, I explore these ideological shifts and compare messages in novel and film not to criticize the movie, which I believe to be a thoughtful and interesting children's film filled with unique complexity and some very positive depictions, especially regarding gender and perhaps even disability. Instead, I am suggesting *How to Train Your Dragon* fits a pattern—one wherein the film adaptation amplifies themes, and especially explicit ideologies and textual conflict, thus widening binaries. Furthermore, I posit that this pattern can be applied to nearly all children's adapted films. While I have thus far suggested thematic amplification as a key cause for this pattern, other adaptation situations offer even more insight into other factors at work, as well as the kinds of ideological implications resulting from the binary polarization I have discussed thus far, which I will continue to explore in subsequent chapters.

CHAPTER THREE

Female Saviors in
Adolescent Film Adaptations

Thus far, I have focused on the causes of binary polarization, describing the ways that filmmakers often focus on a key theme of a source text and make it the central message of the adaptation, and by amplifying a theme, also push concepts like adult/child, independent/dependent, and self/other further apart. While I have concentrated on causes of binary polarization, I have also hinted at some results, pointing out a few of the ideological implications of this polarization. As such, I have contended that the ideological results of widening the divide between such concepts as adult/child and self/other are significant, but in the examples explicated thus far, the effect on ideology varies, depending on what messages the source text includes, what themes were chosen to amplify, and what binaries are affected.

There are, however, some more consistent results of binary polarization, and therefore, in the next several chapters, I will look at three groups of texts in a little more depth, offering examples of patterns I notice in the effect that binary polarization has on certain kinds of children's and young adult adapted films. For although the ideological changes that result from binary polarization in the movies I have discussed so far have depended upon the messages and power dynamics in the original texts, this is not the case within other sets of adaptations for young viewers, and in particular, films adapted from adolescent fiction. In this group of texts, there exists a surprising level of consistency in the ideological ramifications of thematic amplification and binary polarization.

First, while a variety of binaries are polarized in films adapted from young adult texts, male/female binaries are frequently at the center of this polarization and resulting ideological shifts. Not only are concepts of masculinity and femininity more diametrically opposed in the film versions of these novels for teens, but in nearly all of the examples I have studied, binary polarization also shifts depictions of female characters to position them as the emotional and spiritual saviors of their male counterparts. By focusing on the story's romance, a striking number of contemporary YA film adaptations reverse traditional male/female power dynamics by highlighting a man saved by a woman he loves, and yet binary polarization in these cases nonetheless results in a recreation of unequal power structures.

As I started noticing this pattern within the greater trend of binary polarization of film adaptation, my first question was to ask why: what makes adolescent film adaptations unique from others in a way that would mean that binary polarization produces this consistent ideology. Answering this question is part of my focus in this chapter, but it is also something I believe important to interrogate in all of the individual text sets wherein binary polarization affects ideologies. My overall goal is thus twofold in this and subsequent chapters. First, in order to demonstrate that there are commonalities in the kinds of ideological results of thematic amplification and binary polarization, I consider one key result of binary polarization in each chapter. Secondly, I put these results in context by exploring some of the factors unique to the situation in which such films are embedded. While the causes of binary polarization I have examined so far certainly play a role in YA novel to film adaptations, there are also some specific qualities of YA films that may account in part for the consistency of the figure of the female savior. As such, while this and the next two chapters are focused on "results" of binary polarization, they continue to explore causes as well.

To begin this work with YA film adaptations, I first explain the subtrend of the female savior by interrogating an example in which the female hero literally brings the male character back to life: the zombie romance, *Warm Bodies*. I then look at three possible reasons that polarization of binaries leads to this type of ideology. I first use Mike Cadden's discussion of single- and double-voiced discourse in YA literature to suggest that shifts in point of view might contribute to binary polarization causing a consistent focus on the female savior. Subsequently, I posit that contemporary film's investment in strong female heroines acts as an additional contributing factor linking binary polarization to ideologies of the female savior, suggesting that although such a portrayal is a laudable goal, it often actually adds to polarization, repositioning ideologies to consistently suggest that women are the ones to inspire, while men are the ones in need of such inspiration.

Next, I use Laura Mulvey's theory of the male gaze to posit a third factor in the repeated portrayal of the female emotional savior in YA film, suggesting that polarization is often problematically linked to film choices that promote objectification. In young adult movies, and far more than in the novels upon which they are based, the gaze is exemplified by moments with two levels of watching: film choices direct the audience to stare at a teen male who is gazing at a female teen, a move sometimes also paired with characterization linking her to the concept of the Manic Pixie Dream Girl. I then close the chapter by concluding that shifts in point of view, attempts at female empowerment, and traps of the male gaze and Manic Pixie Dream Girl not only create a female savior, but in doing so, also produce a film that is far more single-voiced than its textual predecessor.

Loving Her Makes Me More Human

What strikes me most about the subtrend of the female savior within the greater trend of binary polarization in YA fiction adaptations is that it is not subtle—it is a pattern that surprises me in its consistency and the obvious way films participate in it. Certainly, books participate in this idea as well, but amplification of theme in YA film often also leads to simplified and intensified characterization. In the books upon which these films are based, both male and female characters struggle with questions of self, power, and their place in society. In the film adaptations, far more than in their novel predecessors, women do not seem to require or engage in such introspection, while the men are transformed—often quite literally—because they fall in love with powerful, beautiful young women. This is perhaps most obviously true in the film version of Isaac Marion's *Warm Bodies*, wherein the zombie protagonist, R, comes back to life because he falls in love with a human teen, Julie. R's humanity is restored when they kiss, and this acts as a catalyst for all zombies to regain life through interpersonal interaction.

Marion's *Warm Bodies* has been described as a zombie romance, and the film certainly accentuates this description. This emphasis on romantic elements as part of the shift from book to screen is not a new phenomenon. Whelehan draws from Wagner to suggest that classics like *Wuthering Heights* are often adapted "into heightened love stories" (Whelehan 9), because "a love interest is held to construe to audience interest almost exclusively" (Wagner 234). Rhonda Brock-Servais and Matthew Prickett agree, suggesting that female characters are often "not treated by their narratives as distinct individuals but are rather indicative of something greater—the romance" (224). They suggest that in a visual medium, "it's nearly impossible to show inner development of a character" (217), and they thus build on Hutcheon's description of showing versus telling to note that a focus on a character's romantic interactions allows introspective novels to make inner feelings and character growth visible.

While this is sometimes true, the use of romance to show a character's inner life often also has the opposite effect, so that romantic emphasis can diminish a focus on inner development, instead presenting flattened characters that make gender constructions appear more diametrically opposed. Again, this change results from a thematic amplification—but the themes accentuated in adolescent film are typically romance related, wherein the power of love takes center stage. While romantic development can be indicative of emotional development, most often, romantic amplification in film adaptations replaces character complexity with a binary, wherein men alone require or engage in introspective experiences, perhaps even unaware of their need for such self-questioning until they meet a female heroine. These women, who in the novel versions also question their purpose and role in society, instead seem to have risen above such feelings of powerlessness or insecurity in many film adaptations, thus being able to transform the inner lives of their male paramours and, by extension, sometimes transforming society as well.

It is the polarization of male/female binaries that creates this power dynamic. While male and female characters both display uncertainty and introspection in many teen novels, film adaptations of these texts shift roles to depict men and women as inherently different, so much so that the films seem to reverse traditional gender roles. By simply reversing the "violent hierarchy" that Derrida describes, these films do not eliminate it, but only create a new problematic. Not only do power dynamics continue to be unequal due to this polarization, but women also bear the responsibility to create more balanced and productive societies by civilizing their male counterparts. This may be a different kind of problematic social construction than one in which men save women from physical harm, but it is no less dangerous as an ideology.

The film version of *Warm Bodies* is a poignant example of this power dynamic, particularly because as zombie fiction, it already explores binaries and liminal spaces. As Shawn McIntosh describes, "The unique balancing act that zombies represent between control and enslavement, strength and weakness, us and them, and group versus individual identity offers a window into better understanding of . . . how we perceive ourselves and certain aspects of popular culture" (1). The novel version of *Warm Bodies* fits this assessment well. For example, Julie describes envying R's zombie status, especially after her boyfriend is killed, telling R "things are just . . . I feel things so hard sometimes. When that happened with Perry, I would have loved to be more . . . like you" (52). This sentiment suggests that she and R, although seemingly representing binaries of female/male, human/zombie, and alive/dead, are not so different, further emphasized because Julie's dialogue includes ellipses, a stylistic choice that typically characterizes R's broken zombie speech. Julie asks, "So if existence was just binary, dead or alive, here or not here, what would be the fucking point in anything?" (115), and this questioning of self invites the reader to ask similar questions, unpacking the complexity of liminal spaces.

The film eliminates nearly all of Julie's introspective questioning and instead positions her as the answer to these existential questions for her romantic partner. For R, Julie is the point to everything. This sets up a dynamic wherein she, existing above such liminality, is a goddess set against the monster that R represents. He is the beast, and she the beauty who saves him, a notion that differs from the book's extended meditation on and even celebration of the complexities of liminality. The film adaptation polarizes binaries of the text, separating concepts of alive and dead and male and female.

In the novel version of *Warm Bodies*, introspection not only characterizes Julie, but also the two male characters of the story: R and Julie's deceased boyfriend, Perry. When R eats Perry's brain, he gains the ability to tap into his angst-ridden memories and emotions, an experience that acts as a catalyst for R's self-reflection to take on a new complexity. The two young men eventually begin communicating during these visions, so that Perry actively participates in R's transformation, perhaps even more than Julie, while he also works through his own existential crisis. In fact, R learns that when Perry was alive, he questioned life's futility so deeply that he contemplated suicide, and in the novel, both young men discuss what it means to be alive. Like R, Perry also exists in a liminal space between life and death, and together, they question life, death, and what lies beyond, allowing readers to similarly delve into these complex questions.

Conversely, Perry's role in the film is very different, and like Julie, he lacks an introspective quality. While R does have visions of Perry's life, these focalize almost exclusively on his relationship with Julie, and there is only one scene in which these visions allow R to interact with Perry. In this scene, Perry is flippant and condescending, opening an opportunity for Julie to come to R's defense, saying R "can dream if he wants too" and asking R, "What about you, what do you want to be?" She specifically encourages him, saying, "You can be whatever you want." By replacing the parallel between Perry and R with Julie's articulation of the seeming solution to these questions in a more didactic way, the film not only polarizes the book's alive/dead binary, but it also greatly reduces the questions of self with which these young men struggle. Instead, R's romance with Julie is the focus in the film, rather than simply one part of two young men's more complex existential transformations.

More than love, R expresses in the novel that he yearns to want, to hope, to feel; he thinks, "I long for exclamation marks, but I'm drowning in ellipses" (59). Love may be part of this existential yearning, but falling for Julie acts more as the spark that ignites a host of other desires and feelings. In contrast, the film highlights Julie as the flirty, bright-eyed object of R's fixation. She lacks any of the angst she exhibits in the novel, and he is in awe of her. This begins in their meet-cute, a slow-motion shot set to the lyrics "There is a storm that's ranging through my frozen heart tonight," and extends to the film's climax, when R wants to protect Julie because saving her saves his soul. After R jumps from a skyscraper with Julie in his arms (placing himself so he will endure the impact), Julie pulls him from the pool in which they have landed, kissing him and returning him to his human state.

This is the element I wish to highlight—loving Julie does not simply metaphorically transform this male character, but *literally* brings him back to life. Moreover, while this is a part of both the film and the novel, the movie focalizes on the romantic elements and highlights R and Julie's relationship in order to accentuate this idea. More importantly, this ideological focus defines nearly all adolescent film adaptations I have studied, wherein young men wish to protect beautiful, striking teen women from harm, but it is the women who end up saving them by facilitating an emotional and, in this case, corresponding physical transformation.

By saving R, Julie saves the world. R's transformation into a more human incarnation of himself inspires (or perhaps infects—this point is somewhat unclear) the other zombies with similar hope, and in the end, the entire structure of society that places zombie versus human is dismantled because their love has begun a global change in zombie kind. In some ways, this offers a positive change of pace, and the feminist in me is somewhat pleased to watch a woman save the world. Yet I am also disappointed, for while power dynamics may appear dismantled, they are not; they are simply reversed, and once again, the responsibility is placed on a single individual in a romantic relationship to stand apart as strong, brave, and unwavering. Whether a male or female character, this paradigm is problematic, and it detracts from the work of the text to demonstrate both male and female adolescents as inquisitive, flawed, and strong all at once.

Furthermore, it seems to me that the techniques of character development inherent to film versus those utilized in adolescent novels might also help to unlock my central question of this chapter: why does polarization of binaries so often lead to an enhanced image of the "female savior" in these movies? Certainly, I think it important to problematize this ideology, especially because it reoccurs with such frequency. Far more than evaluating these movies for their merit, I am interested in exploring why this pattern occurs.

Narration and Power at the End of the World

In attempting to answer this question, I find myself drawn to Mike Cadden's distinction between single- and double-voiced discourse in adolescent fiction. Cadden suggests that while single-voiced texts reinforce vertical author/reader power hierarchies by offering only one correct ideology, an adolescent novel that engages double-voiced discourse, "achieved through providing multiple and equal YA consciousnesses and a clearly unreliable singular YA consciousness, provides the YA audience the tools to grow as readers" (153). This is possible even with a single narrator, he asserts, if that narrator offers "sufficient self-consciousness and self-questioning for a young reader to understand that ... [the] story that needs to be considered rather than just swallowed" (149). Cadden also quotes Elizabeth Schuhmann, who notes, "many advocates of novels written for young people have come to consider first-person narration a preferred technique for this kind of literature" (314).

Taken together, these two points can offer significant insight into a key difference between YA novels from their film adaptations. While adolescent fiction is often written in first person or focalized though a character so as to give access to that character's thoughts, film typically involves far less articulating of the self-consciousness or self-questioning Cadden describes as an important component of double-voiced discourse. Viewers watch characters, but almost never hear them think in the way of a novel. Instead, character thoughts must be conveyed visually.

I do not mean to suggest that film can be described simply as a third-person narrative structure; focalization is typically far more complicated than this and includes varying perspectives through the use of camera angles that alternate from overview shots to those shots seemingly (or discretely) focalized through individual character's eyes. In fact, film's use of camera angles and techniques actually suggests that in some ways, it is far more complex than novels in its use of points of view and focalization. As Markus Kuhn and Johann N. Schmidt describe, film "derives its impact from a number of technical, performative, and aesthetic strategies that combine in a syncretizing, largely hybrid medium, establishing interlocking conventions of storytelling" (387).

Nevertheless, the internal dialogue that characterizes adolescent literature is mostly absent in film. When included, character thoughts are frequently presented in voice-over, which is not typically considered by critics to be a preferred technique. As Sarah Kozloff describes, "Only a few [theorists] have found any kind words for the technique, while scores have criticized it" (8). For this reason, such techniques are often used only in limited ways in adolescent film. While I agree that, as Kozloff describes, voice-over has "usefulness in the grand cinematic tool chest," including "underscoring character's flaws" (128), I would suggest it is often less effective in conveying the level of self-consciousness that first-person narration in YA novels achieves. This key difference lies at the heart of the ways adolescent film adaptations shift their characterization so as to result in a polarization of male/female binaries.

For example, in the case of *Warm Bodies*, readers are privy to R's thoughts throughout the text, and although there are moments of voice-over-style narration in the film to replicate a bit of this, filmmakers almost always chose expressions of insecurity rather than introspection when implementing this technique. Conversely, although Julie's introspective and uncertain moments exist in the novel as dialogue, these moments are almost never included in the film. As a result, most of the self-consciousness and self-questioning of the novel is eliminated.

I believe that this removal or minimization of self-consciousness and self-questioning qualities results in a greater polarization of binaries in film adaptations as compared to their source texts. When readers do not have the chance to consider a character's assessments of events in their lives, adolescence appears a very different experience—one wherein turmoil, uncertainty, and angst is replaced by a much more confident quest to unlock the mysteries of self, rather than come to understand that selfhood is ever changing and always evolving.

To consider how this relates to polarization of gender binaries and the production of the female savior, I turn to another YA film adaptation, the 2016 movie version of Rick Yancey's *The 5th Wave*. Like *Warm Bodies*, *The 5th Wave* is told via first person, but in this case, it is polyvocal, narrated by several key characters. Characters describe their hopes and fears as they battle to survive the alien invasion of the Earth, and while alternating sections are focalized through both male and female characters, much of the story is focalized through its female protagonist, Cassie Sullivan. Both Cassie and the second most prominent focalizer, Ben Parish, question whether being thrust into this alien apocalypse has stripped them of their humanity. Another male character, Evan Walker, acts as Cassie's primary love interest, and while his perspective only accounts for a brief section of first-person narration, he too is exceptionally introspective in the novel. Evan, readers come to learn, is an alien/human hybrid, born believing himself human until the alien forces switch him on, and he realizes that he is both human and host to an integrated alien presence. He is both, or so he explains to Cassie, and this duality links him to the other characters; he too grapples with questions of his humanity and purpose.

This element of Evan's character, however, is significantly changed in the film, and viewers are provided with nearly no context regarding his self-reflection or the ways he grapples with a dual self. Instead, when viewers meet Evan in the film, he seems to have reconciled these questions, a transformation attributed almost entirely to Cassie's presence. In the novel, this transformation is a far longer process and the text ends without it being entirely resolved. For example, Evan challenges the intent of his alien brethren even before meeting Cassie, and readers see this not only in the chapter told from his perspective, but also when he explains to Cassie that by inhabiting a human body, he feels freed to "feel something again" (371). His embodied experience as a hybrid has been pivotal, and while part of his newfound emotional experience is the love that Cassie has elicited from him, Evan's questioning of self is far more complex than simply this element.

In contrast, *The 5th Wave* movie—like *Warm Bodies*—focuses primarily on Evan and Cassie's romance, offering an abbreviated development of their relationship. Evan says, "Our kind believes that love is just a trick. An instinct. A way to protect your genetic future," and when Cassie asks if he really believes that, he responds, "I did. But then I saw you." The word "saw" is key here, for the film pairs this line with a flashback wherein Evan looks at Cassie through the scope of his rifle, reacting with surprise and awe as he catches a glimpse of her. He continues, "I don't know how. I don't understand it, but it was like you flipped the switch back. You made me want to be human again." Simply seeing Cassie turns Evan back toward his human side, whereas in the novel, he grapples with both sides of himself and fights against the invasion long before meeting her, explaining that even before he was placed in a human body, he advocated coexistence between aliens and humans. In fact, in the novel, when Evan sees Cassie through the scope of his rifle, he is not transformed—instead, he shoots her, believing she might be a hybrid too.

Additionally, the novel version of Cassie describes Evan as a uniquely liminal creature, using phrases like "human and other" and "both and neither." Evan, like Cassie, is blurring binaries and opening questions of self. In the film, Evan's final line is "I was wrong when I said I was both one of you and one of them. You can't be both. You have to choose. I choose you." The phrase "I choose you" is added here from the novel, for in the movie, Evan's transformation is not about a questioning of his people, purpose, or even his humanity—it is about Cassie, and he is transformed because of her.

Here again, the emotional transformation that this young man experiences is not simply personal; instead, falling in love inspires him to social change on a much grander scale. Like the social change inspired by R and Julie's relationships, *The 5th Wave* film suggests that Evan's relationship with Cassie results in his subsequent efforts to overturn the oppressive regime of the alien invaders. In the novel, Evan already saw himself as part of a resistance movement before he met Cassie, but the movie shows him only fighting against the alien invaders after meeting her . . . he follows her to the alien camp and plants bombs there in order to prove his commitment to her, to demonstrate that he has *chosen* her. She transforms him, and as a result, he works to transform society. In these films and a wide range of other examples I have studied, male characters strive to be a savior, to physically save the powerful women in their lives and affect society, but this impetus comes in part because they are emotionally saved by these heroines. This associates men with external or physical heroism, while linking women with an internal or emotional space, a dichotomy not present to such extremes in the books.

I suggest that it is the narrative style inherent to film that creates this dynamic, in which conceptions and constructions of men and women seem diametrically opposed. The first-person narration and polyphony of *The 5th Wave* allows readers to see a kinship between characters, wherein each teen (whether male or female) questions their decisions and place in society, traversing difficult emotional spaces and complex choices with uncertainty and turmoil. While there are moments in which the actress who plays Cassie, Chloë Grace Moretz, does seem to capture some of this angst in her facial expressions, on the whole, the film is more plot than character driven, and first-person inner dialogue is replaced with a third-person accounting that shifts characters into far more binary positions.

When internal turmoil is removed and binaries are polarized, the result is a male character who requires a woman's influence in order to become more human, more insightful, and perhaps even more adult. Nevertheless, narration alone does not seem to fully account for this trend, and to explore additional contributing factors, I move to another popular YA dystopia series, Suzanne Collins's The Hunger Games series. When adapted into film, these books evidence not only shifts in narration, but also how this aspect combines with contemporary efforts to produce "strong" female characters in film, an impetus that while seemingly positive can also lead to a polarization of binaries with significant ideological results.

"Self-Consciousness and Self Questioning": Dilemmas of a Strong Film Heroine

Collins's The Hunger Games series follows a teen protagonist, Katniss Everdeen, who is forced to participate in a televised competition between children reaped from poverty-stricken outer communities oppressed by the wealthy Capitol, subsequently chronicling her joining of the rebellion against these forces. Katniss is a strong heroine, both in Suzanne Collins's novel and in the film adaptation, wherein she is played by Academy Award–winning actress Jennifer Lawrence. Before joining the cast of *The Hunger Games* (2012), Lawrence was already well known to audiences, nominated for an Oscar for her 2011 role in *Winter's Bone* and starring in the popular X-Men origin story series as Mystique. Between the release of the first and second film in The Hunger

Games series, Lawrence also won an Academy Award for *Silver Lining's Playbook* (2013) and, propelled to stardom, was nominated again in 2014 for *American Hustle* and in 2016 for *Joy*. Even her more recent film, *Passengers*, which was considered unsuccessful by critics (receiving only 31 percent positive reviews on Rotten Tomatoes), was the second-highest grossing original live-action Hollywood release of 2016.

I point out Lawrence's filmmaking history for a simple reason—to establish her as a Hollywood star during the theatrical run of The Hunger Games film series, which was first released on March 23, 2012, and concluded cinema screenings in early 2016. In fact, I would go so far as to associate her with Richard Dyer's concept of "a star image" because she is "made out of media texts that can be grouped together as promotion, publicity, films, and criticism" (60). Like Dyer describes, much of Lawrence's popularity and renown has been built by interviews, her dynamic presence at award shows, and other promotion and publicity, making her a known entity not simply as an actress, but as a media icon. Analyzed through the lens of Saussure's notion of the signifier, Dyer's concept of the star is thus relevant to Jennifer Lawrence's role as Katniss in that her very presence connects her to ideologies regarding "strong" women. In each of the popular films in which she was cast during this timeframe, Lawrence exhibits distinctive strength, whether winning the torturous dystopian games and leading a rebellion against Panem's corrupt Capitol, or enacting one of the other roles that distinguishes her as a Hollywood A-lister.

Dyer's star theory describe the images associated with such individuals as "structured polysemy," wherein they exist not simply in the "multiplicity of meanings and affects they embody," but also in the attempt to "structure them so that some meanings and affects are foregrounded and others masked or displaced" (3). Lawrence's combined roles from 2012 to 2016 offer a meditation on the qualities of female strength, which she herself describes in a 2014 Dior advertisement, claiming, "a powerful woman is someone who exudes confidence and can be tough but fair and kind . . . and also knows how to get what she wants" (Popp). More importantly, Lawrence's role as Katniss Everdeen evidences Hollywood's increased interest in producing contemporary films with strong women. According to San Diego State University's Center for the Study of Women in Television & Film, women comprised 29 percent of protagonists in the top one hundred films at the US box office in 2016, a figure up 7 percent from 2015, which was also a year lauded as a historical high. Yet even though Lawrence can be viewed as participating in this trend, she also demonstrates that what strength comprises in film fundamentally differs from how this characteristic can be manifested in the adolescent literature upon which those films are based.

These differences have been noticed by critics like Iris Shepard and Ian Wojcik-Andrews, who describe the mixed reception to the film, including a seeming absence of "Katniss's political consciousness" (196). They explain, "From Hollywood's point of view, a young adult movie that features thoughtful, reasoned inner monologues from a smart sixteen-year-old about the possibilities of a classless society is not as commercially viable as seeing an attractive female ride into the Capitol on a chariot of fire" (196). I agree, but further suggest that Hollywood's hesitation to delve into inner monologue seems not entirely a product of a disinterest in political considerations. In fact, I believe Hollywood is more interested in these kinds of social and cultural critiques than ever before, perhaps simply because these elements sell. Voice-over inner contemplation does not. Furthermore, if *The Hunger Games* and other recently popular dystopia films are any indication, strong female characters also sell, but an uncertainty about one's place in society expressed though self-conscious angst does not—at least not in fantasy (I will further discuss more realistic views of teens in the latter part of this chapter).

Quite simply, strength in film, especially for women, differs from novels. Katniss appears strong in the movie in great part because she lacks excessive inner turmoil, whereas the novel's first person narration focuses often on her indecision, insecurity, and doubt, paired with intense problem-solving abilities, exceptional skill with a bow and arrow, and courageous leadership in the face of hardship. In the film, however, viewers only see the later qualities, and very rarely see Katniss questioning, uncertain, heartbroken, or afraid. The filmic Katniss is emotional, certainly, and in fact, I would suggest that one success of the film is Lawrence's ability to enact a strong emotionality through body language and facial expressions. However, while she expresses great feeling—whether angry, annoyed, saddened, or fearful—she never seems to express doubt, never demonstrating what Cadden describes as self-consciousness or self-questioning. While I would suggest that these qualities in the book actually add to her overall character strength, the movie posits strength in a very different way, and one that contributes significantly to the polarization of male/female binaries of the film.

For example, after Katniss volunteers for the Games to save her sister, she rides to the departing train with her cocompetitor, Peeta Mellark, who in the film is depicted as crying quite hysterically. In contrast, Lawrence portrays Katniss as stoic, showing emotion only in a single frustrated glance at Effie Trinket, their ridiculous escort. This matches the description of the book, wherein Katniss recounts, "I've had a lot of practice wiping my face clean of emotions and I do this now. I catch a glimpse of myself on the television screen on the wall that's airing my arrival live and feel gratified that I appear almost bored" (*Hunger* 40). This is strategy, but film audiences are not made aware of that fact. Readers see how purposefully she strategizes, forced to push aside emotions, as well as her endless questioning of Peeta, who she believes is strategizing as well, even in his tears. Katniss works hard to put on a brave face to survive, but in the film, viewers only see the face, not the difficulty that goes into maintaining it.

This scene in the film accentuates the binary set up between Peeta and Katniss, reversing traditional power dynamics by positioning him as emotionally stricken. While the book explains that this binary is not so simple, viewers' inability to access Katniss's thoughts creates a binary between her seeming strength and the very different ways that the male character, Peeta, is strong. While the book also includes male/female binaries, the movie accentuates them.

This continues throughout the Games, as when Katniss hears the announcement that the game rules have changed so that both she and Peeta can survive. In the film, Katniss has only just recovered from losing Rue, perhaps the only scene in the film wherein viewers see her truly break down emotionally. When she hears that she might save Peeta (rather than have to kill him to survive), she does not even hesitate, immediately running to his aide and caring for him without reservation, so much so that viewers unfamiliar with the novel may assume that she has developed real feelings for him. This fits the book's description of the plot, but again, Katniss's inner monologue in the novel changes the dynamic significantly. In the novel, Katniss first ponders her reason for going to Peeta: "if either of us took the other's life now we'd be pariahs when we returned to District 12 . . . being one of the star-crossed lovers from District 12—it's [now] an absolute requirement if I want more help from sympathetic sponsors" (*Hunger* 247). She immediately begins to strategize, even looking up at the cameras to smile and support this charade of romance. Here again, readers see a strong heroine, but one not simply brave or filled with compassion—she is a master strategist, but also complex in her exploration of what she must do, and what she is willing to do, to survive.

This is perhaps most evident in the final climactic scene of the novel, when Katniss suggests that she and Peeta kill themselves via the poisoned berries, rather than allow the Capitol to force one of them to kill the other. In the movie, this is clearly an act of political defiance on Katniss's part, as she looks up at the camera with an obvious disdain, even taunting. Meanwhile, Peeta again seems diametrically opposed from her, instead fixating on her and touching her braid. In another stark gender reversal, she is the rebel, and he the boy in love. In the book, this binary between lover/fighter and male/female is far more complex. Katniss is conflicted, first raising her bow by instinct, but then refusing to kill Peeta until pushed into a new line of thought when he threatens to kill himself instead. She cares for him, but this is not her main reason for wanting to save him, for she thinks, "If he dies, I'll never go home, not really. I'll spend the rest of my life in this arena trying to think my way out" (*Hunger* 343). She is neither the hopeless romantic nor the political rebel, but a teenager trying to survive, heartlessly strategic and caring at once.

I do not mean to suggest that these examples demonstrate that the book offers a stronger heroine than the movie; in fact, I believe quite the contrary. Not only do I wish to avoid such a book/film hierarchy, but I would go so far as to also suggest that in some ways, the movie version of Katniss is stronger or, at least, stronger in terms of how American society often defines expressions of strength. In the film, Katniss seemingly lacks much of the uncertainty she displays in the novel, and especially for viewers unfamiliar with the book, she seems to have a great deal of conviction and courage. Those familiar with the book might add in some of their understanding of Katniss's character, but any substantial self-conscious questioning is, as Shepard and Wojcik-Andrews describe, conspicuously absent.

This characterization polarizes the male/female binaries of the film. In the novel, readers only see Peeta and Gale (Katniss's longtime friend and potential love interest) through Katniss's eyes, and via this perspective, they both seem confident, courageous, and socially conscious, drawing a sharp contrast from her own feelings. For example, Katniss feels inferior to Peeta, thinking, "While I've been ruminating on the availability of trees, Peeta has been struggling with how to maintain his identity. His purity of self" (*Hunger* 142). These kinds of contrasts continue throughout the series, with Katniss judging her own indecision and survival instincts against her male counterparts, who she sees as more noble. In the film, Katniss never does this; Lawrence seems a pillar of strength, the same kind of strength that Katniss attributed to Peeta and Gale in the novel, but did not see in herself. Still, rather than balancing the power structures of the text, wherein male/female binaries might be lessened if both Katniss and her male counterparts seem strong, the movie seems more to reverse this dynamic, highlighting her as the hero and Gale/Peeta as defined by their devotion to her.

This shift aligns The Hunger Games film series with the pattern I notice across all YA film adaptations, with the notion of the female savior alive and well. Gale is a great example of this, for while Katniss relies on his strength throughout the series, she also comes to disagree with his participation in the rebellion and the lengths he is willing to go, culminating in her uncertainty whether he bears responsibility for her sister's death. In the novel, this debate opens questions for the reader as well, who might also begin to wonder what lengths are necessary and ethical when it comes to the "greater good." Yet in the film, scenes with Gale almost exclusively surround his being in love with

Katniss, as viewers see him flirting with her, gazing jealously at her romantic interactions with Peeta on the screen during the games, and bemoaning their relationship, attempting to convince her to choose him. While Gale's role in the book fosters questions about the ethics of rebellion, in the film, he is regulated to the role of potential romantic partner, defined only by his love for Katniss.

Peeta's character faces a similar filmic transformation, and again, he becomes a supporting romantic character to Katniss's heroism, rather than an individual himself. In the novel, Katniss repeatedly stresses that Peeta is the one who can lead the rebellion, that he is "truly, deep-down better than the rest of us" (*Fire* 277) and "it's because of that underlying goodness that he can move a crowd—no, a county—to his side with the turn of a simple sentence" (*Fire* 338). This is the reason, more than any other, that she wants so desperately to keep Peeta alive in the novel; she believes him more worthy and important than herself. In contrast, these elements barely come into the film at all. The closest the film comes to this sentiment is Haymitch telling Katniss that she could "live a hundred lifetimes and never deserve that boy," and although Katniss does not respond to this, she does stress that they must save him. This seems, however, to be about her growing feelings for him, again defining him within the context of their romance, rather than his role in the rebellion.

The final novel in the series provides the best example of the amplified "female savior" element, for much of Collins's *Mockingjay* concerns Peeta's rehabilitation after the Capitol brainwashes him to hate Katniss, a plot element kept consistent in the film. In the novel, Katniss faces her greatest indecision, doubt, and self-questioning of the series when faced with this challenge, unsure whether to mourn him or if she might somehow help him find his way back. Here again, similar to *The 5th Wave* and *Warm Bodies*, Peeta is literally transformed from a broken, brainwashed shell back into someone at least akin to his previous self because of his love for this inspiring and remarkable heroine. In the book, this romance exists, but much of Katniss's desire to help Peeta is also because she believes the rebellion needs him. This dynamic is reversed in the film, wherein Peeta's role seems primarily to be about his loving her, including how that love saves him and allows her to save (or at least attempt to save) their society.

Far more than in the novels, the young men of The Hunger Games film series seem to exist in relationship to Katniss—they are not separate individuals, but parts of her storyline. In the books, readers see Katniss idolizing them both, but in the films, viewers only see them idolizing her—she is the one who will save them, but also save Panem. Her strength seems unwavering in the films, and while this might appear a positive quality reflecting an increased investment in strong female protagonists in film, an emphasis on or desire to represent this strength also seems to play into a repeated message of adolescent film: that women are responsible for saving the men in their lives, and by extension, their society.

Still, being a savior is not always so literal as in these zombie, alien, and dystopian novel to film adaptations, and thus to further explore the reasons why this trend emerges across adolescent film, I move to several examples of realistic fiction that similarly follow this paradigm. Before doing so, however, I find it imperative to mention one other ideological implication of the redirection of emphasis and thematic amplification in *The Hunger Games* film. Ebony Elizabeth Thomas suggests that while "readers are positioned by stories to identify with protagonists like Katniss . . . Rue is the story girl who haunts the narrative the most . . . [and] Rue's story, if counterstoried through a critical race lens, is a critique of Katniss's heroism" (43). In the film adaptation, filmmakers shift Rue's role, and in particular, alter Katniss's response to Rue's death in ways that, as Thomas describes, "diminishes Rue's selflessness as the sacrificial mockingjay and as impetus to revolution, and makes Katniss's unselfish devotion the center of the narrative . . . as Katniss shifts her focus to her eventual love interest, Rue fades from the narrative" (55).

This emphasis on romance at the expense of other ideological elements fits with the ways I describe other YA texts, but here, it also serves to undermine the role of a crucial character of color in the text. Furthermore, the violent online response to the film, wherein Rue's "very existence was an affront to audiences when she emerged from the page to appear as dark skinned on the big screen" (Thomas 34) demonstrates the racism of a viewership who finds "the idea of Rue as the slain mockingjay—the symbol of purity and innocence" to be "strange, even alien" (Thomas 62). While Rue's character allows for a unique consideration of race in the novel, in the film, this element is simplified and left uninterrogated as the filmmakers lessen Rue's role and cast black actors as resisting forces without giving time or consideration to the complex intersections between class and race or the idea that powerful institutions oppress certain members of society more than others. Thus, in addition to the gender-based ideological elements of binary polarization that repeat again and again, these racial components also cannot be ignored. In short, it is clear that thematic amplification and binary polarization can have varied and, often very problematic, ideological ramifications.

John Green and "The Patriarchal Lie of the Manic Pixie Dream Girl"

Thus far, I have suggested that consistently, polarized male/female binaries in adolescent novel to film adaptations result in an amplified characterization of male characters who are emotionally or spiritually saved by a strong female protagonist. Further, I have posited two potential ways the nature of film contributes to this pattern emerging so consistently: shifts in narration that limit introspective self-questioning and a growing trend in film to highlight a certain kind of strong female teen character. To illuminate a third contributing factor, I turn to several concepts that theorists associate with gender representation in film, beginning with Laura Mulvey's notion of the male gaze, and more importantly, her writings about the "possessive spectator." While drawing on Mulvey's concept of the gaze has limitations (especially, as critics have noted, because it assumes a heteronormative/male viewership), Mulvey's emphasis on the patriarchal structures reinforced by the very nature of film is useful to considering YA adaptations.

Mulvey writes, "going far beyond highlighting a woman's to-be-looked-at-ness, cinema builds the way she is to be looked at into the spectacle itself . . . cinematic codes create a gaze, a world, and an object, thereby producing an illusion cut to the measure of desire" (25). In particular, I find Mulvey's distinction between "three different looks" especially relevant to adolescent adapted film. While certainly, adolescent females are subjected to both the gaze produced by the camera and the voyeurism of the audience viewing the film, I am surprised by how frequently and obviously adolescent film employs the third kind of looking Mulvey describes, in which a male character observes a female character in a distinctively objectifying way. This set of shots is a strikingly consistent creative choice for representations of teen characters. In such examples, shots alternate between a view of the male character and his viewpoint, often a slow-motion shot of the female, who is frequently backlit. The camera shots of the female teen certainly objectify her, but I am especially interested in the shots of the teen male, and the ideological results of showing the audience prolonged images of this character gazing, as well as the female character being gazed at.

I have already mentioned two examples of this kind of camerawork, explicitly utilized in *Warm Bodies* during Julie and R's meet-cue, and in *The 5th Wave*, when Evan first views Cassie through the scope of his rifle. While *The Hunger Games* does not feature so obvious a shot, one of Gale's key screen moments in the first film is an addition not present in the novel: his watching Katniss in the games on a television screen as she kisses Peeta (a scene that starts to establish him as a jealous third party in the love triangle). In each case, viewers are encouraged to watch the teen men being emotionally moved by watching their female counterparts, and this visual assessment begins the male characters' transformations. The act of watching may seem to afford the young men power over these women, but the context actually reverses this dynamic, showing the men's physical reactions in order to highlight that they are changed through this viewing, whether positively (in *Warm Bodies* or *The 5th Wave*) or negatively (as in *The Hunger Games*).

Moreover, this concept is even more clearly exemplified in realistic novel to film adolescent adaptations, best exemplified in two key scenes of the 2015 film version John Green's *Paper Towns*. In Green's novel, Quentin is madly in love with the elusive Margo, whose legendary adventures culminate in her disappearance and Quentin's subsequent quest to find her by following supposed clues she left behind. This creates a male/female dynamic set up even in the film's opening, a scene that draws much of its voice-over narration directly from the text, but also features a young Quentin staring at Margo as she exits her minivan and turns to glance at him in a slow-motion shot. A key line is then added to the prologue of the novel: "From the moment I saw her I was hopelessly, madly in love." This not only emphasizes that, like the other characters I describe, Quentin seems transformed even in only seeing Margo, but it also emphasizes this "seeing" as viewers watch him gaze at her longingly. This paradigm repeats the last time Quentin sees Margo before she disappears, wherein camerawork includes shots watching her climb into her bedroom window, but emphasizes shots fixating the viewers gaze on a male protagonist watching his beloved.

I point to this scene especially because it both enacts Mulvey's concept and links it directly to the concept of the female savior. Immediately preceding the us-watching-him-watching-her scene, filmmakers added a key piece of dialogue to the textual version, wherein Margo tells Quentin, "Ok, you see this . . . this is your comfort zone. It's this big, Quentin. All of the things you want are way out there. The way you felt tonight—that is the way you should feel your whole life." This line links the watching scene with Margo as a transformative force, altering the male protagonist for the better.

While these elements are set up by the novel, my key point here, and throughout my study, is that filmmakers focus on and amplify such dynamics, thus polarizing binaries in ways that repeatedly create male/female power relationships that empower and objectify women simultaneously. Yet realistic film in particular also seems to frequently engage another concept often called upon and critiqued by film theorists: the Manic Pixie Dream Girl. Introduced by Nathan Rabin in his 2007 review of *Elizabethtown*, the term Manic Pixie Dream Girl "exists solely in the fevered imaginations of sensitive writer-directors to teach broodingly soulful young men to embrace life and its infinite mysteries and adventures." Often associated with realistic teen films, John Green's work engages this paradigm, and more importantly, the adaptations of his work into film amplifies this characterization in problematic ways.

More pop culture than theoretical, the term Manic Pixie Dream Girl has faced criticism for its oversimplification of gender dynamics, so much so that in 2014, Rabin tried to "retract" the term, noting he feels "deeply weird, if not downright ashamed, at having created a cliché that has been trotted out again and again in an infinite Internet feedback loop." In this retraction, however, Rabin references Green's Tumblr post about *Paper Towns*, in which Green states the book is "devoted IN ITS ENTIRETY to destroying the lie of the Manic Pixie Dream Girl . . . I do not know how I could have been less ambiguous about this without calling [*Paper Towns*] The Patriarchal Lie of the Manic Pixie Dream Girl Must Be Stabbed in the Heart and Killed."

While this seems a strong reaction, I agree with Green that *Paper Towns* appears to very purposefully work to dismantle the trope, especially in its conclusion. Margo clearly articulates that she is not a Manic Pixie Dream Girl, and in viewing her in this way, Quentin loses out. She explains, "When did we see each other face-to-face? Not until you saw into my cracks and I saw into yours. Before that, we were just looking at ideas of each other, like looking at your window shade but never seeing inside. But once the vessel cracks, the light can get in" (302). Dripping with metaphor, the point here is clear: Margo wishes to stab Quentin's Manic Pixie Dream Girl vision of her in the heart and kill it.

However, in order to lead readers to this conclusion, Green had to, by very necessity, create a Manic Pixie Dream Girl. Without Margo exemplifying this trope, he could not dismantle it. While I applaud his desire to challenge the cliché, this seemingly didactic message of his novel only comes after over two hundred pages of carefully crafting this figure, thus recreating it and instilling it rather powerfully into the minds of readers. Certainly, the lesson is clear: do not view girls this way. Readers have spent, however, a substantial amount of time developing a connection to a character who absolutely views girls this way, and I wonder if the building of this character trope is perhaps more powerful than the didactic attempt to break from it. At least one reviewer of the film, Anna Leszkiewicz, agrees, asking, "Is a Manic Pixie Dream Girl not a Manic Pixie Dream Girl when her sole function is to teach a brooding, soulful young man that his understanding of women is flawed?"

Furthermore, while I commend an effort to, as Rabin describes, "try to write better, more nuanced, and multidimensional female characters: women with rich inner lives and complicated emotions and total autonomy, who might strum ukuleles or dance in the rain even when there are no men around to marvel at their free-spiritedness," I wish to point out that Margo does not have this kind of rich inner life, or at least, readers do not get to see it. Readers only see Margo through Quentin's eyes, so that while Green promotes the idea that a female character should have a rich inner life in the text's conclusion, he does not go so far as to give readers access to it.

The film adaptation of Green's work takes this even further, similarly lacking any explication of Margo apart from Quentin's view of her, but also eliminating much of the self-questioning and introspective qualities of its male protagonist as well. In doing so, the movie creates a female emotional savior, in part because it engages the Manic Pixie Dream Girl phenomenon in ways that both Rabin and Green problematize. For example, in the final scene between Margo and Quentin, he again stares meaningfully at her, shot in the same style as the other two moments I have explicated, and again utilizing slow motion and emphasizing shots that watch him watching her. After they embrace, Quentin learns that Margo did not leave clues so that he would follow her, and while Quentin is clearly disappointed, he nonetheless professes his love. Margo is skeptical, saying he does not know her, and more importantly, "I don't even know me. I have no idea who I am."

In the novel, this exchange is followed by Margo's clear dismantling of her Manic Pixie Dream Girl status, a concept the film version similarly establishes when Margo says, "People have always looked at me and seen what they wanted to see . . . the myth of Margo Roth Spiegelman. But it's just a fantasy." The following shots, however, contradict this, instead making her seem quite mythical. She describes, "You were my first partner in crime. I wanted you to be my last," and viewers, witnessing a montage of her and Quentin's adventures, are reminded just what she has done for him. She has transformed him, which he affirms by saying that she did not ruin the last few weeks of high school for him, but "in fact, I think they were the best weeks of my life." The film nods to Green's objective, but while Quentin notes she may not be the "myth I made you out to be," he follows this by saying "you're still pretty something," so that while the ending voice-over claims, "what a treacherous thing it is to believe a person is more than a person," this does not seem the true sentiment left to the viewers. The concluding scene instead proves that Margo changed Quentin's life for the better, transforming his emotional self, and she has done this because she is this amazing creature, the Manic Pixie Dream Girl.

Paper Towns is not the only culprit of this filmic emphasis on the Manic Pixie Dream Girl, however, or the ways that young men are shown very purposefully reinforcing the notion of women as objects of the male gaze. Indeed, the idea of the gaze and, in particular, the way teen films seem to direct this gaze toward a Manic Pixie Dream Girl seem a part of adolescent film, perhaps even more strongly than adult film because it is so obviously highlighted. More significant, however, is the way this concept interacts with a binary polarization to further accentuate an amplified representation of the female savior.

Adolescent Film Adaptation and the Death of Double Voice

Earlier in this chapter, I suggest that when adolescent novels are adapted to film, shifts in narrative viewpoints decrease elements of self-questioning that are imperative to creating what Cadden calls double-voiced discourse. This, I posit, factors into a more polarized male/female binary in the adaptations, resulting in a consistent emergence of the female savior. I would like to end this chapter by looking at the other side of this cause-and-effect relationship. On the one hand, a shifted narrative perspective that eliminates self-conscious teen protagonists plays a key role in *causing* male/female binary polarization in adolescent film adaptations. However, I also believe that shifts in single/ double-voiced discourse can also be identified as the *result* of polarized binaries. Because concepts of male and female are consistently delineated into distinctive categories in YA films, these movies are almost always more single-voiced than their novel counterparts.

As a result, the function of these films differs from the novels upon which they are based. While many of the novels I have discussed provide, as Cadden describes, "the tools for identifying potentially debilitating world views in the text" and thus help teens "grow as readers" (153), the films function instead to provide a construction of adolescence that states, often quite definitively, what it means to be a teenager. Furthermore, the consistency in the ideologies of inspiring females and lesson-learning males contributes to this construction, so that instead of the kind of horizontal power relationship that Cadden identifies as characteristic of double-voiced YA texts, film provides a far more vertical power structure, and in some cases, a far more didactic tone.

Thus, Cadden's argument plays a crucial role in understanding the trend of the female savior. In looking for the cause of this pattern, I have thus far contended that three key elements are at work: 1) viewpoint/narration shifts that decrease self-conscious introspection, 2) a contemporary emphasis on the inclusion of "strong" female characters, and 3) film's inherently objectifying nature, illuminated by such concepts as Mulvey's notion of the male gaze and the Manic Pixie Dream Girl phenomenon. These factors polarize male/female binaries, which results in a consistent figuring of women as men's emotional saviors. But single/double-voiced discourse is also the critical middle step that explains why binary polarization results from this paradigm. Binary polarization (facilitated by point of view shifts, a desire to include strong female characters, and the objectifying nature of film) creates a more single-voiced narrative, which in turn causes a consistent ideology to emerge, that of the female savior.

After identifying this cause and effect relationship in an effort to investigate the pattern of the female savior in adolescent adapted film, I am still left with a question, however: what is the consequence of this consistent shift toward single voice and the trend in gender dynamics it creates? I suggest that the answer to this question is best illuminated in the adaptation of a novel that is especially double-voiced, Tim Tharp's *The Spectacular Now*. While the novel participates in double-voiced qualities, these elements are dismantled in the film in great part due to a shifting understanding of the female lead.

In *Spectacular Now*, the novel's protagonist, Sutter, is a teen alcoholic dealing with having been abandoned by his father while pursuing a relationship with the shy and naive Aimee. Although the novel is told from his perspective, the reader sees Sutter in a very different way than he claims to see himself, creating a contrast that fits exactly with Cadden's descriptions of double-voiced YA literature. Sutter is the ultimate unreliable narrator, but the text engages double voice in even more concrete ways than this. Readers can tell from page one that Sutter is a jerk, and it is clear that everyone he encounters knows this. Yet Sutter is also exceedingly charming, and readers may find themselves swept up in this; in fact, it is perhaps what makes the first-person novel so engaging.

In this way, double-voiced discourse emerges—Sutter is charming and seemingly sincere, but his claims also seem utterly wrong in many cases, identified as such by all of the other characters of the story, even if we only see their reactions in the periphery of Sutter's drunken viewpoint. Thus, readers are not only given the chance to contemplate the potential unreliability of Sutter's perspective, but seem invited to do so, creating a contrast between what Sutter says and the ways the novel inherently challenges his ideas.

For example, in the film's opening scene, Sutter aides Walter, a young boy running away from home. Sutter contemplates the situation, noting, "I can see it [the world] like he does—a giant orange sun dripping down into the bluest ocean you ever saw with palm trees genuflecting at its glory" (5). He encourages Walter to "embrace the weird, dude. Enjoy it because it's never going away" (7), and returns him to his mother. However, while Sutter's charm and benevolence here seem engaging, this is immediately challenged when Walter's mother accuses him of drinking and driving (which is true). When Walter "gazes up" at Sutter "with a forlorn expression" (9), the reader might share it, conflicted because Sutter seems a good guy, even though he is also doing something widely understood as exceptionally dangerous.

Later, Sutter starts spending time with Aimee, in part to help her break out of her shell and enjoy the seemingly easygoing life he relishes. Aimee is drawn in, saying, "You bring the magic. I feel it right now. It's like nothing can touch us, like everything else in the world—the problems, the responsibilities—have just disappeared. We're in our own universe" (150). The reader might be similarly drawn in, seeing Aimee as improved by her interactions with Sutter and even seeing merit in these teens' effort to "live in the *right now*" (153). As Sutter falls for Aimee, however, he also causes her pain and lets her down, pulling her into his drinking in ways that have greater and greater consequences. Still, even when he sometimes seems to be trying to convince the reader of the merits of his perspective, with Tharp increasingly using second-person "you" to emphasize this, he never actually learns the lesson that readers might expect.

To take this approach with a topic like teen alcoholism is a risky endeavor. One might expect that there is really only one perspective that an adult author would be willing to suggest to a teen reader when it comes to not simply alcohol consumption, but ramped alcoholism and drunk driving. Certainly, I do not suggest that Tharp avoids this entirely or suggests that alcoholism is positive; I do think, however, that Sutter's charm complicates didacticism, asking the reader if it is possible that this "spectacular now" in which he resides actually has merit.

Furthermore, Tharp also reworks the tropes that are common in books about teen drinking, as when Aimee and Sutter are in a car accident directly resulting from Sutter's drinking. Unlike in other examples of YA fiction, Aimee emerges with only minor injuries, and Sutter is "transformed from a semivillain into a real hero" (279) with her family when she tells them that he saved her. Moreover, this incident acts as a catalyst not for him to stop drinking, but to view Aimee differently, noting "I've never loved anyone as much as I love her right now. That's how I know I'll have to give her up" (277). Sutter does this, and the reader almost respects him for it—he loves her and finally puts her first. Yet this means the book also evades any "happily ever after"—to "save" Aimee, Sutter abandons her and ends the story in a bar, where several drunken patrons call him a hero and a king, and he disappears into "the middle of the middle of my own spectacular now" (294).

Sutter's complexly charming but also deeply flawed character is especially evident in ambiguity of message in this ending scene of the novel, wherein he has not learned any lesson and does not seem to plan to change his behavior. He also sees a beauty that the reader might almost envy, describing, "The night is almost too beautifully pure for my soul to contain. I walk with arms spread open under the big fat moon. Heroic weeds rise up from the cracks in the sidewalk, and the colored lights of the Hawaiian Breeze ignite the broken glass in the gutter" (294). This is a bit heartbreaking, and the reader might feel badly for this protagonist who still seems to only be avoiding the losses he has faced. Nevertheless, the way Sutter sees the world here is also a bit beautiful, complicating a clear didactic message that would condemn him.

The ending of the film is dramatically different and results directly from a more polarized binary that enacts the female savior. Aimee similarly survives the car accident and Sutter seems to intend to let her go by leaving her waiting at the bus stop. Sutter then visits the bar described in the novel, but after this scene (the last in the book), ten additional minutes are added, beginning with a scene in which Sutter drives home and collides with the mailbox, sparking a fight with his mother. They have a frank discussion about his father, and she holds him as he cries, admitting that he believes no one loves him. As Sutter's mother says that he is so very wrong, they have a genuine moment of connection, with the scene then cutting to Sutter writing his admissions essay to college.

This is a crucial final moment of the film, not only because it is a clear indication of Sutter learning his lesson, thus promoting the single-voiced discourse of the film, but also because it clearly identifies Aimee as a crucial part of this emotional growth. Sutter focuses on the words "challenge," "hardships," and "future," on the screen of his computer, and in a voice-over monologue admits that the real challenge or hardship of his life has been himself—his fear of failure, letting people down, hurting people, and getting hurt. These words align with a montage of images of the men in his life that correspond to these fears as well as the people he has "shut out" because of that fear. He says he "screwed up," and concludes, "It's fine to just live in the now, but the best part about now is that there's another one tomorrow. And I'm going to start making them count." He ends the voice-over by saying "It's not too late for me," a sentiment that shows him approaching Aimee on a college campus. She smiles, tucks her hair back, and the screen cuts to black. He has been changed, and Aimee was instrumental in this transformation.

I suspect that movie producers chose this ending in order to fit with the conventions and patterns in other adolescent film, but also because its single-voiced didacticism is very satisfying in this case. In fact, when Sutter breaks up with Aimee in the novel, thinking "I do have a future to give her after all, just not one that includes me" (286), readers may feel conflicted, wanting to believe that Sutter can change and that loving Aimee will make him a better person. By depriving readers of this resolution, Tharp evades the problem-resolution model that we so often come to expect from fiction, perhaps in great part because film so consistently employs it.

In addition to the far more clearly didactic happily-ever-after message that this ending offers viewers of the film, Aimee's role in Sutter's conversion in the film cannot be understated. She is the reason for this transformation, a change that is not a part of the novel. This alone casts her as the savior in the same way as the other women I have discussed, but it also seems interesting to note that in the novel, Sutter believes himself to be in the position to save Aimee, something he contemplates throughout the narrative. He tells his friend, that Aimee needs "moral support . . . she lets her family run all over her. You can see it in her eyes. It's like she doesn't think she's important enough to even stand up for herself" (85). This is something that Sutter does provide, and although he sometimes treats her badly, he does help Aimee transform, finally deciding to go live with her sister and escape her emotionally abusive home life. These elements are by and large eliminated from the movie, shifting Aimee from a truly insecure teen to a force to be reckoned with.

Like Jennifer Lawrence in the role of Katniss, the actress playing Aimee was also cast in several key roles as a strong female protagonist around nearly the same time as *The Spectacular Now*, released in 2013. In the next year, Shailene Woodley went on to star in the film adaptations of the Divergent dystopian series (beginning in 2014) as well as the popular adaptation of John Green's *The Fault in Our Stars* (2014). While these roles were very different, her quiet strength is clear in each of them, as it is in *The Spectacular Now*. For example, in the novel, when Sutter tells Aimee that he has been lying about his Dad, she simply says, "Don't worry . . . I'll never throw you away" (204), but in the movie, this scene is expanded into her encouraging him to face his fears, saying, "I'll make you a deal: I'll stand up to my mom if you stand up to yours," to which he responds, "you're spectacular."

In another scene not present in the novel, Aimee has dinner with Sutter's mother and sister, and again tries to bolster his confidence and convince him to face his baggage with his father. She says, "You can do it, Sutter. I know you can," after which he takes her advice and talks to his mother. In scenes added or altered in the film, she is consistently the catalyst for him to change. What is more, much of her insecurity is cut from the film, and while readers must often rely on Sutter's description of her, her dialogue is consistently characterized by self-doubt, almost so much so that it might make sense that Sutter wishes to save her. The movie includes almost no emphasis on these character traits, instead painting her as a quiet, but nonetheless stunningly beautiful and confident young woman.

This contributes to the shift from double to single voice in the adaptation. While in the film, Aimee seems to be slowly but surely converting Sutter to see the error of his ways, in the novel, he is a corrupting influence on her, despite his inability to see this. The reader is invited to challenge this concept—seeing Aimee both as improved by Sutter's influence, but also diminished. Even if readers might characterize Sutter as a more negative than positive force, first-person narration complicates this, creating a double voice because of both his unreliability and the contrasts in the texts between how he claims to see the world and the ways those around him see him. These elements combine and create double voice, but in the film, shifts in narration combined with the dramatic change to the story's end sway the narrative back, more concretely aligning it with single voice.

I end my consideration of this shift from double to single-voiced discourse by returning to the idea of consequences, suggesting that readers might question whether such a shift is a bad move for the adaptation to make. Might it actually be ethical to offer more didacticism when it comes to issues as serious as teen alcoholism and drunk driving? Might it be useful to have Sutter meet more frightening consequences of his actions to prove the danger of his behavior, and might it be similarly fruitful to show him learning the error of his ways?

In fact, the rave reviews of the film by critics seem to support that this more didactic approach is favorable. For example, Roger Ebert seems certainly to like this aspect of the film, reviewing it by writing, "Here is a lovely film about two high school seniors who look, speak and feel like real 18-year-old middle-American human beings. Do you have any idea how rare that is?" and continuing, "What an affecting film this is. It respects its characters and doesn't use them for its own shabby purposes. How deeply we care about them ... We have known them. We have been them." I wonder if what Ebert is drawing attention to here is truly authenticity of the teen experience, or if he is actually highlighting the way the film adheres to a constructed notion of adolescence, depicting not real teens, but precisely what adults want to believe about how teenagers struggle with complex issues, only to resolve them as they draw closer to adulthood.

Perhaps a case could be made for a more didactic tone for the movie, creating a text that delves into alcoholism with some nuance, but also emerges with a clear message. Still, I think that the novel version, with its ambiguity and complexly flawed narrator, might, as Cadden describes, more fully give "the young reader the chance to navigate her way through these contrasts" (152). The film eliminates the opportunity, but it does so in a very specific way—by introducing a more didactic influence through the female character. As Aimee saves Sutter in the film, the increase in single voice shifts the ideologies surrounding alcohol use, but also changes the ideologies about gender, including who does the saving and who must be saved.

Thus, the film offers a more conservative ideology, but also one that posits women as the civilizing force, reflecting two elements. First, this movie indicates filmmakers' lack of trust in teen viewers to unpack complex and contrasting ideologies, instead sticking to a more concrete problem-solution model. Perhaps this comes back to perspective, and perhaps it would be impossible to capture Sutter's personality and charisma, balancing it with his lack of reliability as a narrator in the medium of film. But in making this change, the movie also exemplifies a second element—that such single-voiced adolescent films often deliver their didactic messages by positioning women as the emotional saviors of the men who love them.

CHAPTER FOUR

Audience and Aetonormativity in Picturebook to Film Adaptations

Just as films adapted from young adult novels polarize especially male/female binaries, leading to a consistent emphasis on a female savior, other kinds of texts similarly demonstrate common results of binary polarization. For example, when picturebooks are made into movies, amplified themes typically foreground the adult/child binary, thus making it the primary site of polarization. This makes sense, given picturebooks' positionality within children's culture. While the experience of adolescence suits itself to an exploration of male/female dynamics, picturebooks, which are typically read by especially young readers, explore what it means to be a child in a world filled with adults. Moreover, the power dynamics inherent to the form play a significant role in the consistent ideological results of adult/child binary polarization, for while novels like the ones I have described so far are often read independently by young people, picturebooks are frequently read to children, a situation that positions adults differently than many other kinds of children's literature.

While picturebooks adapted into feature length films reproduce the pattern of thematic amplification and binary polarization I identify across all children's and YA films, these films are also uniquely embedded in a system with distinctive characteristics, such as the need to add additional content in order to fit the expectations regarding length in feature films. Picturebooks usually have physically fewer pages than a children's novel, and thus developing the story to stretch across the typical ninety-plus minutes of a feature-length film requires not only more content but, in particular, more events to occur. Certainly, there are novel adaptations that have a great deal of new content (such as *How to Train Your Dragon*), but in those cases, the adaptation choices are frequently to change, rather than to add. In the examples I explore in this chapter, the addition of content is required, rather than a choice.

More important than having simply "more" content, however, are the choices filmmakers make about how to craft this new content. While many of these decisions align with the attempts to amplify a theme that I have thus far described, the particular differences between picturebooks and picturebook films also plays an additional role. Picturebook films create a different viewing experience than most instances of picturebook reading, which usually positions the adult as teacher and the child as learner. Instead, when children watch a film, adults often accompany them; this is a necessary part of the form because children need adults to facilitate the activity. In order to persuade adults to engage in such a viewing experience, filmmakers and production companies have to think about an audience that is different than the audience of a picturebook. Both audiences include children and adults, but in a picturebook film, the adult is a different kind of participant, positioned alongside a child instead in a more vertical power structure.

Maria Nikolajeva terms this power dynamic aetonormativity, or the "adult normativity that governs the way children's literature has been patterned from its emergence until the present day," a concept she builds out of heterology, or the "inquiry of imbalance, inequality, asymmetry between different social groups" (8). Adult/child power imbalances perhaps seem less damaging than self/other or male/female binaries, for children eventually grow into adults and assume power (a key distinction from other aspects of heterology, wherein a disenfranchised group rarely becomes the group in power). Nevertheless, when adult/child binaries are polarized and power imbalances increase, ideologies are impacted in important ways, and most important of these, I suggest, is how these films depict not the children they portray, but the adults.

This shift in portrayals of adults represents the key effect I have observed resulting from polarization of adult/child binaries in picturebook films: additional content highlights adult roles and presence within the story far more than the films' textual counterparts, foregrounding adult characters and featuring adults learning lessons from children. Additionally, this pattern of more prominent adults and adult-centered references is combined with reinforcement of aetonormativity, so that even when power dynamics seem disrupted, they are also reestablished more strongly than in their source text counterparts. Again, just as in the effects of binary polarization I describe in YA film, this ideological shift is one of degree; there is an increase in adult presence, an increase in the portrayal of the adult as lesson-learner, and an increase in aetonormativity. However, because these increases are facilitated by the addition of new content that does not exist in the source text, the resulting ideological shifts are especially noticeable.

Moreover, in the case of picturebook films, investigating these factors is especially enlightening, as it also allows for a deeper consideration of the ways that dual audience and didacticism—two key elements of children's fiction—differ from book to film. Dual audience in children's literature is certainly not a new concept, explored many times from Jacqueline Rose's provocative claims in *The Case of Peter Pan, or The Impossibility of Children's Fiction* (1984) to Nodelman's 2008 discussion, *The Hidden Adult: Defining Children's Literature*. A study of picturebook adaptations, however, can offer a more in-depth understanding of how the dual audience of a film differs from the dual audience of its source text, a difference exemplified even in the terminology used to describe such films, often called "family" rather than "children's" film.

When filmmakers consider their audience in a family film, they perceive it as different from the dual audience of a picturebook, and this perceived difference, I suggest, accounts for decisions about greater adult emphasis as a key part of additional content added to a picturebook film. This emphasis also typically overturns adult/child binaries, placing children in increased power positions for a time, but eventually reestablishing aetonormative power structures. I explore this concept further by examining the 2012 film adaptation of Dr. Seuss's famed text, *The Lorax* (1971). By looking at these ideological implications of binary polarization, *The Lorax* film speaks to the perceptions about dual audience that shape filmmakers' choices.

Furthermore, increased separation between concepts like adult/child inherently creates a greater hierarchy, and thus, it would make sense that the texts are also more didactic—more "teaching" centered because this kind of content puts adults in a power position over children. Yet the question of who is teacher and who is learner is one picturebook film adaptations often appear to dismantle, a characteristic that is especially evident in the 1995 film adaptation of Chris Van Allsburg's *Jumanji* (1981). This film emphasizes a trend I note across all picturebook films, wherein filmmakers reposition adults as learners while also increasing didacticism in ways that simultaneously increased aetonormativity. By focusing on and repositioning adults as learners, the family film precipitates a viewing experience in which adults might feel like their power is challenged or overturned. This, I suggest, creates an impetus for more didacticism to establish adult/child hierarchies more forcefully, thus increasing aetonormativity.

I end the chapter by extending this discussion with a somewhat controversial family film, Spike Jonze's 2009 adaptation of Maurice Sendak's *Where the Wild Things Are* (1963). This movie offers a distinctive example of how filmmaking choices can contribute to binary polarization, but also emphasizes a common ideology that results, wherein adults are portrayed as feeling powerless despite their seeming position of power. I suggest this not only disrupts aetonormativity only to ultimately reinforce it, but also suggests important and deeply rooted ideologies related to childhood and adulthood.

"Unless Someone like You" Buys a Ticket to This Movie

Films made from picturebooks written and illustrated by Dr. Seuss offer a useful first step to understanding how polarization of adult/child binaries affects ideologies because the books exemplify the power dynamics Nikolajeva describes. Nikolajeva calls children's literature "a unique art and communication form, deliberately created by those in power for the powerless" and yet still capable of "subvert[ing] its own oppressive function, as it can describe situations in which the established power structures are interrogated without necessarily being overthrown" (8–9). This characterization can certainly be applied to Seuss's *The Lorax* (1971), which focuses on a message of environmentalism delivered by the adult Once-ler, who relays to a young unnamed protagonist that his greed and disregard for nature led to the destruction of the beautiful Truffula Trees and their corresponding ecosystem. The film reproduces this plot, but develops the unnamed child into Ted, a boy who must also save his community from being overrun by forces of corporate greed. Learning from the Once-ler's mistakes, young Ted is able to overturn problematic ideologies in his society, but only within aetonormative structures. While both the book and its adaptation represent a carnivalesque overturning and return to aetonormativity, additional content in the film shifts the nature of the dual audience by adding elements that disrupt power dynamics in more direct ways and balancing this disruption by more tangibly reinforcing adult/child power hierarchies.

In addition to the often teaching-related and/or didactic quality of these texts, the Seuss books (like all children's books) engage a dual audience because they are purchased, published, and written by adults. Yet for a family film like *The Lorax* (2012), adults typically play one of two additional roles: in a movie theater, an adult must purchase a ticket and view the film alongside the child, and in the case of a home/mobile viewing, a nearby adult often supervises the child watching the film. In either case, the adult acts as the facilitator of the activity, as would be the case if the adult were to read the picturebook source text to a child. Still, the power dynamics inherent in reading a picturebook differ greatly from those of a film viewing, wherein adults may facilitate the activity, but also participate in ways far more similar to the experience of the child viewer. Adults and children often watch a film together, while an adult reading a picturebook to a child creates a far more vertical power dynamic.

Joe Sutliff Sanders considers this difference when comparing picturebooks to comics, noting that "because the speaking reader of picture books has both initial and performative access to the words in those books, a great deal of the power in the meaning-making process of picture books lies outside the immediate purview of the listening reader," going on to describe power being held by the person "who chaperones the words as the words fix the meaning of the images" (79–80). Although film works differently than comics, it similarly takes on the role of "chaperone." Especially at the movie theater, adults watch the film with the children they have brought to this space, and rather than interacting with the text from the position of storyteller, they are positioned as a viewer/listener of the story just like the child. These experiences of being co-viewers disrupt the power dynamic of the text, placing adult and child viewers in more equal power positions than they might be in reading situations involving Seuss picturebooks.

This adult viewership is especially evident in the controversy over *The Lorax*'s marketing campaigns, which critics claimed conflicted with the movie's messages about problematic notions of consumerism. Among its over seventy product tie-ins (as reported by the Campaign for a Commercial-Free Childhood) were promotions surrounding Mazda SUVs, Xfinity TV service, Target, DoubleTree Hotels, and IHOP restaurants, leading news outlets like the *Washington Post* to run headlines such as "The Lorax Helps Market Mazda SUVs to Elementary School Children Nationwide" (Brown). As several online journalists noted, SUVs, television service, and a family breakfast at the local pancake house are not products typically sold to children, but to the families that will also be the purchasing power of movie tickets to *The Lorax* screening and, eventually, DVD copies of the film. While not new (Nathalie op de Beeck's 2005 article, "Speaking for the Trees: Environmental Ethics in the Rhetoric and Production of Picturebook" makes similar claims about the book itself), this controversy reflects the concepts surrounding audience that I believe are crucial to a consideration of picturebook adaptation. Films made from Dr. Seuss movies are seemingly intended for children, but these viewers require a parent to drive them to the movie theater and purchase the ticket.

Additionally, the film version of *The Lorax* acknowledges a dual viewership in how it frames its opening scene and shifts the perspective of the story. To see this distinction, it is useful to return to the context of the picturebook. In many cases, a parent, teacher, librarian, or other invested adult will read *The Lorax* to children, creating a power dynamic and an element of didacticism that is not only adult mediated, as in all children's literature written by adults, but also mediated again by an adult reader. Even when the story is read independently by a child, the structure of the text still places the adult author/narrator in a position of teacher and authority. The text includes an adult storyteller; the Once-ler is telling the story to a young listener, figured as a tiny unnamed child. This exemplifies Nikolajeva's commentary that "the child/adult imbalance is most tangibly manifested in the relationship between the ostensibly adult narrative voice and the child focalizing character" (8).

Moreover, Seuss's *The Lorax* goes even further, using direct address ("Ask him. He knows.") and second person to associate the reader with this young observer. This move allows the "you" of the story to be imposed on the reader, making the ending all the more direct: "Now that you're here, the word of the Lorax seems perfectly clear. UNLESS someone like you cares a whole awful lot, nothing is going to get better. It's not." Thus, whether read by or to a child, there are several levels of adult presence in this text—adult writer/publisher and possible adult reading aloud, as well as an adult within the story dictating the lesson or moral to a child. The statement of "UNLESS" clarifies this power dynamic even further, for readers are left with the idea that to stop a terrible future, they must "care a whole awful lot." This is something a child can accomplish—caring about the environment.

By incorporating a new secondary narrative, the additional content in *The Lorax* film shifts this dynamic, polarizing the binary between children and adults by presenting them as conceptually different and, as a result, repositioning the story away from a directive provided to children toward a message that more fully includes the adult viewer. In *The Lorax* film, the unnamed child in Seuss's picturebook is expanded into Ted, a boy who lives in Thneedville and wishes to impress his childhood crush, Audrey, by finding a way to plant a real tree, something that Audrey has always dreamed about. Thneedville, viewers come to discover, is the town that remained after the Once-ler's decimation of the Truffula trees and is now run by a corporate megalomaniac named O'Hare, who sells bottled clean air and thus has a vested interest in preventing Ted from realizing his desire to plant a tree for Audrey.

Here viewers can see both thematic amplification and a resulting binary polarization. First, this new storyline emphasizes the destructive effects of valuing individual wealth amassed through the production of goods, both in the new character O'Hare and his problematically commercialized town of Thneedville, as well as in the expanded backstory of the Once-ler, who learns the value of a pro-environment stance from the Lorax and comes to understand the importance of keeping his word. By expanding and emphasizing these themes, filmmakers also polarize binaries, making Ted and Audrey especially seem entirely set apart from the clueless or malicious adults of their world. Just as in other examples I describe, this binary polarization does not stand alone, but intertwines with others, such as good/evil and autonomy/dependence. Furthermore, the Once-ler's story exemplifies Nikolajeva's description of young people moving from one side of this binary to another, for at the start, the Once-ler is a young man who grapples with his limited power, growing into the adult who now imparts the wisdom of his experience to Ted, a representative of a new generation who might have the ability to evoke real change.

This binary polarization combines with storytelling techniques inherent in the form of film to result in an overturning and subsequent reestablishment of aetonormativity. In contrast to the book, which uses techniques of framing, direct address, and second person to direct the story to the child reader, the film opens by addressing a wider audience. In the initial scene, the Lorax himself frames the film as a story he is about to tell; he stands in front of a curtain, saying, "There's more to the story than what's on the page, so please pay attention while I set the stage." The Lorax is the chaperone of meaning, to use Sanders's term, but he is not simply addressing children. Instead, this comment seems to directly address the changed power dynamic of the cinema experience, for now the viewer is not positioned as a child listener, but as part of a wider audience—which includes adults and children—sitting in a theater and listening to the Lorax.

While the book builds to the powerful final "Unless," the framing of the film instead highlights the story of Thneedville, wherein adults learn lessons about environmentalism and corporate greed, just as the adult Once-ler learns the same lessons in the flashback sequences. Conversely, the film uses the distinct space of the theater to foreground the adult's role both as moviegoer and learner, for while the Once-ler's message is directed toward a child (Ted), the Lorax speaks to adults who have the power to not simply "care a whole awful lot," but actually take action to stop the destruction they perpetuate. This shift, reinforced through content as much as framing, reflects the changing power dynamics inherent in a theater or similar group viewing experience. The vertical power structures typical to instances of reading are replaced with a more horizontal structure, wherein the film itself is the authority, and that authority (through the narrator of the Lorax) speaks to both children and adults.

Additionally, while in Seuss's *The Lorax*, adult power/presence is implied, adults themselves (other than the Lorax) are almost never explicitly pictured or described. In fact, while the unnamed child appears on nearly all pages in the story's frame, the Once-ler (a presumed adult) is only ever represented with arms and occasionally eyes, and the only other adult, an unnamed consumer, holds the thneed to obscure his face. This reinforces the story's focus on the child learner. In contrast, adults play a large role in both Ted's experience in Thneedville and the fleshing out of the Once-ler's tale. Unlike the passive child character in Seuss's version, Ted uses what he learns from the Once-ler to encourage the adults of his town (wholly new characters in the adaptation), and as a result, they reform their belief systems to take a more environmentally friendly approach. This foregrounds the additional adult characters, but also puts them in position as learners, a move similarly exemplified in the additional elements of the Once-ler's story. While the Once-ler in the film seems to hold a power position similar to the book version as storyteller, because his character is also enhanced by additional content, audiences see him too in the position of adult learner. In both instances, adults are more central to the story, and these adults all learn lessons, with the biggest addition to the story focusing on Ted and Audrey (children) teaching lessons to adults.

While this change seems to disrupt adult/child hierarchies, family films frequently feature adult characters (especially in Disney's animated fairy tales, which typically star older protagonists), indicating that film producers might believe children are interested in stories about adults, a perception supported by the popularity of these films among child viewers. In addition to this element, however, new content in *The Lorax* film, and especially the conflict between an adult villain (O'Hare) set against a heroic youthful protagonist, also amplifies Seuss's more understated critique of commercial culture, doing so in a way that relies on adult understanding of these kinds of social structures in order to resonate fully.

In *The Lorax* movie, amplification of the commentary on consumerism, evident in the additional narrative and several of the film's musical numbers, shifts the book's message to place more blame on corporate, commercialized power structures. While Seuss's *The Lorax* certainly alludes to the consumers at work in the system of thneed production, this concept is only emphasized once, and as I have mentioned, the face of the consumer is hidden from view. The film gives a face to consumerism and those who perpetuate it; in addition to expanding the Once-ler's character into a young entrepreneur with a vivid backstory, the film also depicts a second level of out-of-control consumerism in Thneedville, headed by the villainous O'Hare. These additional elements offer more than just a subtle indictment of the consumer, whose purchase of the thneed is what eventually leads to widespread devastation of the natural world. Instead, viewers see direct examples of corporate greed and corruption, and a resulting city where synthetic products replace all natural entities. The critique here is not particularly subtle, although it is sold to consumers who purchase a movie ticket, DVD, video download, or soundtrack to hear it.

The message of the dangers of consumer culture run amok has relevancy to children, who one day will be consumers and make decisions about the future of these power structures in society. However, the bulk of the references that offer such a criticism are provided to viewers without explanation, and thus adults, who have greater prior familiarity with such social structures, may take more from these brief references. As Jeanne Klein describes by applying reception studies to children's theater, "'Children's aesthetics,' their perceived interpretations of theatre, differ from that of adults' theorized postulations, based in part on their shorter life experiences with this medium" (40). Because of this, she posits theatrical performances "more likely affirm and reinforce conceptual ideas *already learned* than 'teach' youngsters any 'new' information that they don't already know and recognize" (50, emphasis original). The same is true of film. If movie producers wished to present these ideas in ways children would understand, they would need to offer more scaffolding, similar to how they present the environmental aspects of the film.

Herein lies a crucial distinction. When it comes to the message related to the environment and the importance of saving the trees, the film provides ample scaffolding to teach this lesson to children, thus mimicking the didactic approach of the book. First, viewers see Audrey's desire for a tree and her visually stunning painting of the Truffula trees that have been extinct since long before she was born. Then, the Lorax highlights the importance of nature to the Once-ler in repeated instances, set in visual contrast to the horrors that result when he does not heed the Lorax's warning. The cause-and-effect relationship is clear; the Once-ler's behavior causes terrible destruction and occurs because he promises the Lorax not to cut down a single tree and then breaks that vow. Finally, in a climactic ending back in Thneedville, Audrey and Ted engage in a high-speed chase with Ted's spunky grandmother (who has also reinforced the messages regarding the environment throughout) in order to escape O'Hare's attempt to destroy the last remaining Truffula seed. The movie ends with a song titled "Let It Grow," so that if viewers have not yet received the message about the environment, it is certainly clear in the concluding lyrics: "It's just one tiny seed / But it's all we really need / It's time to banish all your greed / Imagine Thneedville flowered and treed / Let this be our solemn creed / We say let it grow."

In contrast, the criticism of consumerism and corporate culture in the film is presented not through such step-by-step explanation, and it is not the lesson learned by the child protagonist. Rather, this message is mostly presented through a series of allusions and references that adults have more access to than children. For example, adults might recognize that the advertising staff pitches O'Hare a commercial for bottled air that follows the exact conventions of a beer ad. Adults might also make connections that would pose greater difficulty for children, as in the scene featuring indigenous Brown Bar-ba-loots' placid appeasement by the Once-ler's offering of marshmallows in exchange for taking their land. Adults with knowledge of historical and contemporary instances of such behavior on the part of powerful nations or invaders might see this reference as critical, while some younger children might simply be engaged by the Brown Bar-ba-loots catching the marshmallows in their mouths in slow motion.

These adult-centered allusions are most evident in the film's song lyrics, which require particular foreknowledge to interpret. For example, the musical number "How Bad Can I Possibly Be" presents exceedingly clear images of environmental destruction, but does far less to explain the corporate critique, instead relying on lyric references that viewers unfamiliar with the specifics of consumerist culture would likely not recognize. To add an additional level of complexity, some of these references rely on identifying visual allusions that contradict what the Once-ler is saying. For example, the Once-ler justifies his actions by saying "I'm just building an economy," followed by "a portion of proceeds goes to charity," while his disguised uncle pockets the money and winks. The rhyme then changes to "all the customers are buying . . . the money's multiplying . . . [and] the PR people are lying," juxtaposed with a snapshot of the Lorax mistakenly holding the thneed, which ends up on a billboard labeled "Lorax approved," as the montage ends with "and the lawyers are denying." Again, I am not saying that such images and lyrical iterations would be overlooked by all children, but without more detailed explanation, they seem more directed to adults, most of whom would not require scaffolding to understand the critique. Thus, the film's additional content becomes more adult-centered in several key ways: framing directed toward adults, greater prominence of adult characters, and comical/critical references that would likely be more clearly understood by adult viewers.

These additional content elements work in tandem to complicate aetonormativity. First, by creating a more horizontal viewing relationship between children and adults, the film challenges adult/child power structures. No longer is the adult teaching the lesson in the story, whether as reader or through framing/address. Instead, children and adults are both learners. Furthermore, in the film, it is the children who are able to assert the necessary power to solve problems. Far more than in the picturebook source text, child characters actively and passionately fight for their beliefs, and especially in the case of Audrey, this seems to also suggest a child's (and in particular, a female child's) exceptional insight into the problems of society. Children, in the film version far more than the source, hold the power and bear the responsibility to enact social change, thus positioning them as powerful, a notion intensified by clear binary between them and the either clueless or callous adults.

While aetonormativity appears disrupted in the movie adaptation, this element is also balanced by an amplified reinforcement of adult/child power hierarchies. Ted's carnivalesque disruption of aetonormativity is short lived, and the final song shifts power back to adults. It is an adult's disagreement with O'Hare that begins the final musical number, and in subsequent lines, other adults add their voices. Ted and Audrey may have been the catalyst for this movement, but adults take center stage in its final moment. The biggest exception to this is a young child's line in the song, "My name's Marie, and I am three / and I would really like to see a tree." Still, the condescending "Awww" response of the adult audience does significant work to reinstate aetonormativity. Children, in this final sequence, are portrayed as cute and innocent, rather than in a position of power. Furthermore, because the adult Once-ler is telling Ted the story, it might be argued that Ted never actually leaves an adult/child hierarchy, emphasizing that a child might change society, but only through adult intervention. While Ted is given more power within the film than the unnamed child of Seuss's picturebook, by so dramatically reversing this dynamic, the return to aetonormativity seems especially forceful. Adults and children are allowed to engage more horizontal power dynamics as viewers, but only within the confines of an increased aetonormativity inserted to balance and counteract these elements.

It seems important to highlight, however, that this increased aetonormativity resulting from intensified adult/child binaries also lines up with another binary polarization, for male/female binaries are more polarized in the film adaptation as well. Moreover, this polarization is striking in its connection to YA film adaptations, and in some ways, Audrey's role in the story seems a precursor to the kinds of interactions one might expect if the adaptation were to highlight her and Ted as teenagers, rather than children. The addition of a distinctive male/female binary into the adult/child discussion adds a new ideology about who is in need of "fixing"—the adult, but especially the male adult. While I have thus far described this as a result of binary polarization in YA film adaptations, it is also something Trites identifies in films for much younger audiences, including the fourteen Pixar animated films that can "serve as a case study of how one cultural narrative—'women are more mature than men'—persists and in turn contributes to the perpetuation of such additional cultural narratives as sexism, ageism, and reverse discrimination" (*Cognition* 105). She chronicles how "Pixar's immature, insensitive, conflict-ridden, funny characters" are usually men and "easily contrasted to Pixar's mature characters, who are usually female" (*Cognition* 109).

This repositioning of adult characters, as well as its pairing with a subsequent reinforcement of aetonormativity, represents a trend that adaptations of other Seuss picturebooks also emphasize, despite their differing release dates and styles of production. Similar to *The Lorax*, the film adaptation of *How the Grinch Stole Christmas* (2000) amplifies a critique of commercialism, developed through additional content that does more than highlight the true meaning of the holidays, but specifically critiques corporate greed. Moreover, the film locates this social problematic within the purview of adults. While viewers are privy to the Grinch's childhood backstory, this seems in service of commenting on the bullying perpetuated by adult characters who torment the Grinch, leading him to engage in a rant about Whoville's greed at Christmas and then plot to steal all evidence of the celebration (as in the picturebook). This bullying scene of the film changes the text's message, for while the Grinch of Seuss's tale learns that "maybe Christmas doesn't come from a store," but "perhaps means a little bit more," the Grinch in the film seems to already know this, and it is a lesson the adults of Whoville need to learn. Cindy Lou (again, a female child character) sees the greed of Christmas and the wrongness in the way the Grinch is bullied, while the adults of the story are the ones who must change.

Nel comments on this element of *The Grinch* film adaptation by noting the emphasis on Seuss's moral, but writing that the film also "stresses the values of self-improvement, emphasizing a quintessentially American narrative: if you work hard, anything is possible" (133). Yet Nel is actually identifying two distinctive lessons of the film: self-improvement and working hard. Cindy Lou Who exemplifies the latter, presented as "equal parts social worker, therapist, and investigative reporter" (Nel 133). The Grinch and the Whos, all adult characters, are the ones to engage in self-improvement. Nonetheless, aetonormativity is restored by the end of the film, for while Cindy Lou Who acts as an inspiration or catalyst, the final scenes set up the Grinch as the most powerful voice of change. Binary polarization has resulted in adults portrayed as lesson learners, but only while maintaining aetonormative structures.

Another Dr. Seuss film adaptation, *Horton Hears a Who*, also matches the adult/child dynamic of *Lorax* and *Grinch* in several ways. For example, the Sour Kangaroo represents adult forces that must embrace new ways of thinking, and her baby kangaroo tries throughout to rebel against her, in the end standing with Horton instead of his mother. Also, the mayor of Whoville learns a valuable insight from his son when he realizes that he was not really listening to what Jojo was trying to say to him about his unique views and interests. Thus, as in the *Lorax* and *Grinch*, these instances showcase lessons learned by adults.

Additionally, *Horton* provides an example of the use of allusions to offer social critique that seems more accessible to adult viewers than children, much like *The Lorax*. Two main institutions are criticized in many of the less explained allusions of the text: the Whoville Council who refuses to believe the mayor and instead wishes to ignore the impending danger and preserve the status quo, and an educational system based on conformity and censorship, vocalized through the Sour Kangaroo. These institutional critiques are the product of additional content, but neither is explained in the film in any direct way, instead relying on references that will resonate more with adult audience members already familiar with these social structures. Again, added content seems to offer messages and ideologies about adults learning to be better adults but also, more than their picturebook source texts, presents this material in ways directed to adult viewers, evidencing the filmmakers' acknowledgment of the differences of dual audience that are inherent to the form of film.

"Acting like a Man" in the Family Film

In addition to a rethinking of dual audience, the role of didacticism also changes in film adaptations as a result of polarized binaries leading to adult-centered overturning and reinstatement of aetonormativity. In a film like *The Lorax*, book to movie changes related to didacticism may go unnoticed, as Seuss's picturebook is already a very obviously didactic tale. Allsburg's *Jumanji* (1981) eludes such clearly didactic imperatives, so that when altered to fit the disruption-resolution model, didacticism becomes far more explicit in the film adaptation. One might imagine such changes would result in a more child-centered narrative, wherein a child would learn a lesson to resolve the story's conflict. This is not the case; just as in *The Lorax*, additional content in the film *Jumanji* (1995) plays out the disruption-resolution model by featuring lessons learned by adults in the film, rather than lessons learned by children (as in the picturebook). Additionally, the resolution of this model amplifies aetonormativity's seeming disruption, so that while children appear to be given more power than in the picturebook, adult/child hierarchies are also more forcefully reinstated than in this source text.

Van Allsburg's picturebook *Jumanji* follows two children who embark on a magical adventure when they play a board game that brings to life a set of jungle-themed challenges, creating a chaos that subverts the adult authority of the text mandated by their parents. In a true example of aetonormativity, power hierarchies are reestablished when the children return order by completing the game, narrowly avoiding the crisis of having their parents return to a home overrun by the treacherous jungle. The book aligns with Nikolajeva's discussion of the carnivalesque; in playing Jumanji, the children are empowered to assert control over fantastic elements, all while also held to the authority of the game. Just as Chaston describes in connecting *Jumanji* to the Seuss's *Cat in the Hat*, in both stories, parents leave and chaos ensues, only to disappear by the time the parents return. The Cat's arrival and the game of *Jumanji* provide frightening and troubling amounts of chaos, presenting ideologies regarding children's independence and expressions of power within adult mediated systems.

Playing the game of Jumanji also constitutes rebellion against adult authority, albeit initially unknowingly. The story begins with the children's mother saying, "Now remember . . . your father and I are bringing some guests by after the opera, so please keep the house neat," a sentiment that Father follows up with "Quite so." Chaston considers this element in comparing the picturebook and film versions of *Jumanji*, drawing on John Gardner to note that a key question of this picturebook is "What if disobedience had consequences?" (cited in Chaston, "Ozification" 17). I would add to Chaston's discussion of this element by pointing out that, unlike the film, the *Jumanji* picturebook explores disobedience and consequences in a way that resists didacticism. Although playing Jumanji does result in disobedience from the parents' mandate to "keep the house neat," Peter and Judy make every attempt to follow instructions provided by adult authority. Even though Peter worries it will be "boring," they play a board game, an exceptionally calm and mess-free activity. These children can hardly be blamed for the resulting chaos, for who could possibly imagine that a board game would create the forbidden mess? Further, although the next set of children who find Jumanji at the end of Van Allsburg's story are criticized for never reading instructions, Peter and Judy do not exhibit this behavior, immediately reviewing the game's parameters. In fact, Judy makes a point of articulating this, telling Peter to put down the pieces and listen while she reads the instructions. Peter obeys, and it is clear that these children seek to follow the adult authority of both their parents and the game makers. They do not need to learn this lesson.

This point is important because it sets up a key element of the adaptation. While *The Lorax* book begins as a clearly didactic tale, *Jumanji* does not and must be altered to fit the disruption-resolution model. As a result, the film version centers its additional content around this question of disobedience and adult authority. This is established most concretely in a secondary storyline wherein young Alan is swept into the world of Jumanji for decades. He returns to the contemporary world as an adult who must work through his beliefs about power and parenting as he aids a new generation of children playing the game. Thus, at its heart, this movie is a story about a father and son, and the son's subsequent journey to understand the positionality of his father, but only once he becomes an adult himself.

This, again, exemplifies a binary polarization. While adults in the picturebook, though only briefly present, offer a directive to their children, the adult role in the film is far expanded, but also in ways that create a greater conceptual dichotomy between the adults and children. There is increased adult/child conflict between Peter and his father, which like the conflict in *Coraline*, serves to create a greater conceptual difference between them. Furthermore, when adults take on a more central role in the film adaptation, their interactions with children show that children actually have unique insights, so that like *The Lorax* film, children are portrayed as inherently different than adults, and thus able to teach them valuable lessons, if, that is, aetonormative structures are maintained.

This is the central element in the *Jumanji* adaptation, because a stronger degree of aetonormativity also affects the text's didacticism. Although the film occasionally seems to criticize adult behavior, it actually reinforces aetonormativity even more strongly than the picturebook, especially in the movie's end, when Alan takes up the ideologies laid out for him by adult authority. This structure also results in a more clearly didactic message about how to face one's fears, presenting this concept by depicting an adult, rather than a child, learning a lesson.

The film *Jumanji* begins with young Alan hiding out in his father's factory to avoid a group of bullies taunting him below. Alan's father scoffs at his predicament, saying, "Look, if you're afraid of something, you've got to stand and face it." While he eventually backtracks this idea upon realizing that his son was being attacked by not one but several older boys, the crux of the film surrounds Alan's coming to terms with whether he ascribes to this belief or not. This growth happens, however, when he is an adult. After the instance of bullying, Alan and Sarah begin playing Jumanji, but they are interrupted when Alan is sucked into the game. Sarah runs away screaming, and twenty-six years later, Peter and Judy free an adult Alan from the terrifying jungle of Jumanji. They then coax Alan into seeking out the adult Sarah to help them all to finish the game. In the process, the child characters teach the adult characters, and the focus of the narrative shifts from one centered on children to one centered on adults.

While the film seems to suggest that the authority-driven parenting approach of Alan's father is a problem, the movie actually reinforces his "men aren't afraid" sentiment; in fact, this seems to be the film's primary lesson. For example, when Peter is turned into a monkey, Alan tells him, "What, are you crying? You don't cry, all right? You keep your chin up. . . . Crying never helped anybody do anything, okay? You have a problem, you face it like a man." He immediately sees the pattern this scolding reinforces, saying, "I'm sorry. Twenty-six years buried in the jungle, and I still became my father." He seems to acknowledge that Peter was right about this in his previous commentary on fear: "Remember what you told me? It's alright to be afraid." Still, the next comedic line contradicts this, for Peter admits he was not crying out of fear, but because his newly acquired monkey tail is causing him pain while stuck in his jeans.

Rather than suggesting that Alan has learned that his father's beliefs about what "makes a man" are problematic, the film undercuts this idea because when they initially met, Peter has not actually told Alan that it was all right to be afraid. In the line that Alan is referring to, Peter was using reverse psychology (as he later admits to Judy). He expresses the opposite of what he believes in order to get Alan to respond in exactly the way that he does—saying that he is not afraid. This is a manipulation, and one that reinforces the notion that a person (and especially a man) should not be afraid, or at the very least, should not show fear. Peter believes this and uses it to shame Alan into joining them in order to prove that he is not afraid.

When it comes to ideologies surrounding fear, the messages of the film are also very gendered, again bringing in male/female binaries to pair with the adult/child polarization. When the female and maternal figure of the story, Sarah, makes a point to suggest to Alan that he might reconsider the way he "parents" Peter, Alan seems to take her up on this advice, again suggesting the role of the female to provide insight in a male's development of self. Nonetheless, the overall story actually supports the opposite ideology about fear when it comes to men, whereas Sarah's fear is far more condoned. In fact, Sarah's fear of Jumanji has controlled her life, and she describes the extensive therapy she has undergone in an attempt to move past the trauma she faced as a child. While this at times is portrayed as silly (which is certainly problematic in terms of the movie's depiction of trauma and resulting PTSD and mental health options), overall, Sarah's fear seems more acceptable, and she relays this to the children, noting, "It's ok. We're scared too." Still, while the question of fear's merit is more flexible for women than men, the overall theme of the film shines through when this statement is followed by a distinctive "but," and even Sarah makes clear that they must conquer their fear by finishing the game.

The main lesson of the film (and one that is not subtle to any degree) is about conquering fear. More importantly, the movie is not really about how Peter and Judy (the children) respond to fear, and in fact, viewers really never see any instance in which they are afraid or being instructed about fear (since Peter's crying was actually not about fear at all). Instead, viewers see adults dealing with fear, coming to grips with how they should approach situations that frighten them, and thinking about how they should talk about fear with children.

This is perhaps most true in the interactions Alan has with the movie's main antagonist, a hunter who has pursued him both during his time in the jungle and upon his return. It is no coincidence that this figure is played by the same actor who plays Alan's father. This casting especially resonates in the final climatic moment of the film, when Alan's father in his Jumanji hunter form asks him, "Aren't you afraid?" Alan responds by articulating a key theme of the movie, thus establishing the film's didactic message: "I'm terrified. But my father told me . . . you should always face what you're afraid of," to which the hunter/father responds, "Good lad. You're finally acting like a man." This is the lesson Alan has learned, and the hunter (i.e., his father's jungle alter ego) has taught it to him.

Additionally, Alan actively reinforces an adult/child power hierarchy when he returns home as a child. As Alan and his father both apologize to each other, his father says, "Let's talk it over tomorrow . . . man-to-man," conceding his position of power in this statement to some degree. Alan responds, "How about father-to-son?" reestablishing and reinforcing the original adult/child dynamic. Even more importantly, he also admits to being responsible for causing the earlier ruckus at the factory that results in an employee losing his job, and in doing so, Alan shows that even at home, he has conquered his fear and accepted his father's position of power.

While initially the film seems to offer a critique of the father's behavior, going so far as to figure him in the role of the violent hunter, in the end, Alan adopts his "be a man—don't be afraid" belief system, seemingly to his benefit. The adult Alan is the central character of the story, and the one who learns something from the experience of Jumanji. The children in the film are secondary, which is a substantial shift from the picturebook, wherein there is adult presence, but adults only appear in the text in their brief initial instruction, accompanied by an illustration in which only their legs are shown.

Chaston notes this distinction, writing, "The triumph of defeating the game is taken away from the children and put into the hands of the (admittedly childlike) adults, Alan and Sarah. Whereas Van Allsburg's children solve their problems without adult help, Judy and Peter no longer have the ability to save themselves. It is an adult male figure, not Judy, who shakes the dice at the end of the movie and rescues them" ("Ozification" 18). Again, just as in *The Lorax*, this places adults in the foreground of the adaptation far more than in the source text, but it also disrupts power dynamics by placing adults in the position of lesson learner. In this way, just as the viewing experience creates more horizontal adult/child power dynamics than the reading experience, the content of the film also reinforces this seeming disruption of aetonormativity. The adult reader of the source text is not only placed in a greater position of power than the adult viewer of the film, but the text itself also reinforces this relationship. Adults in the picturebook hold a role of absent authority, but by featuring adults more prominently as characters who grow and develop, the movie puts adults in the position of learner alongside the child, even while it also strongly reinforces aetonormativity. This is even more the case in *Jumanji* than in *The Lorax*, for the whole story seems to revolve around the reinstatement of the adult/child power hierarchy established in the film's onset, wherein Alan's father so forcefully positions himself as the authority figure. While the film seems to at times push back against this structure, in the climactic final moments, aetonormativity is very strongly reinstated, and far more so than is demonstrated in the return of the parents in the picturebook's conclusion.

Like the elements I have described with regard to audience in *The Lorax*, these differences in the *Jumanji* film adaptation also have to do with adaptive practice and expectation—the perceptions filmmakers have about a movie's unique dual audience work with perceived audience expectations with regards to filmic conventions to shape content additions. This is especially true in a live-action film like *Jumanji* (1995), which is marketed as an action-packed spectacle starring a famous comedic actor. Positioned this way, *Jumanji* perhaps appeals to adults even more than an animated film like *The Lorax*. The picturebook *Jumanji* certainly has a dual audience, but because the film is not only mediated through adults, but in part directed toward them, the adaptation reflects a very different perceived dual audience by increasing both disruption and reinstatement of aetonormativity.

Additionally, this distinct dual audience of film has interesting implications in how critics might consider audience in children's literature more broadly. The adaptive changes facilitated by the need for additional content support contemporary considerations of children's literature that focus on the relevancy of textual messages to both adults and children. Marah Gubar writes of such perspectives in describing a kinship model of childhood, "premised on the idea that children and adults are akin to one another, which means they are neither exactly the same nor radically dissimilar. The concept of kinship indicates relatedness, connection, and similarity without implying homogeneity, uniformity, and equality" (453). I would suggest the same concept is at play in the production of a family film, in which both potential child and adult viewers play an important role in determinations related to content additions.

From this perspective, the seemingly "dual" nature of a film's dual audience seems to fade away a bit, so that as Gubar describes, "children and adults are separated by differences of degree, not of kind, meaning that we should eschew difference-model discourse that depicts children as a separate species in favor of emphasizing that growth is a messy and unpredictable continuum" (453). Still, while *The Lorax* and *Jumanji* both engage the more horizontal power dynamics of a film's dual audience, they also do so while reinforcing and even amplifying aetonormativity as compared to their source texts. This leads me to believe that the ways adults envision the "child" and the power structures that define adult/child binaries still exist as a strong part of not only children's literature, but especially adaptations of those texts into film.

Powerful and Powerless Adults

Filmmakers also emphasize adult/child binaries in a film adapted from one of the most famous picturebooks of all time: Maurice Sendak's *Where the Wild*

Things Are (1963). Adapted in 2009 under the direction of Spike Jonze, the film met with controversy, as Ebert alludes to in describing the somewhat unsettling wild things, noting "I don't find them particularly lovely, nor should I; they're not fuzzy toys but characters in a dream that slides in and out of nightmares." Ebert mirrors other reviewers in attributing this to audience, commenting that the film will "play better for older audiences remembering a much-loved book from childhood."

This mirrors my arguments about *The Lorax* and *Jumanji* that the distinctive dual audience of film plays an important role in how filmmakers craft new content, for they take adults viewers into account. Still, I would further suggest that portrayal of adult/child binaries in *Where the Wild Things Are* evidences another consistent ideological effect of binary polarization. When adaptations position adults as lesson learners within a system that nonetheless reinforces aetonormativity, these films reinforce a view of adulthood that emphasizes its challenges. In doing so, adaptations like *Where the Wild Things Are* not only polarizes concepts of adulthood and childhood, but also posit adults as individuals who hold power but feel powerless.

This representation of powerful adults who express feelings of powerlessness is another ideological ramification of binary polarization, which is alive and well in the *Where the Wild Things Are* film adaptation. Like in the picturebook *Jumanji*, parental authority plays a significant role in Sendak's *Where the Wild Things Are*, but the source of this authority always exists outside of the page. Although Max's mother calls him "Wild Thing," even her subsequent action is displaced through passive voice: "so he was sent to bed without eating anything." Max finds a way to express his need for a "wild rumpus" by traveling to an imaginary world, only to realize he wishes to return to a place where "someone loves him best of all," and again, his mother's presence exists (in the "still hot" supper), but she is never shown. Just as in *Jumanji* and *Cat in the Hat*, the child's carnivalesque adventure is temporary, and Max returns to the safety of home where power structures remain the same. Like Alan, Max (though considerably younger) ends his story by returning to the adult/child power dynamic that he initially sought to rebel against, a plot development that Spike Jonze follows in his film adaptation.

Because Nikolajeva's aetonormativity is so keenly a part of this source, it is difficult to believe that it might be even stronger in the film. Yet just as in the other texts I have explicated, power structures in Jonze's adaptation first appear to be more strongly overturned in the film, only to be more forcefully reinforced than the picturebook version. This, again, comes from new content, for to achieve the necessary length for a feature-length film, Jonze engages in significant restructuring, beginning by giving Max's wild behavior a set of specific causes. Viewers witness two turbulent conflicts in the first scenes of the film: first, when Max's sister wishes to play with her friends instead of him, prompting him to attempt to destroy her room and, second, when his mother's new boyfriend tells her that she should not stand for Max's behavior.

The more important addition to the film, however, is the fully formed personalities of the wild things and, especially, Carol, whose portrayal mimics Max's pre-island perspectives and behavior. While Max still takes on a power position over the wild things by becoming their king, the film refigures this reversal by also positioning him in the role of parent over Carol and the other wild things, thus learning that his mother's frustration is well founded. Max sees himself in the conflict Carol has with K.W. and the other wild things and thus learns to identify the problem of his own temper. This is true of the book as well, wherein Max adopts his mother's role and learns of her frustration, but this overcoming is made far more explicit in the film, moving from a subtle subtext to the central focus of the additional content.

This thematic amplification is perhaps most noticeable in a poignant scene in which Max tells K.W. that Carol "doesn't mean to be that way . . . he's just scared," to which she responds, "Well, he only makes it harder. And it's hard enough already." In replying to this, Max makes a clear connection to his own dilemma, saying "but he loves you. You're his family. It's hard being a family." He later applies even more direct self-analysis, saying "I wish you guys had a mom," and immediately following this sentiment with his decision: "I'm gonna go home." This discussion makes it clear that Max has learned something about himself. While certainly true in the picturebook as well, the film adaptation amplifies this concept and makes it far more explicit.

Nonetheless, the binary polarization that results from this thematic amplification is a bit different in *Where the Wild Things Are* than other films I have explored. Thus far, I have posited that in films adapted from picturebooks, adults and children are depicted as wholly different from one another, figuring "adult" as the absence of childlike characteristics and "child" as lacking adult characteristics. This harkens back to Gubar's discussion of the kinship model, wherein this stark contrast and contradiction between adults and children fits far more with the difference and deficit models she outlines. In the case of Jonze's film, Max begins in the position of child, but then not only wields authority, but also takes on the role of a parent, deciding to return only after having both expressed his desire for power and learned something about adult perspectives, coming to view himself through adult eyes. While this represents an overturning followed by a reinforcement of aetonormativity, the adult/child binary stems from Max's movement from child to adult and back again, rather than a more obvious distinction between actual adult and child characters in the text. By using additional content to develop Carol into a Max-proxy, Max becomes a stand-in for his mother, so that the film is not centered on adult characters or even adult institutions, but instead on a child learning about what it means to be an adult. This, however, nonetheless polarizes the dichotomy of adult and child, for the two concepts are kept consistently separate in order to achieve the film's thematic message.

Furthermore, I would suggest that the film adaptation still highlights adults and adult perspectives in more explicit ways than its source text counterpart, only in a different way. In Sendak's text, Max's experience shows a child taking on adult power for a short time, but in Jonze's film, Max also learns to see things as his mother does, thus prompting him to return contrite and compassionate. Max realizes that his mother loves him even when she yells, because "it is hard being a family." On one level, this idea resonates with children, socializing them to similarly see the perspective of their parents through Max's eyes. Yet the additions of the film not only reinforce adult/child power structures in purposeful ways; they also affirm to parents and adults that their behaviors and reactions to children in these moments are a normative part of the adult/child paradigm. The film thus explores the complex nature of adulthood and parenting while reinforcing to adults that their struggles and challenges are valid and normalized.

The film is consequently focused on the relationship of parent to child as one built on power; it suggests that an adult's frustration with a child overturning these power structures in destructive ways is justified. The book also presents this concept, for Max makes the same decision as his mother, sending the wild things to bed without supper. This part of the text's message is more subtle, overshadowed perhaps by the next line, where the reader learns that Max was "lonely and wanted to be where someone loved him best of all." In the film, Max learns both lessons about power and love as well, but the additional content focuses on the power dynamic between Max and the wild things by explicitly voicing Max's role as the adult in the situation. By creating a Max proxy in the character of Carol, the filmmakers make Max's role as the adult more explicit than in the source by featuring adult perspectives in more obvious or prominent ways.

In Sendak's book, Max follows Nikolajeva's notions of the carnivalesque informing aetonormativity in that he disrupts the power dynamic between adult and child temporarily, but returns to it in the end. In the movie, this is also true, but the disruption is more purposeful; it is meant for Max to gain insight into the adult/child power dynamics. This emphasizes these dynamics for the child viewer, but it does so for the adult moviegoer as well, reinforcing that this adult/child power position is correct. In this way, the film balances the adult and child viewer as its potential audience, offering something to both children and adults in ways more pronounced or explicit than source text.

In addition to evidencing binary polarization's effect on aetonormativity, the *Where the Wild Things Are* adaptation also demonstrates another ideological ramification of this seeming overturning and ultimately increased aetonormativity. The film emphasizes that even though they are powerful, adults often feel powerless, a notion achieved through filmic techniques that create a sense of juxtaposition. By juxtaposing distinctively childlike characteristics, such as innocence, with a tone that is far more dark and chaotic than the picturebook source text, the film highlights the powerful/powerless dynamic adults experience.

For example, in the opening scene, viewers alternate between frantic shots of Max running with shots from his perspective as he chases the dog, with both camera angles exhibiting jarring movements until he catches the canine, quite roughly, and the camera pauses on the film's title, displaying white lettering as if it is etched violently into the screen. The tone immediately shifts, however, to a more static scene of a lonely Max making a snow igloo, which is paired with sweet, childlike music. Here, Max is remarkably calmer, and when his sister refuses to join him, his imaginative play becomes no more violent than kicking a fence in order to reject it, enacting the rejection he feels. After a boisterous snowball fight, however, Max is rejected again and frightened by being caught in the collapsed snow fort, after which the tone shifts again suddenly as the music from the opening returns and Max ransacks his sister's room, destroying a homemade gift he made for her. He immediately regrets it, and the next scene returns to the quieter music with Max in his bed.

This set of scenes alternating from chaotic and violent to calm and regretful sets up the contrast and complexity of Max's emotions, but in ways that seem more strikingly polarized than the book—he quickly goes from sweet/sad to angry/violent repeatedly in the opening ten minutes of the film, but also proves he is capable of calm independent imaginative play, which he demonstrates several times before donning his wolf suit in an attempt to garner attention from his mother, who is entertaining a male guest. This leads to a violent conflict between Max and his mother, which not only includes a physical struggle between them, but ends in his running away into the night, screaming and throwing things in the darkness until he finds the boat that takes him to the land of the wild things. At first the ocean scene is as calm as the picturebook, but his arrival is skewed as chaotic by quick alternating shots and camera movement as he essentially crashes into the rocky shore. This journey does not take place in the safety of his room, but is surrounded by the anxiety of his physically running away.

Juxtaposition continues when Max first arrives to the land of the wild things, when he (and the viewer) observes these giant creatures from hiding, with camera shots alternating between Max and Carol, demonstrating that he realizes the connection between them. The scene is ominous, achieved through a mostly dark set, lit primarily with flickering light sources positioned to create the look of low burning fire. Carol is destroying giant wicker spheres, and he appears visibly upset, prompting Max to join in the destruction, a move Carol accepts when the two sniff one another and Carol exclaims, "See, this guy gets it." Viewers may breathe a sigh of relief in this shift to a more lighthearted tone, but the mood shifts again immediately when the other wild things approach Max and rebuke him for destroying their homes. Shot/reverse-shot angles come closer and closer as they crowd him, with shots of Max positioned from above and those of the wild things taken from below to further create a feeling of intimidation. The wild things threaten to eat him, and this seems a serious concern, with dark lighting and strained music combined with growling sounds to emphasize Max's anxiety.

An especially interesting aspect of this final part of the nighttime forest scene is its juxtaposition of intense, anxiety-producing imagery with an emphasis on Max's childlike nature. The lighting choices, music, and camera angles produce a sense of anxiety and foreboding far darker than anything of Sendak's text, but the action of the scene emphasizes Max as a quintessential child, thus also commenting on the innocence and imagination of childhood. Max stops the wild things from eating him by retelling the story of his interaction with his sister's friends, recasting himself as an all-powerful victor over a group of Vikings. The details of this story highlight him as childlike, but the adult directorial hand is also very present in the construction of the scene and its commentary on childhood. While visually interesting and poignant in its consideration of childhood, the scene seems far more *about* childhood than *for* child viewers.

This, I suggest, aligns the *Where the Wild Things Are* film with the same kinds of considerations of dual audience that I have noted in other picturebook adaptations. While certainly a film that could be enjoyed by children, the movie takes adult viewers into account in significant ways as well. The shifts in tone associate the film more concretely with filmmaking choices in adult films, and this combines with additional dialogue and plot content to produce a sense of commentary on childhood, further connecting the film with its adult audience. These elements are supported by choices that again seem to overturn aetonormativity but actually reinforce it, for while Max seems to be in the power position in the text, this happens only when he takes on the role of adult.

Specific camerawork choices, lighting, sound, and other elements of form continue throughout the film toward these ends, creating a tone that might be described as somber and deep but also, at times, anxious and disturbing. This also speaks to an adult perception of childhood, trying to relay the chaos of feeling out of control that is often associated with being a child. Here, visual juxtaposition emphasizes this kind of commentary about the nature of childhood but with an intensity that also gives the film a more adult feel. Even when filmic choices create a lighter tone, emulating sunshine and more jovial music, for example, there is still a sense of intensity and violence, as the wild things pull down and destroy trees or engage in extremely physical play, throwing themselves into trees or hitting each other. There is a roughness to even the most playful or beautiful scenes brought about in part by the huge size of the wild things, enhanced by visual and editing choices.

This juxtaposition of lighter, more jovial components with dark and intense elements does not produce a seamless melding, but actually serves to highlight a clash, making the beautiful, light parts of the story and the violent, disturbing components more noticeable. For example, when the conflict between Carol and K.W. intensifies, Max's suggestion of a dirt-clod fight seems in some ways playful and rambunctious, meant to ease the building tension. The subsequent scene is jarring in its visual juxtapositions. Increased lighting brightens the scene, but a more barren, desert-like setting makes this brightness almost too intense. The play is silly, but also violent, with the wild things striking each other roughly, yet inflicting little physical harm. Even the music shifts abruptly from exciting and fun to a faster, more anxiety-producing intensity, and the juxtaposition of these elements builds a tension of the scene that comes to a head when Carol and K.W. confront one another, acting out the emotions Max seemingly feels toward his sister. Max watches this confrontation and, through him, so does the viewer, positioned to observe this interaction but in no position to remedy it. Viewers, like Max, are thus made to experience what it is like to be an adult in a film that repeatedly emphasizes how difficult it is to be one. Adults may seem to be powerful, but the film emphasizes the powerlessness that they feel by using a chaotic juxtaposition, including an intense and unsettling tone that builds as Max comes to understand what it means to be an adult.

These visual and tone juxtapositions are themselves a polarization, but also serve to reinforce an adult/child binary. Max feels wholly set apart from his mother and sister in the film, a disconnect primarily located in his positionality as a child—a foreign entity that critics use the term "radically other" to describe. Gubar, for example, references Rose and Nodelman in suggesting that far too often, critics emphasize the "radical alterity or otherness of children" (451). This idea plays a part in the dichotomy of the film; while Gubar's kinship model seems reinforced by the idea that Max is learning what his mother experiences, he does so only by coming to understand the wide divide between his perspective and hers. When Max gains power in the land of the wild things, aetonormative structures seem reversed, but are even more polarized, and the disconnect between him and the wild things grows as he finds himself increasingly in the adult position. The tone of the film reinforces this, growing more intense the more that he disappoints the wild things, coming to realize that being the parent is very difficult.

Filmmakers make specific choices to increase this anxious tone, emphasizing that Max feels powerless, and viewers are meant to thus see how his mother must have felt the same. This becomes extremely clear when Max confides to Douglas that he is not really a king, and Douglas warns him not to "ever let Carol find out," a sentiment followed by a sharp high-pitched tone one might associate with a horror film. The subsequent night scene shows Carol suffering from a violent nightmare, and Max appears afraid, the next day suggesting that he needs a secret chamber, perhaps to protect himself. Carol is noticeably distraught by this, again becoming violent. This violence is far from lighthearted or jovial, and music choices in particular serve to associate it with a tone of fear. Here again, the film comments on what it means to be an adult by showing a child (or childlike wild thing) acting in a radical and unpredictable way, making this the primary focus of the movie. In doing so, the film highlights the difficulties and powerlessness that goes along with the seemingly powerful position of adulthood.

This presents a clear ideology about adults that stems from the binaries of the film. Furthermore, the notion of powerful adults experiencing a sense of powerlessness is an ideology that other picturebook adaptations emphasize as well, albeit in more subtle ways. In *The Lorax*, and frequently in other texts that suggest that children must be the catalyst for social change, adults are positioned as ultimately in the power position of society, but also are simultaneously viewed as ineffectual—unable or unwilling to make positive change happen, even if they see the need for it. The Once-ler's being hidden away as he tells Ted his story certainly reinforces this, but *Jumanji*'s focus on Alan's conversion does so to an even greater degree. Alan, but also Sarah and the other adults in *Jumanji*, are consistently frustrated and dismayed at how little power they can assert over the children in their lives and, more strikingly, how little power they have over the game. These adults—and adults consistently across films for children—express that they feel very powerless, despite their position of power over the children in their lives. While this ideology represents a pattern across not just picturebook adaptations, but children's film more broadly, it is especially striking in picturebook adaptations, wherein additional content positions adults in more noticeable ways than their source text.

This portrayal of adults feeling powerless, more than just a disruption of aetonormativity, represents deeply seeded ideologies of childhood and adulthood. In fact, the ways children's film so often seems to explore this aspect of the adult experience might even be part of the reason why filmmakers in picturebook adaptations utilize additional content to pair foregrounded adult roles and perspectives with increased aetonormativity, seeking to prove that although they feel powerless, adults can, indeed, take solace in their power. In this way, the commonality of these kinds of ideologies in children's film suggests that as a society, we are entirely comfortable with the adult/child hierarchy—it is not one we seek to change, disrupt, or dismantle as we do with hierarchies like male/female or self/other. Whether this is good or bad, I would not suppose to answer, but it is worth noting how distinctive the adult/child binary seems, and how often it lies at the center of especially picturebook to film adaptations.

CHAPTER FIVE

Adaptive Dissonance in Wizard of Oz Films

In previous chapters, I have theorized that in films adapted from children's and young adult texts, there seems a consistent change from the source text to the new movie: binary polarization. In considering the causes of this pattern, I have suggested that filmmakers often latch onto a single theme of the source and intensify or amplify it, and this pushes key concepts apart, erasing the complexity of a middle ground in ways that separate notions of independence/dependence, self/other, male/female, and adult/child. In the last two chapters, I have focused on the results, examining the effect of polarizing male/female binaries in YA texts and the reworking of adult/child in films made from picturebooks. Still, there is a key factor that I have thus far set aside—what happens when not one, but many films are made from a children's book? While I believe binary polarization still happens in these texts, they also have unique characteristics, and as such, the result of binary polarization is a bit different as well.

To explore how repeated adaptation changes binary polarization's effect on the ideologies presented by each new movie, I use a representative example—L. Frank Baum's *The Wonderful Wizard of Oz* (1900) and several of its film adaptations. The results of binary polarization are different here because they are not tied to an emphasis on a particular trope or character (such as the female savior in YA films or the adult lesson-learner in picturebook adaptations). Rather, more polarized binaries—no matter what those binaries are—affect the very way that ideologies and messages are presented. Each time a new movie is made from a source text that is repeatedly adapted, there is more tension between ideas in the film itself—more conflict between the ideologies within the new movie. I term this internal tension or conflict *adaptive dissonance*.

To understand adaptive dissonance, it is important to first recognize the difference between a single film adapted from a children's book and instances of multiple adaptations. Like a lot of the aspects I have discussed about adaptation so far, this characteristic of the new films is pretty straightforward: when more than one movie is made from a children's book, each new film is affected by the films that came before. This results in something more complicated than one-to-one adaptation (wherein just one movie is made from the source text), a difference that might be most easily conceptualized by thinking about a web of adaptations that influence any new movie produced. This is crucially important, for although a comparative study between source text and adaptation is useful, analyzing a group of films adapted from a single source requires a consideration of how adaptations affect each other and what effect this has on textual messages. Every time a new adaptation of a book like *The Wonderful Wizard of Oz* hits theaters, television, or even the stage, it necessarily engages and is influenced by not only the original literary source text, but also by the other adaptations of that text. Even when such a film appears to draw from the source text or bears a strong resemblance to another previous film, there always exists a web of adaptations influencing the new work, including how it presents ideologies.

This distinctive quality changes the way binary polarization works. Filmmakers often still focus on a key theme and make it stronger, which is especially true in Wizard of Oz adaptations, but they are not simply focused on how that theme or message works in the source text. Instead, they are also influenced by the ways that other adaptors have interpreted and often amplified that theme, and the ways messages are presented in the other adaptations affects decisions made about the new adaptation. Like the other kinds of adaptations I have discussed, this has a lot to do with audience expectation—the adaptors have to assume that at least some movie viewers will be familiar with the source text, and others are likely to have seen the other film adaptations. This is especially true with the Wizard of Oz because one of its adaptations— the 1939 MGM film starring Judy Garland—is such a famous and well-known movie in the history of children's film. Thus, when filmmakers are influenced by the source text as well as other adaptations forming a web around it and each new film produced, binary polarization creates ideological tension, so that the result of multiple influencing adaptations is a greater degree of conflicting ideologies in these new films. Messages become muddled or confusing, or sometimes, concepts becoming more starkly opposed to one another will mean that messages seem in conflict with one another. Instead of presenting a unified theme, the film presents a mash-up of ideologies, which can have problematic or concerning results in the overall messages of the film. This ambiguity, confusion, or conflict between the messages and ideologies of the new movie produced is the phenomenon I term adaptive dissonance, which I argue represents a consistent pattern in instances of multiple adaptations.

I want to take moment to clarify here, because while there usually is a lot of conflict or tension between the messages, themes, or ideologies of each movie in a web of adaptations from a single source, this is not what I call adaptive dissonance. Instead, adaptive dissonance is something that exists within each film—it is an internal tension or conflict between the messages of just that one adaptation. In this way, an examination of adaptive dissonance suggests not only a text's divergence from or conflict with the ideologies of a precursor text, but also a conflict *within* each new adaptation, creating an internal discord that intensifies through multiple adaptations. This differentiates these texts from one-to-one adaptations like the ones I have studied in earlier chapters. When a single adaptation is made from a source text, ideological shifts typically still result in a clear set of textual messages presented by the film, even if those messages differ from its textual predecessor. However, this is not the case in instances of multiple films adapted from a single source, which are not simply ideologically opposed to each other, but consistently evidence a heightened degree of internal ideological tension. Although it would be expected that multiple adaptations might result in tensions between ideologies presented in individual texts, my claim takes this idea of conflicting ideologies one step further, suggesting that the influence of multiple textual precedents also results in adaptive dissonance, or increased *internal* ideological tensions.

Furthermore, just as I have described in identifying some of the consistent results of binary polarization in young adult novels and picturebooks made into films, adaptive dissonance is not a randomly occurring phenomenon, but happens because binaries are polarized. In this way, adaptive dissonance is its own trend—a consistent pattern across texts in a set that share similar contextual factors—but it is also a key consequence of a wider trend in filmic adaptation.

As I have described with other sets of adaptations, the unique factors of this group of texts is something that critics have explored, but what I add to this discussion is a look at these ideas through the lens of binary polarization. In the case of multiple films made from one source, this examination means thinking about the textual web, and the most useful way of doing this for many adaptation studies scholars has been to use Bakhtin's concept of dialogism, or the idea that texts are constantly affected by other texts, but are also always affecting other texts too. Critics use this idea of a continual dialogue between texts to note, as Stam does, that film adaptations are "caught up in the ongoing whirl of intertextual reference and transformation, of texts generating other texts in an endless process of recycling, transformation, and transmutation, with no clear point of origin" ("Beyond" 66). However, while I build on Bakhtin, as well as Julia Kristeva and Gérard Genette's *transtextuality*, I wish to not just look at the web of intertextuality itself, but also interrogate something that I see as a consistent result of that intertextual, transtextual, or dialogic web, at least in all of the examples of children's film adaptations that I have studied. In each of those examples, and perhaps most strongly in the Wizard of Oz adaptations (which is why I have chosen this example to describe this trend), there is far more conflict between messages and ideologies in the movie adaptations than in the source. The forces outside the text (forces that are part of the intertextual, transtextual, dialogic web) create a greater amount of conflict within the text: the text's themes and ideologies conflict more with one another than in the source, and often in increasing amounts with each new adaptation.

Bakhtin's dialogism may play a role in this adaptive dissonance, but in instances of multiple adaptations of a single source, the ongoing intertextual whirl has a consistent result: more ideological conflict in the adaptation than its precursor texts. This point represents a distinction that warrants a new term, necessary to describe this pattern. I have chosen "adaptive dissonance" because it seems to best capture the internal discord or disharmony that consistently exists in cases of multiple films being made from a single source.

Dialogism suggests that all texts include an element of dissonance in that there are often multiple voices and perspectives presented (although, as I use Cadden to explore in my discussion of YA film adaptation, some texts are far more single-voiced and double-voiced than others). In fact, the premise of the work of Bakhtin, Derrida, and much of poststructuralism is that language itself is dialogic; this is also the foundation of my exploration of binaries. Yet just as my contention that binaries are more polarized in adaptation tracks an increase, so too does my use of the term adaptive dissonance. In this case, I note an increase in ideological tension. Adaptive dissonance is primarily different than dialogism in terms of degree: there is more ideological tension in multiple adaptations of a single source than is produced by the fundamental inconsistency/instability of all texts. Furthermore, while tension between ideologies can be a productive part of literature, a point Cadden stresses when applying Bakhtin to the ethics of the YA novel, too much tension can also have negative results, which is what I wish to explore in adaptations of Oz adaptations.

In developing the term adaptive dissonance, I also draw from several observations critics make about instances of multiple adaptations. Katherine A. Fowkes, for example, notes that "the popularity and staying power of Wizard and other classic films may lie precisely in their myth-like ability to juggle conflicting ideas and impulses, thereby providing possibility of various and sometimes opposite interpretations" (61). This idea of "juggling" conflicting ideas leads me back to questions I have explored throughout my study and, in particular, the reasons for this adaptive choice. Kate Newell begins to explore this question by studying how, in Wizard of Oz films, "fidelity is deployed in service of specific arguments" (90), and similarly, Leitch suggests that in Sherlock Holmes retellings, because "every adaptation wants to claim the authority . . . [they] often disagree with each other and sometimes with themselves" (*Discontents* 216). It is this brief point in Leitch's assessment that I believe is worthy of far greater consideration: the notion that adaptations do not simply disagree with each other, but sometimes with themselves. For while I am interested in the question of why adaptors "deploy" fidelity or infidelity, I am also interested in the result, and I find it striking that in children's adapted film, it is not simply "sometimes" that this kind of internal discord occurs; instead, it is the norm. Regardless of their agenda or relative success in engaging with what Newell describes as fidelity and infidelity to various cultural, historical, and textual entities, adaptors who build from a web of previous adaptations consistently produce texts with a sense of internal ideological conflict that is far more profound than in the initial source text. This internal adaptive dissonance, I suggest, constitutes a trend worthy of a second look.

I thus begin my study of adaptive dissonance in Oz adaptations by focusing on the notable 1939 film, setting up the context of an internal ideological discord by describing how the popularity of the song "Somewhere over the Rainbow" as a cultural artifact interacts with critics' interpretation of the concept of "no place like home." I then trace adaptive dissonance in *The Wiz: The Super Soul Musical* (1978), its recent remake, *The Wiz Live!* (2015), and *The Muppets' Wizard of Oz* (2005) to suggest that these films engage previous adaptations, including the 1939 film, in ways that hinder the depth and complexity of the race-related messages that they are able to send. Finally, while adaptive dissonance leads to ambiguity with potentially concerning ideological implications in all of these examples, I end by comparing Disney's *Oz the Great and Powerful* (2013) with the smash musical *Wicked* (2003) to demonstrate that adaptive dissonance can lead to negative ideological representation, evidenced by the troubling gender depictions that result from ideological tension in Disney's Oz movie prequel.

Difficulty in Deciphering the "Dreams That You Dare to Dream"

While I believe adaptive dissonance exists in all instances of multiple adaptations created from a single source, I have chosen Baum's *The Wonderful Wizard of Oz* and its adaptations in part because of the extraordinary impact of its most popular and notable film version, MGM's 1939 *Wizard of Oz*. As Douglas Street, Mark Evan Swartz, and others have attested, "so influential is this film that it, and not the novel, is generally the source of people's familiarity with *The Wizard of Oz* story" (Swartz 91). The influence of this film is vast, and while in subsequent sections, I will detail some of the unique ways it affects other adaptations, I first wish to establish how binary polarization plays a critical role in not only the ideological shifts of the adaptation, but also the subsequent emergence of adaptive dissonance in all Oz film adaptations.

Adaptive dissonance seems particularly pronounced when one adaptation stands out as having a widespread impact and importance, and as such, the Oz adaptations make a great example because the 1939 MGM film is culturally significant, remaining both popular and acclaimed for the better part of a century. When one adaptation, such as the 1939 *Wizard of Oz* film, begins to rival the source text in significance, later adaptations are likely to include adaptive dissonance to an even greater degree. Thus, while pre-1939 Oz adaptations—such as *The Fairylogue and Radio-Plays* (1908), *The Wonderful Wizard of Oz* (1910) based on the 1902 stage musical, *The Patchwork Girl of Oz* (1914), and *Wizard of Oz* (1925), directed by Larry Semon and Frank Joslyn Baum—certainly play a role in the adaptive dissonance of the 1939 film, later examples demonstrate it in more pronounced ways. Similarly, instances of multiple adaptations with a well-known Disney film also reflect a heightened amount of adaptive dissonance, which I will discuss a bit more in the chapter that follows.

Although one film might have an especially profound impact on the degree of adaptive dissonance, this phenomenon also cannot be traced through adaptations via a straight line based only on chronology. Instead, multiple adaptations act more as a web, wherein some new adaptations are influenced by certain variants more than others. Oz adaptations provide great examples of the complexity of this web. For example, *The Wiz Live!* draws especially from *The Wiz* and the 1939 MGM film, but that does not mean that it should be interpreted apart from Baum's source text; even if there exists primarily an indirect relationship between this film and the novel, Baum's influence is still part of what causes that internal ideological tension. In the same way, while the influence of the Muppets adaptation on *The Wiz Live!* is less pronounced, it still exists, especially when considering that Queen Latifah moves from the position of Aunt Em to a Wizard who seems to espouse many of the same principles. On the other hand, although the Muppets film is strongly influenced by the MGM movie, it draws on source text references absent from the 1939 film as well and is not even wholly separate from *The Wiz*; the choice to cast the human characters with African American actors certainly connects the films. Tracing all of these connecting filaments could go on forever, and I am not even sure one could ever truly claim to have done so completely. My goal here is therefore not to map the web of connections within this adaptation corpus, but consider the result this web has on new adaptations. That result is adaptive dissonance.

Few would debate the lasting impact of the MGM film, however, and critics have identified a key distinction between the messages of Baum's text and its

MGM adaptation, with Chaston perhaps best articulating a crucial concern, which he calls (and I have referenced previously as) "Ozification." Examining several children's films including *The Blue Bird, Alice in Wonderland*, and *Jumanji*, Chaston writes that "through their Ozification, those aspects of the original stories that empower child protagonists, especially girls, and that seem to critique the adult world are transformed into a sentimental message that 'there is no place like home,' encouraging young viewers to conform to adult expectations" ("Ozification" 13). While Chaston suggests "the novel and its sequels often include images and characters that subtly undercut the message that there is 'no place like home'" ("Home" 217, 210), the lesson of the MGM film is perhaps summed up best in Dorothy's iconic line: "if I ever go looking for my heart's desire again, I won't look any further than my own backyard. Because if it isn't there, I never really lost it to begin with." Thus, the film's suggestion that Dorothy has learned not to venture out of the domestic sphere into the world of adventure undercuts, as Chaston argues, Baum's message and portrayal of a distinctively adventurous female hero.

Filmmakers amplify the theme of "no place like home" purposefully, for as Michael Patrick Hearn relays in *The Annotated Wizard of Oz*, members of the film's production team stressed that adaptation choices should reflect the idea that "Dorothy is only motivated by one object in Oz; that is, how to get back home to her Aunt Em, and every situation should be related to this main drive" (12). This represents exactly the type of thematic amplification I describe in other adapted children's films, which here again results in a polarization of binaries. I believe that what Chaston calls Ozification results from a purposeful focus on a theme that sets home/away and adult/child binaries further from one another conceptually.

Thus, two elements seem at work in this example. First, this repetition of binary polarization in the 1939 *Wizard of Oz* film reinforces this as a key pattern in children's film adaptation overall. Secondly, I suggest the film not only exhibits this quality, but that in instances of multiple adaptations from a single source text, polarization of binaries *results* in adaptive dissonance. To explain this, I examine several binaries at work in the text.

Perhaps most notably, the binary of adult/child is far more explicitly dichotomous in the film *Wizard of Oz*. The opening Kansas sequences focus specifically on adult/child conflict, as Dorothy finds herself opposed to not only Miss Gulch (who wants to kill Toto), but consequently her Aunt Em and the farmhands. This conflict hinges on the fact that the powerful forces in this space are adults, while Dorothy is very much a child. Although her Aunt and Uncle are too busy with adult problems to assist her, the farmhands suggest she needs to use her brain, heart, and courage to solve her difficulty with Miss

Gulch, setting up the notion that her subsequent interactions with their Oz counterparts, who do not possess these elements, are representative of her own childlike lack of these qualities.

This element of overlaying the Kansas world onto Oz is not a part of Baum's text, in which the description of Dorothy's home lasts only one short chapter, and does not include Dorothy's attempt to run away, inspired to seek "somewhere over the rainbow" beyond the farm. The film's addition of Professor Marvel (who later plays Oz) sets up a key adult power figure, for in frightening Dorothy into returning home by telling her that he sees Aunt Em sick and brokenhearted in his crystal, he effectively squashes her attempt to disturb the adult/child binary, providing another example of increased filmic aetonormativity.

This continues in Oz, where unlike in Baum's text, Dorothy is made to seem silly in inquiring about good and bad witches as the Munchkins giggle in the background, and her introduction from Glinda is an instruction to "meet the young lady who fell from a star." Her status as child becomes even more clear when the Wicked Witch appears, calling Dorothy "my little lady" and threatening her "little dog too," placing her in the same adult/child paradigm of her relationship with Miss Gulch (played by the same actress as the witch). The film's Wicked Witch then seeks out opportunities to similarly terrorize Dorothy, in contrast to Baum's text, wherein the Witch only concerns herself with Dorothy when she approaches her kingdom.

This shift in the adult/child binary relates to another key dichotomy in the text: the notion of home versus away. Again, Baum's text sets these concepts in tension, for while Kansas is gray, Oz is filled with "strange and beautiful sights" (34). The visual nature of film, however, and in particular, the use of a new technology, allows MGM's *Wizard of Oz* to accentuate this, creating one of the most stunning visual dichotomies in film history when Dorothy steps into a world of stunning Technicolor, which provides a striking contrast to the earlier sequences, filmed in sepia. Like the physical film elements that are utilized to contrast Coraline's real and other worlds, here we see a striking visual contrast between home and away.

Despite the striking and even magical quality of Oz, Dorothy nonetheless ends the film claiming she should never have looked for her happiness beyond the dulled tones of Kansas. This in itself is a conflict, and one identified in 1939 by such writers as reporter Howard Rushmore, who wrote that "no place like home" was "a moral that falls a trifle flat[,] for no tot (or adult) doesn't wish for at least a roundtrip ticket to the land of Oz after seeing how attractive Mervyn LeRoy has made it" (qtd. in Hearn *Annotated* 77). Yet by linking the hierarchical presentation of a polarized adult/child binary with a similarly dichotomous home/away binary, filmmakers also amplify another important theme of Baum's text: that individuals often already possess those qualities they seek, but cannot see in themselves.

While Baum presents this idea of already possessing what one desires through Dorothy's companions, the filmmakers add weight to this theme and reinforce Dorothy's status as a child by presenting her as in need of learning this lesson as well. Baum describes Dorothy's influence as crucial in other characters finding their own power, but the film portrays Dorothy learning the lesson that she did not see, or at least appreciate, what she already had: friendship, community, and family. Having the same actors who play the farmhands in Kansas transform into her newfound Oz friends reinforces this, amplifying Baum's theme that a person may already have what she desires by polarizing binaries of adult/child and home/away to result in a problematic ideological shift that devalues female power and autonomy.

It is in this ideological implication of the polarized binaries of the film that viewers can see a crucial connection that ties the binary polarization with a resulting adaptive dissonance, for what interests me most about how this theme is changed is the way it does not seem to fit with other key elements of the film, creating an internal discord within the MGM movie. If filmmakers wished to simply shift the story toward a new ideological focus on the importance of home, family, and domesticity, it would stand to reason that the ways they amplified the themes of the source text would align with this endeavor. Furthermore, it would seem that this thematic amplification and alignment, which subsequently polarizes binaries between adult/child and home/away, would also result in a clear message related to home and domestic life. This could not be further from the truth. Instead of a clear, "no place like home" emphasis, the film seems wrought with internal conflict, with home and away in even more conflict than in Baum's novel.

The final scenes of the film seem to offer a clear take-away, as Dorothy espouses the importance of realizing that "there is no place like home." Still, this is not the part of the movie most often remembered; instead Judy Garland's performance of the iconic ballad "Somewhere over the Rainbow" represents a singularly memorable aspect of the film. When Garland expresses her longing for a place where "troubles melt like lemon drops," and her hope that "someday I'll wish upon a star / And wake up where the clouds are far / Behind me," this memorable rendition resonates powerfully, evident by its Oscar win in 1939 and the countless subsequent renditions that artists have made into chart-topping successes.

This song certainly suggests Dorothy's profound sense of longing, but it does not appear that she longs for that which she already possesses (home and family) in the way that the musical numbers of her comrades represent these elements. "If I Only Had a Brain," "If I Only Had a Heart," and "If I Were King of the Forest" each shows that her comrades desire something they already have, which sets them in direct contrast to Dorothy. Although Dorothy struggles to fit into her life in Kansas, where adults criticize or terrorize her, reinforcing her powerlessness, she traverses Oz far move deftly, behaving bravely and solving problems faced by her companions. The key point here is that Dorothy does not seem to recognize these aspects of her journey as she reflects on it in the final scenes of the film, so that while she initially sings of a longing that is profoundly meaningful to viewers, the final message of the movie discourages this longing.

Nonetheless, when I hear the heartfelt words and rich melody of "Somewhere over the Rainbow," I am not discouraged from longing; instead I am encouraged to believe in the possibility of a place where dreams come true. Salman Rushdie shares this sentiment, writing that those who buy into the "no place like home" theme of the movie:

> would do well to listen to the yearning in Garland's voice . . . What she expresses here, what she embodies with the purity of an archetype, is the human dream of leaving, a dream at least as powerful as its countervailing dream of roots. At the heart of The Wizard of Oz is a great tension between these two dreams; but as the music swells and that big, clean voice flies into the anguished longings of the song, can anyone doubt which message is the stronger? (23)

While the song "Somewhere over the Rainbow" is perhaps the most iconic and profoundly meaningful element of the film, the movie itself amplifies this element of longing only to call it problematic. The film does not overtly support this sense of longing in its overall message, but the meaning of the song itself, conveyed as much through Garland's wistful tone and memorable performance, resonates independently from the film. Thus, the message of the song and the lesson of the film's ending seem to not only be in tension, but are somewhat contradictory—and this internal discord represents adaptive dissonance.

While the iconic nature of Garland's ballad as set in conflict with the other elements of the film produces adaptive dissonance even within this early adaptation, I would suggest that as additional elements are added to the adaptive web with each new adaptation, this kind of internal tension increases. To explore this, I now turn to other key Oz adaptations.

Cultural Context and the Implications of Ideological Ambivalence

Binary polarization leads to adaptive dissonance with perhaps even more weighty ideological implications when the context of an adaptation takes on new elements, as is the case with *The Wiz*, transformed from its Broadway musical production to a film in 1978. Rhonda Williams considers the cultural and historical contexts of *The Wiz*, writing that "given America's politically and socially heightened sensitivities to gender and race" in 1978, the film "highlights Dorothy's position of power within the Black family unit and community as the giver, nurturer, and taker of life for Black men and women" (195). Williams also notes that the film is limited in its successful portrayal of this message, for "nothing that happens in Oz motivates her change of attitude" and in "the midst of all the originality and sparkle, the message is ultimately lost" (203). I suggest that adaptive dissonance causes this loss of the adaptation's presumed message about Dorothy's potential role as a leader in the African American community. Furthermore, adaptive dissonance also plays a meaningful role in a subsequent adaptation of *The Wiz*, NBC's primetime television special *The Wiz Live!* (2015). This new film replaces the ideological ambivalence of the 1978 version with more message clarity, but also demonstrates an internal conflict that sidesteps issues of culture in some concerning ways.

Set in 1970s Harlem, *The Wiz* utilizes a polarized home/away dichotomy to explore the question of whether twenty-four-year-old Dorothy, played by Diana Ross, should leave home to explore new possibilities. Dorothy teaches kindergarten in New York City, but her Aunt Em prompts her to consider a potential suitor and encourages her to take a more promising high school teaching position, suggesting that her family believes "it's time you got out of that sandbox and into some new people, new neighborhood." Williams describes the context for this push, noting that Aunt Em essentially encourages Dorothy to consider her role as a "responsible black woman who is working to rebuild the moral fiber of the Black family and community by getting out on her own and starting a family" (196). Still, this scene also sets up an increased home/away dichotomy that reinterprets the idea of "Somewhere over the Rainbow." Like Garland's character, Ross's Dorothy seems consumed by fear, but her fear has a very different cause, expressed when she sings, "What am I afraid of? / Don't know what I'm made of / Why am I afraid of feeling? Feelings? / If I dare to take a chance / Would someone lead me?" Like Garland's ballad, this song is positioned just after the opening sequence, but while both speak of longing and a wish to escape fear, Ross's rendition seems to offer an attempt to explain her perspective that "I can't see how goin' south of 125th Street ever made anybody's life better." Rather than longing for "somewhere over the rainbow," Ross's Dorothy is already afraid of seeking anything outside of her own backyard at the beginning of the film.

It is worth pointing to this distinction because, even though the films suggest different interpretations of Dorothy's character, they both open with an exploration of longing and the tension between home and away—something that demonstrates the influence of the MGM *Wizard of Oz* on *The Wiz*, and also highlights the ways that the binaries of the source text are more polarized in the film adaptation. In *The Wiz*, as in the MGM version, the question of leaving home to seek something better leads Dorothy to express a profound longing which highlights that home and away cannot be overlapping or inter-mingling concepts, but are opposed to such a degree that they cause these women conflict and pain.

Additionally, in both films this polarization shifts ideas about appreciat-ing that which one already possesses, and in *The Wiz,* this ideology is focal-ized through Dorothy perhaps even more than her comrades. The difference between the 1939 *Wizard of Oz* and *The Wiz*, however, lies in what Dorothy has overlooked, for while Glinda prompts Dorothy to attest that her heart's desire lies in her own backyard in 1939, in *The Wiz*, Glinda tells Dorothy that she must believe in herself, saying, "I don't know what's in you, [but] you'll never find it in the safety of this room . . . there's a whole world out there." While Garland's Dorothy learns to seek her heart's desire at home, *The Wiz* reshapes "no place like home" into encouragement that women can create meaningful community and shape people's lives in positive ways if they venture away from the security of their home, whether to Oz or south of 125th Street.

In this reshaped view of home facilitated by binary polarization, viewers see the impact of a web of adaptations in producing adaptive dissonance. Post-1939 reworkings of the Oz narrative tend to depend upon the MGM film, often understood in relation to it. Just as in the 1939 film, polarizing home/away in *The Wiz* results in adaptive dissonance, seen in particular at the end of the film. As the story concludes, Ross's Dorothy clearly values home, sing-ing, "Now that I have some direction, / It would sure be nice to be back home / Where there's love and affection." Even so, she has learned to value a life that expands beyond traditional conceptions of home, overcoming her fears to embrace the idea that a loving family could exist outside her own backyard. Unlike the MGM film, wherein the farmhands and Dorothy's Oz companions are one and the same, the family that Dorothy meets in *The Wiz*'s version of Oz incorporates relationships beyond those in her Harlem family. While this discovery prompts Garland's Dorothy to espouse the notion of "no place like home" at the ideological expense of "somewhere over the rainbow," Ross's character proves in Oz that she can leave her comfort zone, reconciling this tension in a more pronounced way than in the MGM film.

Still, just as viewers are left with a sense of tension as to whether the MGM film supports seeking "somewhere over the rainbow" only as a means of learn-ing to "look no further than your own backyard," *The Wiz* concludes without resolving whether Ross's Dorothy pursues the new teaching position or a romantic relationship, leaving the viewer with a similar ambivalence at the end of the film. In fact, in the closing song, Dorothy asks God to "Tell us, should we run away, / Should we try and stay, / Or would it be better just to let things be?" Though less afraid, she still seems uncertain about how far she should venture. Like Garland's Dorothy, Ross's character has changed, but while Dorothy in the MGM version makes clear how this change will affect her (creating adaptive dissonance between what she longs for and what she believes at the end), Ross's Dorothy has less clarity. This ambiguous ending, while different from the conflict of the MGM film, reflects just as much adaptive dissonance. While Dorothy's decision about where to seek her heart's desire produces tension in the 1939 film, Dorothy's indecision in the 1978 version reverses the terms of the dilemma, but nevertheless sustains it.

Why the ambivalence about the film's end and about the value of home versus the potential of building a new life elsewhere? Why not have Dorothy return triumphantly from Oz to accept the challenges that Aunt Em presented to her? If Dorothy's journey has demonstrated that her aunt was correct, and she is capable of overcoming her fears to build a new community away from the safety of her family in Harlem, it seems odd that Ross's character continues to doubt this point. If viewers are meant to see the positive impact that this strong, capable African American woman can have on her society if she faces these fears, why the ambiguity in the film's conclusion? The answer to these questions lies in the unavoidable adaptive dissonance that emerges when there are multiple adaptations of a single source text. While Dorothy certainly grapples with and learns about this conflict in Oz, neither film can resolve it because both are influenced by complex cultural contexts (the Great Depression and impending war, the challenges facing the African American community in the late twentieth century) *and* earlier variants, making it difficult, if not impossible, to fully reconcile these ideologies.

Just as adaptive dissonance in the 1978 version of *The Wiz* results in ambivalence, a similar internal tension caused by binary polarization exists in the 2015 remake, *The Wiz Live!* While *The Wiz Live!* features most of the same musical score as the 1978 version, the story's framing changes dramatically, taking the premise out of Harlem to align more closely with the 1939 MGM film. While Ross's character seems to struggle with a fear of leaving home, a decision with particular cultural weight in the 1970s, *The Wiz Live!* begins with Dorothy, played by Shanice Williams, mimicking Garland's portrayal as she attempts to run away from her home in Kansas. Here again, binaries are polarized, with adult/child and home/away hierarchies more firmly established than in Baum's novel. Yet in this new reworking of the story, the lesson Aunt Em wishes to teach (providing a thematic framework for the film) shifts back to "no place like home," rather than an encouragement to seek opportunities and family elsewhere. In the 2015 version, Aunt Em sings "The Feeling We Once Had" to convince Dorothy not to run away from home, and the production then cuts Dorothy's initial ballad, eliminating the chance for Williams's Dorothy to describe her longing or conflicting emotions as Ross or Garland do in their opening musical numbers.

The Wiz, played by Queen Latifah in the 2015 remake, also reinforces a "no place like home" perspective in offering Dorothy her own cautionary tale, describing her exile in Oz as an unfortunate consequence of angrily running away from her family. Her regret is clear, and very different from *The Wiz's* sentiment that there comes a time "when we must stop holding on to the things that make us feel safe! ...And embrace what we fear ...We have got to know in our hearts that the things that we hold up as sacred are sometimes holding us d-d-d-down!" Similarly, in the 2015 version, Glinda does not tell Dorothy that "there's a whole world out there," but instead mimics the 1939 film by encouraging Williams's character to articulate her concluding lesson, that home is not "where you live, but where you love." Williams's Dorothy, like Garland's version, has learned to seek her heart's desire in her own backyard.

The adaptive dissonance of *The Wiz Live!*, then, does not derive from an ambivalent message, but from a conflict between the frame of the film, which promotes the importance of home, and the other musical numbers, which reflect some of the more complex themes related to race presented in 1978. By connecting so concretely to the theme of the 1939 MGM film while also maintaining so much of a story that, as Neil Earle writes, "coming as it did after a period of advance and renewed confidence on the part of the black bourgeoisie, may well live on as an artifact of the embattled but still hopeful African American experience of the 1970s" (168), the film presents a discord between its messages regarding race and its commentary on the home/away binary.

While the 1978 version presents the home/away conflict as related to the possible responsibilities of an African American woman living in Harlem, the 2015 version eliminates this frame, keeping ideologies related to race and the message of "no place like home" entirely separate. As a result, the remake loses out on the chance to offer meaningful commentary on race and culture; and in some ways, when the polarization of home/away is held at arm's length from the ideologies of race explored in other elements of the movie, the implications of this polarization seem even more substantial than the concluding ambivalence in the 1978 film. The earlier film may not clearly articulate the role Dorothy is meant to play in her community, but its adaptive dissonance leaves the viewer with fruitful questions to ask about the challenges faced by young African American women in the 1970s. In 2015, viewers are left only questioning how "no place like home" fits with the cultural components of the story, if it does at all.

More importantly, by reverting to the model of the 1939 version, *The Wiz Live!* eliminates some of the cultural focus of the film, despite its African American cast. Again, I ask why. Did filmmakers believe that viewers would respond more positively to the "no place like home" premise of the Judy Garland version? Or did they simply wish to avoid tackling the challenge of repositioning the film, moving it out of 1970s Harlem and into a setting that would reflect contemporary ideological issues related to race? If this is the case, filmmakers (whether intentionally or unintentionally) sidestepped a discussion of race by keeping only the casting choices and song lyrics from the 1978 version and adjusting the contextual and plot elements to fit the 1939 version. This circumstance may reflect an acknowledgment of what scholar Robin DiAngelo terms *white fragility*, or "a state in which even a minimum amount of racial stress becomes intolerable, triggering a range of defensive moves" among white viewers (57). Even as written, the film garnered a "social media backlash," evidenced by the Neilson ratings, which reflected that *The Wiz Live!* saw "a 74% increase in racist tweets from the previous 3-hour block" (Seymour). Perhaps the filmmakers—or other individuals who held power in production decisions—feared that a more direct social statement would have raised even louder voices against the film.

Another possibility, however, is that if *The Wiz Live!* falls short of its 1978 predecessor in asking a new audience to productively consider a cultural experience, its avoidance of complexity results from having taken on what Newell might describe as too many agendas. The text responds to many sources, and in this case, the tension created by engaging not only with Baum's novel, but also with the MGM version and the 1978 *The Wiz* film clearly results in discord. The point I would like to make here is that whereas ambiguity may open discussion in the 1978 version, ambivalence and discord in the 2015 remake seem a way of avoiding opportunities for discussion. As Michelle Martin writes in discussing why it is important to read and teach African American children's picturebooks, "silence perpetuates ignorance and prejudice" (181). She notes her commitment to doing "all that I can to expose my students to ethnic texts so that they will not also perpetuate, because of ignorance or neglect, the damning message that people of color don't count" (183). If *The Wiz Live!* responds to adaptive dissonance by removing as much of the cultural essence of *The Wiz* as possible, this example seems another version of the damning neglect that Martin describes.

Muppets, Pop Stars, and Pastiche . . . Oh My!

While *The Wiz* and its 2015 remake represent adaptation examples wherein cultural context combines with binary polarization to result in conflicting internal messages and unclear ideological resolution, the effect of a web of influencing factors can perhaps be seen even more clearly in another Oz adaptation, *The Muppets' Wizard of Oz*. This film, which has received primarily negative criticism, demonstrates another key element of adaptive dissonance—the idea that the more complex the web of contextual factors and adaptive influences, the stronger the ideological tension, and perhaps more concerning, the greater the weight of the ideological implications of that tension. Examining some of the material and contextual factors of *The Muppets' Wizard of Oz*, as well as the way the film works as pastiche, makes clear that even when tensions simply lead to ideological ambivalence, the results can still be profound.

In *The Muppets' Wizard of Oz*, viewers again see Dorothy's story fit to a new context, but as Newell describes, "whereas *The Wiz* appropriates signifiers of 1970s Harlem to create an adaptation reflective of an urban Black American experience, *The Muppets'* appropriates signifiers of American popular culture to create an adaptation reflective of a twenty-first-century postmodern experience . . . evaluated in terms of its fidelity to the 1939 film and to other Muppets' or Disney productions" (86–87). Newell's commentary speaks to the idea of an adaptation web, a distinguishing characteristic of multiple films adapted from a single source that I suggest creates the secondary trend of adaptive dissonance within these works. For certainly, the Muppets come with a set of expectations that strongly influences the adaptive choices that can be made. When *The Muppets' Wizard of Oz* was produced, there was already a long history of Muppet movies, and those who see the film are likely familiar with its cast of puppet characters. What is more, *The Muppets' Wizard of Oz* was one of the first films produced after the Walt Disney Corporation purchased the rights and trademarks of the Muppets from the Jim Henson Company, subsequently attempting to revive the franchise under its umbrella.

Like Newell, I find it intriguing to track these influences, a study which supports the idea that this new Muppets rendition of the Oz story is influenced by the source text, the 1939 film, other Muppets or Disney productions, and a "myriad [of other] intertexts" (89). Still, I think the way Newell describes this web of influence is even more relevant, for she focuses on how the film is distinguished by "its overt use of pastiche" (88). Terms like pastiche or parody are often associated with the Muppets, as when Alissa Burger notes that the film reimagines the Oz story "in a way only the Muppets could achieve, bringing their spirit of self-reflexive parody and contemporary cultural relevance from the stage of *The Muppet Show* into a Kansas twister" ("Myth" 114–15). The subtle difference between the terms parody and pastiche speaks to a key element of how a web of influencing factors and texts can lead to adaptive dissonance.

While Burger points out the critical nature of the Muppets' humor, which she notes speaks to the "more sordid, exploitative side" of reality television and celebrity culture ("Myth" 107), I agree more fully with Newell's use of the term pastiche. As Fredric Jameson describes, unlike parody, pastiche is "a neutral practice of such mimicry, without any of parody's ulterior motives, amputated of the satiric impulse" (17). This definition seems to align with the style of humor and visual antics for which the Muppets are known; they poke fun, but they do so in such a way that seems to celebrate their subject while critiquing it. While certainly on the edge of satire, Muppet humor is not as critical as such, and especially when it comes to stardom and fame, the Muppets promote an investment in comedy, entertainment, and the arts far more than they mock these elements (or perhaps, even as they mock them).

If pastiche is about celebrating, rather than satirizing, then it also has a differing kind of result. Satire is often very clear in its thematic or ideological motive—it is meant to highlight a problematic in its use of criticism. Thus, if *The Muppets' Wizard of Oz* were acting as a parody in order to critique fame and stardom, then it would follow that this would be a clear thematic motive—Ashanti would travel to Oz in search of celebrity status, only to recognize "there is no place like home." Upon closer examination, however, this does not really seem the concluding message or theme of the film, and at best, viewers are left with a sense of confusion and ambiguity when it comes to the film's commentary on fame. This lack of thematic clarity reflects the same kind of adaptive dissonance I identify in *The Wiz.*

What differentiates *The Muppets' Wizard of Oz* from *The Wiz*, however, is the way pastiche plays a key role in creating adaptive dissonance, wherein the nature of the somewhat celebratory intertextual melding combines with another case of binary polarization to create an ambiguity with concerning implications, especially given that this film, like *The Wiz,* is multiculturally committed in a way that other Oz retellings are not. The casting of African American actors in the principle human roles in *The Muppets' Wizard of Oz* suggests at least some element of social commentary at work, and yet when this element is combined with adaptive dissonance, the result is some problematic textual messages.

Viewers can see this adaptive dissonance and lack of clear thematic direction in the very premise of movie. Ashanti, playing Dorothy, is clearly disillusioned with her life in Kansas, and in far more obvious ways than either Ross or Garland, both of whom seem at least conflicted about whether or not they wish to venture outside their backyards. Ashanti faces no such indecision, and her rendition of "Somewhere over the Rainbow" reflects this. Instead of questioning why she cannot fly beyond the rainbow, Ashanti sings (in music video fashion) that "Everybody tellin' me there's nowhere like home. Oh no . . . there's somewhere else for me. I need to take the opportunity and go." The refrain of this song reinforces this, claiming, "Sometimes you gotta get out of Kansas (gotta get out) / And sometimes you gotta take your chances (to find the answers) / Cuz no one ever made it just waitin' around." Ashanti does not desire a place where she won't get into any trouble, but a place where she can be a musical pop star, and she believes her audition with the Muppets will allow her this chance.

Moreover, the viewer likely sympathizes with Dorothy's longing because her life is not portrayed as appealing. She describes her future as one "serving meatloaf to truckers and living in a Kansas trailer park," and Aunt Em's advice that "you never gonna get to where you wanna be until you're happy with who you are" falls a bit flat. Ashanti may not be chased by a wicked neighbor, but unlike Garland, she also does not have a network of friends in the farmhands (later Oz characters); instead, her only friend is her King Prawn, Toto, a companion that substitutes the dog her aunt will not let her have. Instead of *The Wiz*'s emphasis on the values of family as presented in conjunction with the opportunity to leave, this Dorothy seems correct that her life lacks possibilities, and her family does not appear overly supportive.

While distressingly bleak, these circumstances are also fodder for the film's initial attempts at humor. For example, Aunt Em and Uncle Henry describe how Los Angeles is not safe "like here," only to hear the crash of thunder signaling that the tornado is about to sweep their trailer away. This moment achieves a quick laugh in its irony, but it also reinforces the idea that Kansas is not where Dorothy *should* want to be. Although the preceding argument between Dorothy and her aunt seems to hold meaning in such lines as Dorothy's proclamation that "all I know is that I hate living here, and I don't want to end up like you," this widened binary dissolves into jokes and puns, so that the conflict loses some of its complexity and the viewer is simply left with the notion that Dorothy is right—she has "gotta get out of Kansas."

Even in these initial scenes, viewers can see thematic amplification. On the one hand, the messages presented by her aunt allude to the importance of home, but even more importantly, the need for Dorothy to like herself instead of seeking approval from fame. This feeds right into the notion that individuals already possess what they desire, and while not exactly the same message, it certainly suggests a related theme. Dorothy, according to her Aunt Em, needs to learn to value herself without being validated by others, which is not only a theme relevant to a twenty-first-century female protagonist, but one that seems to appropriate the notion that we possess what we seek to a more modern mentality. Furthermore, the longing of "Somewhere over the Rainbow" is alive and well here too, as is the binary polarization created by emphasizing a conflict of valuing home versus a desire for the opportunities that may lie in leaving it. All of these messages have a basis in the other Oz stories, and all seem to swirl around Dorothy as she leaves Kansas and falls into a Muppet-infested Oz.

These varied messages are not resolved in clear ways, primarily because the movie shifts Dorothy's goals from previous film retellings. Upon her arrival in Oz, Ashanti's Dorothy does not want to go home (at least initially); she wants to be a star, a wish that the Wizard eventually grants by allowing her to sing on live television. Dorothy finds this experience unfulfilling, deciding that the joy fame can provide is nothing more than an illusion and, more importantly, that she misses her family. Again, we see the theme that Dorothy already possesses what she really desires (her home), and just as in the MGM film, Dorothy returns having learned her lesson and ready to reestablish the power structure she once wished to overturn, reinforcing aetonormativity once again. Just like Garland, Ashanti makes this idea exceptionally clear when she tells her aunt, "I just want to say . . . you were right. Wanting to be a big star made me forget what I really love about singing. When you're doing it right, I mean really singing, you don't notice where you are anyway."

Because the movie also sets up the actual lack of opportunities for Dorothy to do what she loves in Kansas, however, the story cannot simply end like this, and so Kermit arrives on the scene to offer her the chance to leave her family and go on tour with the Muppets. Although she initially hesitates, Aunt Em intervenes and offers her permission under the guise that she too learned something in Dorothy's absence: "you'll always be home with us, no matter where you are." While this is a touching sentiment reminiscent of Glinda's advice in *The Wiz*, it does not seem to ring true with the rest of the film.

This is most evident in the final musical number. More confusing than catchy, the lyrics praise family as part of the "the good life" and sometimes fit the notion of no place like home ("all you need is right here" and "who said happiness is so far away / closer than you might think, find it every day"). Yet Ashanti's "good life" is one on tour singing with the Muppets, achieved only through her attempts to leave her home and family. The lines "see what happens when you take your chances" and "come on in and find what I found" encourage seeking opportunity away from home, and while the movie alludes to the idea that you can take home with you because it lies within you, the commentary on fame is ambiguous.

The plot of *The Muppets' Wizard of Oz* offers more resolution than *The Wiz*, but Dorothy's final scenes touring as a "big star" seem to sit in contrast with her proclamation that wanting to be famous made her lose sight of what is important. She never learns to love herself apart from the approval of her family or the acclaim of stardom, and it does not appear that singing is more important to her than fame. The film certainly criticizes what Burger calls the "darker side of reality television and instant celebrity" ("Myth" 107), especially in linking these elements with the falsity of the Wizard and Emerald City, but fame is also what Ashanti achieves at the movie's end, thus seeming to simultaneously critique and celebrate its importance.

Even the idea that "you'll always be home with us, no matter where you are" is called into question by the tangible lack of opportunities and the limited emphasis on Dorothy's part in the Kansas community. In fact, the final song suggests her family is now the Muppets, who emphasize that their conglomerate of performers is its own family in several of their films, including *Muppets' Most Wanted*. Is the film thus suggesting that family is important, but we decide our own family? This then seems similar to the lesson Dorothy learns in *The Wiz*, but while Ross at least presumably returns to apply the concept to her life in Harlem, Ashanti does not learn to appreciate her family. Instead, she seeks a new community away from her home in Kansas simply because fame is what she truly desires. Thus, although she initially seems to learn that she always possessed what she truly desired, the concluding message returns to the idea that she was right to seek a life somewhere over the rainbow. Rather than (or perhaps in addition to) learning to love herself, Ashanti highlights another ideology: that leaving home in pursuit of fame is the right choice for this poverty-stricken, African American waitress-turned-singer.

The implications of this idea might lead critics to question the ideological weight of adaptive dissonance in *The Muppets' Wizard of Oz* even more than is necessary when it comes to *The Wiz*. For more than simply another example of adaptive dissonance, I suggest that in this case, ideological tension sends a message itself. In *The Wiz*, the context of the film plays a key role in softening the implications of adaptive dissonance, for although there is ambiguity in the film's ending, the purpose of the film remains clear. Although *The Wiz* may not offer a clear lesson about the role Dorothy is meant to play in her community, the adaptive dissonance of the film leaves the viewer with an opportunity to consider Dorothy's situation further, even after the film concludes. This can include a questioning about how Dorothy's choices—as well as the difficulty she faces in making those choices—might offer insight into the challenges faced by young African American women in the 1970s. This is less true for *The Wiz Live!*, but even in this case, lack of clarity seems a sidestepping of issues, which while certainly damaging, seems less explicitly or overtly problematic than *The Muppets' Wizard of Oz*. In the Muppets version, adaptive dissonance creates a new message in the conflict it creates, one which suggests that fame, despite its concerning elements, is the way to "get out of Kansas"—at least for this young, poor, African American woman. This is a message that feeds into racial stereotypes, and the film fails to empower its black protagonist in meaningful ways or acknowledge the complex interplay between race, class, and gender.

Just as in *The Wiz*, the adaptive dissonance of *The Muppets' Wizard of Oz* also reflects a specific context, but in this case, the use of pastiche complicates its goal and thematic objective. The purpose of Muppets movies generally revolves around humor, but usually in a good-natured way. On the one hand, the line between parody and pastiche is a thin one, for as Michelle Ann Abate notes, "while *The Muppet Show* is commonly seen as containing innocuous comedic content, it often encoded sharp cultural critiques and, at times, even subversive social commentary" (601–2). This is also why Newell's use of the word pastiche offers an intriguing insight into the Muppets, for the social commentary of *The Muppets' Wizard of Oz* is achieved through a relatively amiable style of humor which blurs the lines between celebration and critique in much the same way as the film's ending obscures the distinction between its criticism of fame and a celebration of it.

Nevertheless, this tongue-in-cheek humor, achieved because the Muppet characters most often poke fun at themselves and, by extension, the forms and texts they engage, clashes with other adaptive influences and, most notably, the goal and purpose of other Oz films with which the Muppets version engages. In *The Muppets' Wizard of Oz*, viewers are not meant to simply laugh at Miss Piggy or even the concept of Oz; they are also meant to see Ashanti learning a lesson, much like other film adaptations of Baum's source text. By engaging not only the Muppets tradition, but also previous Oz texts, multiple influencing forces seem to crash into one another in a way that takes adaptive dissonance down a darker road.

This darker ideological implication is not readily apparent, however, because on its surface, the text seems focused on an intertextual interplay that leads to both humor and a sense of play, wherein readers "in the know" can catch even more subtle references to both the sources texts and other cultural referents. In fact, much like other recent Muppet adaptations, such as *The Muppets' Christmas Carol* or *The Muppets' Treasure Island*, much of the humor of these movies lies in making fun of the source texts, doing so with a combination of reverence and humor. In *The Muppets' Wizard of Oz,* this is especially evident in cases such as Miss Piggy's role as all four witches (which eventually results in Ashanti commenting "another witch?" in frustration) and the running commentary of Toto (played by Pepe the Prawn), who often makes offhand, fourth-wall-breaking jokes about Oz. These jokes dovetail with Baum's concept that the power and majesty of the Wizard and Emerald City is actually an illusion, so that while Pepe seems to be making fun of the Oz storyline, he is actually reinforcing and praising it, setting up Ashanti's version of Dorothy to learn this very lesson about fame. Still, even though the film seems to do this ideological work, it also does so within a very Muppets context, which balances both a positive and negative view of celebrity most in the character of Miss Piggy, who Andrew Leal describes as representing "the desire for wealth and fame, embodying its allure (without always possessing its trapping), and showing the pitfalls" (210). Here again, there is ambivalence—a good-hearted critique that not only characterizes pastiche, but in this case, contributes to adaptive dissonance.

In addition to evidencing another case of adaptive dissonance, *The Muppets' Wizard of Oz* also again demonstrates that ambiguity can be problematic. Fitting a seeming commentary about fame to an already complex push and pull between "no place like home" and "Somewhere over the Rainbow" does not simply present a set of unresolved ideological questions related to culture and race (as in *The Wiz*) or even a resistance to engage these ideas altogether (as in *The Wiz Live!*). In the Muppets version, viewers are left with an ambiguity that does more than sidestep questions of fame versus family with regards to the aspirations of young African American women; it reinforces stereotypes instead of questioning ideologies or acknowledging the complexity of these issues. Indeed, not every case of conflicting messages resulting from a web of adaptations will be problematic, but it is certainly worth considering both whether ideological conflict exists and what the result is.

The Masculine Dilemma of "No Place like Home"

To further contemplate possible ramifications of adaptive dissonance, I draw upon an example in which the filmmakers do not reproduce the original *Wonderful Wizard of Oz*, but rather delve into its fantasy world—a world that extends beyond the one that Baum created. While the world of Disney's 2013 live-action Oz prequel, *Oz the Great and Powerful*, presents a separate entity of Oz created both from Baum's text and out of its multiple adaptations, it nonetheless evidences adaptive dissonance. Again, this ideological tension emerges from binary polarization, but in this case, it is not only home and away that are pushed conceptually apart, but also greatness/goodness, and even male/female. By polarizing binaries and drawing from a complex web of previous Oz adaptations, this new version is wrought with tension and laden with ideological implications of that discord. Furthermore, just as adaptive dissonance has ideological implications in Oz adaptations that are multiculturally committed, such as *The Wiz* and *The Wiz Live!*, internal ideological tension in *Oz the Great and Powerful* results in troubling depictions—in this case, with regards to gender.

Again engaging a web of previous adaptations as well as a complex cultural context, *Oz the Great and Powerful* primarily considers the notion of "greatness" versus "goodness." While certainly inspired by Baum's collected works, this film has no clear individual source text; like Gregory Maguire's *Wicked* (1995), it is a new story attempting to explain what happened in Oz before Dorothy arrived. In fact, *Oz the Great and Powerful* seems in some ways most similar to the widely popular Broadway musical version of Maguire's work, first staged in 2003. Still, the film is perhaps best described as a prequel to the 1939 MGM movie, despite the fact that copyright infringement laws forced producers to make several key choices to differentiate their film from the earlier version (such as eliminating the ruby slippers and slightly changing the Wicked Witch's green hue). There exists a distinctive link between the two films, such as shifting from the use of sepia and an old-fashioned 1.33:1 Academy ratio in the Kansas scenes to a brilliant widescreen 3D Technicolor when Oscar Diggs (aka Oz) is swept away by balloon. Additionally, the Wicked Witch's fireball and broomstick, Glinda's bubble, the multicolored horses in the Emerald City, the design of and reference to the Yellow Brick Road, and other costuming and set choices allude not to descriptions found in Baum's work, but to the MGM film. These elements make clear that the film responds to a host of other adaptations, and as a result, it demonstrates the same adaptive dissonance I have thus far described.

Additionally, this adaptive dissonance is directly linked to the polarization of binaries and amplification of theme that I track in other Oz adaptations. Like other adaptations, *Oz the Great and Powerful* explores the theme that an individual already has what he/she desires but simply does not realize it, presenting this message not through the secondary characters (as in Baum's tale), but rather through the text's protagonist. Like Garland's and Williams's Dorothys, Oscar Diggs meets three characters in Oz who teach him valuable lessons and correspond to people and events in his Kansas life. First, Michelle Williams plays both Annie and Glinda, prompting Oz (as Glinda does for Dorothy in the MGM film) to make clear what he has learned at the end of his journey. He tells her, "I want to thank you for opening my eyes," then responds to her question "And what do you see?" by answering, "That I have everything I ever wanted." She wisely notes, "For the record, I knew you had it in you all along," but when he asks whether she means "Greatness?" she tells him, "No. Better than that. Goodness." In response, he kisses her, demonstrating that he has also found love, and even though he was unable to recognize it with Annie, he can more fully appreciate her Oz counterpart.

Similarly, Zach Braff's CGI-enhanced character, Finley, also shows Oz that he already possesses something that he has been unable to recognize: friendship. Braff plays Oz's loyal (and much abused) human assistant, Frank, in Kansas, and he takes on a similar role of servitude in Oz as a flying monkey whom Oz saves from a "cowardly" lion. In Kansas, Oz tells Frank that he does not need a friend, but at the conclusion of the film, he tells Finley, "To you, I give something that I've never given to anyone. My friendship. Now you're my partner. You're my friend," to which a delighted Finley responds, "That's all I ever really wanted."

Also in Kansas, Diggs is booed by his audience because he is unable to heal a girl in a wheelchair, played by the same actress whose voice and likeness are used to create the CGI China Girl, whom Oz glues back together. The China Girl insists on traveling with Oz, and in the end, the gift that he gives her is recognition that he considers her part of his newfound family. Yet in addition to family, the China Girl also shows Oz that he is capable of compassion, and while he could not help the Kansas girl to walk, he can do more than glue the China Girl back together: he can also show her the compassion that she desperately needs. Oz learns to recognize and appreciate love, family, and friends, but the film also suggests that Oz was capable of having these relationships all along and simply needed the majesty of the land of Oz to help him access these elements of his own humanity.

In all three of these examples, the binary of home/away acts as a central focus, for while Oz did not appreciate the merits of his life in Kansas, wanting instead to reach beyond his life to bigger and better adventures, he now sees these elements of family and friendship as valuable. However, another binary is also polarized in this Oz adaptation, for while Oz may have had meaningful relationships all along, they are not what he is looking for when he expresses his own "Somewhere over the Rainbow" longing. Like Dorothy, Diggs yearns for something more than he has, and although the film is not a musical, he is clear about what he desires, telling Annie, "I don't want to be a good man, I want to be a great one. I want to be Harry Houdini and Thomas Edison all rolled into one." Annie responds that this is all she ever wanted for him: "greatness." This point sets up Glinda's final comments, which differentiate the good witch from Annie; unlike Annie, Glinda emphasizes Oz's goodness over his greatness. Like Dorothy in the MGM film, this exchange sets up a conflict between what Oz desires and what he comes to learn to appreciate, polarizing the binary between goodness/

greatness to create adaptive dissonance between "somewhere over the rainbow" and "there's no place like home." In fact, goodness/greatness might even be seen as the masculine version of home/away, wherein goodness relates directly to relationships and family, and greatness correlates to something more—a set of opportunities available if one is willing to sacrifice those more domestic roots.

The key ideological difference between *Oz the Great and Powerful* and the 1939 *Wizard of Oz*, however, is that while these binaries are polarized, Oz is able to have that which he longs for (greatness) and that which he learns to value (goodness) simultaneously. Oz resembles Garland's Dorothy in that he realizes he always possessed something he did not appreciate, but unlike Dorothy, Oz does not return home. For him, "somewhere over the rainbow" and "no place like home" are one and the same. This results in an important ideological implication of adaptive dissonance: unlike any of the female Dorothy characters in previous adaptations I have discussed, Oz, a male character, can enjoy both adventure and the benefits of family and security.

When applied to a female Dorothy, home consistently occupies a more constrained physical space and includes a more defined group of people. Garland's Dorothy chooses to seek her heart's desire in her own backyard, and if in *The Wiz* Dorothy ventures south of 125th Street, she may make friends and form new positive connections, but she also has to leave her family, giving up the comfort and security of a community with shared heritage and experience. *The Wiz Live!* goes even further, replacing the depth of longing expressed when Garland sings "Somewhere over the Rainbow" or the conflicting emotions Ross sings about in "Can I Go On?" with a desire that seems misguided from the beginning, thus firmly espousing an emphasis on family and the domesticity of "no place like home" without any other real considerations.

In contrast, while Diggs's experience reproduces the journey of self-discovery that Dorothy takes in many of the other Oz adaptations, he is not limited like his female counterparts. When Diggs pursues fame, he not only achieves it without any real condemnation, but he also is allowed the chance to essentially reproduce his family from Kansas. By utilizing the convention of the 1939 MGM film that uses the same Kansas characters in Oz, Diggs does not have to give up family, or even the specific people that he failed to appreciate. In *Oz the Great and Powerful*, the message is clear: by leaving home, the male protagonist can have both the greatness he desires and the family he did not know he wanted. By refiguring the dichotomy of home/away for a male character, the film reinforces the idea that while women must choose between home and adventure, men can have both.

This ideology, just as in the other films, results from adaptive dissonance. In this case, because applying the Oz story arc to a male character actually lessens the conflict between home and adventure, viewers see this binary polarized, but also dismantled in favor of another binary more relevant to this male character, described in the text by contrasting good versus great. The focus shifts away from the binary of home/away because for Diggs, home and away can coexist. Instead, the influencing web of adaptations surrounding the production of *Oz the Great and Powerful* draws from the idea of appreciating what one already possesses to explore the dichotomy of fame versus compassion. This, perhaps, seems to filmmakers a binary more suited to a male protagonist, which makes an interesting commentary on male/female dichotomies as well. By reinterpreting home/away in this new context, and even linking fame/compassion or good/great oppositions with home/away, the movie not only engages in a polarization of binaries, but also suggests what kinds of binaries are relevant for male versus female characters.

Nevertheless, what viewers end up with is an even more complex web of factors influencing the film, wherein polarization of multiple binary systems add to a host of other elements contributed by previous adaptations. And again, the result is a discord in the ideologies presented. While the movie sometimes seems to present the notion that goodness is more important than greatness, allowing Diggs to achieve both causes more adaptive dissonance to ensue, so that the film does not put forth a single central message, but conflicting ideologies.

While Oz does come to value love, family, and friends more than he once did, he is also presumably the same Oz character portrayed in the 1939 film—someone whom Kevin Durand describes as "not only a poor wizard, but a man who also fails at what a reasonable person might call 'goodness'" (176). If the young Oscar Diggs grows into the 1939 film's version of Oz, he seems to have focused far more on greatness than on the goodness that Glinda points out. Furthermore, Oz has achieved greatness—the fame of a wizard like Houdini and Edison combined—through deception, and he continues this dishonesty in his ruling of the Emerald City. Glinda may suggest that "greatness" is less important than "goodness," but Oz does not overtly agree because he has no need to do so. In Oz, this talented showman can have both.

Additionally, viewers might believe at the beginning of *Oz the Great and Powerful* that one ideological objective of the film is to criticize the deception that Oz uses to consolidate this power, for in both Kansas and Oz, Diggs's dishonesty and obsession with fame cause harm to himself and others. Yet here again, the film's end creates adaptive dissonance because it too does not adhere to this message. As the story is resolved, Oz's skill at deception is the very attribute that allows him to triumph, leaving viewers to question whether the film critiques Oz, or rather suggests that his ability to deceive is actually a virtue. This question of Oz's goodness versus his greatness is never fully resolved, for while Glinda tells Oz that he is good, he also proves himself to be great, and in some ways, these two concepts seem in conflict.

The consequence of these conflicting messages has ideological weight. Offering a commentary on contemporary masculinity, the film shifts to men the question of leaving home, and imposes a problematic paradigm in which these men must prove themselves both good and great while finding or creating a family of their own. This culturally constructed mandate seems just as disconcerting as women being told to remain in the domestic sphere and taught to find their heart's desire in their own backyard. Moreover, Oscar is not the only one affected by adaptive dissonance in *Oz the Great and Powerful*; the women of this Oz adaptation do not fare much better. Just as polarization of goodness/greatness has ideological weight for the masculine protagonist, adaptive dissonance similarly evokes unanswered questions about power and manipulation, and what it means to be good or great for its female cast as well.

The three main women of the film—Theodora, Evanora, and Glinda—also evidence the influence of the 1939 film on this new adaptation, especially because Theodora transforms from a good (although naïve) Witch of the South into a figure closely resembling MGM's Wicked Witch of the West, explaining why, when Garland's Dorothy travels to Oz, she encounters only three witches. Additionally, *Oz the Great and Powerful* seems clearly inspired by the popular musical, *Wicked*. However, unlike in *Wicked*, wherein as Burger writes that "rather than perpetuating the good/evil dichotomy of female characters that distinguished the earlier versions of Baum and MGM, Maguire populates his novel with fragmented and flawed female characters" ("Witches" 128), *Oz the Great and Powerful* polarizes binaries of good and evil to produce additional discord, and this adaptive dissonance results in one-dimensional women and problematic ideological representations.

Annie/Glinda, for example, is entirely "good," offering a stereotypically supportive and almost sickeningly sweet love interest who, despite her claim that Oz has changed, continually facilitates his ability to pursue his greatness in addition to his goodness and supports his use of deception to achieve his ends. Even more problematic is the double standard of Glinda's polar opposite, Evanora, who—similar to Oz—manipulates those around her to seize power. Like Oz, the film seems to critique Evanora's manipulation, presenting her with very few redeeming qualities. In fact, if the film *were* critiquing Oz for a similar deceptive quality, then these two elements would seem to work together toward a clear message. Unfortunately, while Evanora is a villain because she uses manipulation to seize power, Oz becomes the powerful hero through his ability to deceive. This point not only further problematizes the film's overall statement on power through deception, but also suggests that manipulation is acceptable for the male character, but not the female.

Nonetheless, it is Theodora's story that provides the most troubling depiction of femininity, especially when compared to *Wicked*. *Wicked* asks viewers to rethink their impressions about what it means to be "good" and "wicked," for although society sees Elphaba as the latter, the musical suggests that this is a characterization imposed upon her, one that does not accurately reflect her true story and experience. *Oz the Great and Powerful* might seem to promote the same idea, but while Theodora may not be responsible for her own misery, which results from Oz's selfish disregard for her feelings and Evanora's manipulation, she transforms from being exceptionally naïve to becoming completely driven by rage and vengeance. Her wickedness is not a judgment imposed upon her by society, as in Elphaba's case, but an identity that she physically embodies because of her hatred of one man.

As a result, Theodora herself begins to represent adaptive dissonance. Viewers may wish to sympathize with her because her wickedness is inflicted upon her, but it is difficult to do so because she behaves so badly. The jealousy and heartbreak that cause her wickedness lack a sense of gravity, perhaps in part because viewers' connection to her situation is hindered by her extreme naiveté. She is easily manipulated, the result of a toxic relationship with a jealous older sister. In this conflict, viewers can see another adaptive influence, for critics have identified this paradigm within Disney films even as early as *Snow White and the Seven Dwarfs* (1937). As Sandra Gilbert and Susan Gubar note of this film, "The central action of the tale—indeed, its only real action—arises from the relationship between these two women: the one fair, young, pale, the other just as fair, but older, fiercer . . . the one sweet, ignorant, passive, the other both artful and active" (36). This contrast describes exactly Evanora and Theodora's relationship, but also reproduces a dynamic presented by Disney time and again, in films including *Cinderella* (1950), *Alice in Wonderland* (1951), *Sleeping Beauty* (1959), *The Little Mermaid* (1989), and more recently, the Rapunzel retelling *Tangled* (2010).

Perhaps the most troubling element of Theodora's story is its end. Oz patronizingly tells her, "Theodora, I know your wickedness is not your doing and should you ever again find the goodness within you, you are welcome to return," but he is unwilling to apologize for any part he has played in her becoming wicked. Since his proclamation is made far more for the benefit of the townspeople below than it is for Theodora, his compassion seems just part of the show; moreover, the suggestion that he has the power to forgive and redeem her undercuts her power and perhaps even her very character. And we cannot forget that the very next interaction in their relationship (as far as the movie intimates) is when he sends Dorothy to kill her.

I suggest that these problematic depictions result not only from the web of adaptations upon which *Oz the Great and Powerful* draws, but also from the adaptive dissonance that results from this web of influence. Drawing from Baum, attempting to fit with the MGM film and other adaptations, and reproducing an approach similar to that of the popular *Wicked*, the film muddies the potential complexity a backstory might provide. In *Wicked*, Elphaba and Glinda sing that because of each other, they both have been "changed for good," but Glinda and Evanora undergo no change in *Oz the Great and Powerful*, and Theodora's transformation is only from exceptionally naïve to wholly wicked. These women's relationships seem to make them all far less good, and they are poor models of complex and nuanced femininity. Certainly, film and musical theater are different mediums with divergent audiences, and the middle step of Maguire's novel retelling complicates *Wicked* as a direct adaptation of *Wizard of Oz*. Nonetheless, for audiences expecting *Oz the Great and Powerful* to fulfill Buchbinder's notion of a critical adaptation, the adaptive dissonance of the film results in disappointment.

Disappointment runs as a thread throughout my reading of Oz adaptations, but I do not mean to suggest that all instances of multiple adaptations only offer problems. Moreover, while there are problematic aspects in these texts, there are also wonderfully interesting and complex elements as well. The dazzling use of set design and exceptional song lyrics to comment on the African American experience in *The Wiz*, the gender reworking of Queen Latifah's Oz character in *The Wiz Live!*, the funny and culturally critical pastiche of *The Muppets Wizard of Oz*—these are ideologies that work. Still, what *Oz the Great and Powerful*—which I find harder to praise—hints at is that while each new adaptation might be interesting and complex in unique ways, some binaries are especially fraught with problematics. Home/away might not seem like a socio-politically charged binary, but as Chaston suggests, and as I extend here, home/away is extraordinarily gendered and in these adaptations also racially bound. When widened binaries between home/away cause white/black or male/female to become polarized, this is a problem. As such, polarization in this case, and unfortunately, also in great frequency, is negative.

Nonetheless, adaptive dissonance is obviously not the only reason an adaptation is potentially problematic, and I do not want to diminish the historical and cultural factors that contribute to negative ideologies or even ideological tension itself. Fully exploring the tensions and problematics of gendered representation in *Oz the Great and Powerful* requires a look at the cultural conflicts surrounding contemporary manhood. Representation—whether related to gender, race, or another ideologically grounded cultural construct—results from a host of social and theoretical factors, with adaptive dissonance playing just one part in the mix.

Nonetheless, whether the messages in conflict are concerning or simply complex, *Oz the Great and Powerful* (2013), *The Wiz Live!* (2015), *The Wiz* (1978), and *Wizard of Oz* (1939) all demonstrate that in cases of multiple film adaptations of a single children's text, adaptive dissonance is the consistent result. While ideological tensions exist in many children's stories, as we see from the concept of home/away in Baum's *Wonderful Wizard of Oz*, across these and other examples of multiple adaptations, film versions increase the conflict between messages.

I will thus end by noting that although Oz film adaptations might provide a particularly strong example of adaptive dissonance, other cases of multiple films adapted from a source text do similar work. It would be interesting to further consider, for example, how the tension between nonsense and logic manifests in *Alice in Wonderland* adaptations or how critics might question of the merits of "growing up" by articulating the tensions in *Peter Pan* film and play versions. These other texts follow a similar pattern, for while ideological tensions exist in many children's texts, just like the concept of home/away in the *Wonderful Wizard of Oz*, film adaptations increase the conflict in these messages, and this heightened conflict has profound ideological implications, especially concerning race, gender, and other culturally constructed elements of selfhood. As a result, the adaptive dissonance emerging from the complex web created when multiple films are adapted from a single source suggests the importance of considering how film adaptations relate to one another in addition to their source and, in the case of Oz retellings, begs the question of how we reimagine the dreams that we dare to dream.

CHAPTER SIX

Theory and Pedagogy: A Disney Approach

While my exploration of binary polarization in children's and young adult adapted film identifies a key aspect of the adaptive process, I also find it an especially useful approach in my teaching, chiefly because an examination of binaries illuminates ideologies in ways my students find very accessible. One of my key pedagogical goals is to help students consider textual ideology, and by articulating comparative analysis based in literary theory, my students are able to make meaning from texts, a skill that pedagogy theorists suggest is central to literary study. Elaine Showalter, for example, writes that "at some level, whether we believe in pleasure, politics, or philosophy as the goal, all of us who teach literature believe that it is important not only in education but in life" (24). Learning about children's adapted film and, indeed, children's film more broadly can allow students to dig into literary analysis in these kinds of meaningful ways, and my theory of binary polarization offers a tool to do this.

For some teachers, the importance of literary analysis surrounds self-awareness, as in Marcel Cornis-Pope's description of his goal to help students "examine and correct their own reading habits and assumptions . . . [to become] more aware of the naturalized conventions that participate in their construction of meanings" (154). Others, like Mark Bracher, take this self-awareness in a more "radical" direction, writing that "there is no more legitimate aim or feasible function for education than the development of students' identities . . . to promote learning and understanding, foster intelligence, enhance our students' capacities for success and fulfillment, and contribute significantly to the general welfare" (xiv). Scholars frequently use this kind of rhetoric to emphasize that making meaning out of literary texts can translate into a more robust engagement with the world in personally enriching and socially responsible ways. No matter the overall goal, I believe students are able to make meaning from texts when they consider how a text reinforces, works against, or complicates the dominant belief systems of our society. Ideology lies at the heart of literary study, and my theory of binary polarization in children's film allows students to engage this kind of complex interpretative work.

In particular, an emphasis on binary polarization in children's adapted film blends opportunities for close reading with a theoretical framework, opening the chance to engage with critical perspectives and work toward common analytical course objectives. In writing about adaptation pedagogy, for example, Leitch builds from the work of Gerald Graff and Matthew Arnold to emphasize that he requires students to be "not merely literate, but critically literate, capable not only of absorbing and summarizing what they have read but of questioning, analyzing, contextualizing, extending, and synthesizing" ("How" 4). My theory of adaptation draws on all of these skills, but also incorporates criticism and theory, so that students at a variety of levels can more fully hone their skills of critical reading and scholarly engagement.

This is especially true when I focus my pedagogy around adapted films produced by the Walt Disney Corporation. Perhaps more than any other corpus of films, Disney movies have inspired a significant amount of ideologically based literary criticism, and they also demonstrate the key tenants of my theory in accessible ways, making them the perfect textual base for teaching adapted film through a lens of binary polarization. Films produced by the Disney Corporation are not only commonly taught but also widely known to students, and because students frequently have a strong emotional investment in them, thinking about such popular movies in new ways offers a strong entry point into a critical and theoretically driven approach.

Two key objectives define my approach to teaching Disney adaptations. First, I encourage students to find their voice in relation to contemporary critical scholarship, whether this means applying theory or articulating their own ideas within a critical context. Second, I ask students to think critically by evaluating the films, wielding close reading to make claims about the messages texts send and the ways they reinforce or challenge dominant belief systems. Because this manifests in varying ways depending on the unique needs of my students, in this chapter I will offer three potential classroom approaches, each utilizing a theory of binary polarization in children's adapted film in a different classroom space.

First, I apply my theory of adaptation of children's film to an especially criticized text that can inspire discussion in a foundational children's literature or introductory literary analysis class: Disney's 2009 *The Princess and the Frog*. Then, I suggest the 2014 film *Maleficent* is especially relevant when teaching young adult literature. I end the chapter with pedagogical approaches to the 2016 live-action remake of Disney's *The Jungle Book*, which I believe is particularly useful in a more specialized literature class, such as one focused on canonical literature or texts for middle-grade readers. By offering varying approaches to teaching each of these films, I also posit that these pedagogical techniques can be adapted to consider other Disney films as well, and my theory of adaptation can be a productive way to do so.

Introducing Binaries and the Disney Hegemony with *The Princess and the Frog*

Especially in a course wherein students have limited previous experience with texts for young readers, *The Princess and the Frog* (2009) offers a strong entry point to explore a theoretically driven discussion of ideologies based in binary polarization. Disney films find particular traction in the classroom as part of the teaching of fairy tales, especially in situations when, as Naomi Wood recounts, "students will often politely tell me that these new versions are all very well, but that they prefer the 'original,' by which they mean Disney" (25). Because this is an attitude many students new to literary analysis hold, a movie like *The Princess and the Frog*, which differs greatly from its source and has been the subject of often scathing literary criticism, offers a strong opening into a discussion of ideologies presented by fairy tales and the power of the Disney hegemony. The film is also one that seems especially defined by binary oppositions, making it a perfect movie to consider in light of this theoretical framework.

To begin this study, I ask students to review several versions, including the Grimms' tale "The Frog King." Students are surprised by how different this early variant and some of its picturebook retellings are from their expectations, and they express shock at the princess's dramatic flinging of the frog against the wall and the lack of a kiss to transform the gallant amphibian. As we use these versions to define fairy tales as a genre, I encourage students to consider critical approaches, drawing from Wolfgang Mieder's "You Have to Kiss a Lot of Frogs (Toads) Before You Meet Your Handsome Prince": From Fairy-Tale Motif to Modern Proverb" and Jack Zipes's "What Makes a Repulsive Frog So Appealing: Memetics and Fairy Tales" to discuss why contemporary perceptions of the tale differ from this early variant.

I combine introduction of these perspectives with critical background about Disney in order to help students work toward the first of my two key pedagogical objectives, and Disney films provide no shortage of critical viewpoints from which to build. I assign articles such as "Using Critical Race Theory to Analyze How Disney Constructs Diversity" by Amy Cappiccie, Janice Chadha, Muh Bi Lin, and Frank Snyder; "Images of Animated Others: The Orientalization of Disney's Cartoon Heroines from *The Little Mermaid* to *The Hunchback of*

Notre Dame" by Celeste Lacroix; and "Strange Faces in the Mirror: The Ethics of Diversity in Children's Films" by Heather Neff, and I reference the plethora of critical texts available, such as *Multiculturalism and the Mouse: Race and Sex in Disney Entertainment* by Douglas Brode; *From Mouse to Mermaid: The Politics of Film, Gender, and Culture,* edited by Elizabeth Bell, Lynda Haas, and Laura Sells; *Diversity in Disney Films: Critical Essays on Race, Ethnicity, Gender, Sexuality, and Disability,* edited by Johnson Cheu; *Mouse Morality: The Rhetoric of Disney Animated Film* by Annalee R. Ward; *The Mouse That Roared: Disney and the End of Innocence* by Henry A. Giroux and Grace Pollock; *Deconstructing Disney* by Eleanor Byrne and Martin McQuillan; and *Good Girls and Wicked Witches: Women in Disney's Feature Animation* by Amy M. Davis.

From this cache of sources, I draw several key ideas specific to *The Princess and the Frog,* including Sarah E. Turner's use of David Roediger's term "racial inbetweenness" to describe scholars' frustration that Tiana—whom many consider the first African American Disney princess—is transformed into a frog for more than two-thirds of the film. Turner describes Tiana as a "safe and sanitized" character (93), "simply a princess who 'happens' to have black skin but is not representational of blackness or racially prescribed tropes" (84), demonstrating "once again [Disney's] adherence to the politics of colorblindness" (90). Pairing this idea with Kheli Willetts's sentiment that "the arrival of a Disney-born black princess—more than 70 years after the appearance of their first effort to create an animated fairytale with Snow White—offers little consolation to people like me who spent their childhood on a quest for a reflection of myself in the world of Disney" (9), I help students to see why so many critics do not believe Tiana does enough productive ideological work.

Students are amazed by the overwhelming evidence of Disney's racist tendencies, and their mouths drop at my description of *Song of the South* (1946) or the horrifying musical number "What Makes the Red Man Red" in *Peter Pan* (1953), about which David Martínez, in his *Peter Pan* critique in *Seeing Red—Hollywood's Pixeled Skins: American Indians and Film,* writes, "My jaw hit the ground when I heard this song and saw these 'redskins' hopping around and making fools of themselves. Granted it was only a cartoon, but it was one in which the animators took the liberty of demeaning an entire race in the name of entertainment" (39). Students cannot believe they did not notice King Louie as an African American caricature in *The Jungle Book* (1967) or the problematics of *Dumbo,* wherein stereotypical crows seem tame in comparison to the "Song of the Roustabouts," which features faceless dark-skinned circus workers who sing "We slave until we're almost dead / We're happy-hearted roustabout" and "Keep on working / Stop that shirking / Pull that rope, you hairy ape."

Once we have established this critical perspective, I invite students to become the critics themselves, thinking about *The Princess and the Frog* by considering the messages the story sends, and I find that the concept of binaries offers an accessible theoretical framework from which to build. I first explain that twentieth-century academics like Claude Levi-Strauss and Roland Barthes believed that how we understand language depends on our understanding of the *difference* between the word and its "opposite," and as such, the meaning of words is more about a relationship than a fixed definition. While structuralism focuses on these systems of relationships that act as the foundation of our understanding of the world through language, theorists like Saussure emphasize that language is therefore arbitrary because the signs that make up language derive their meaning from their relationships and contrasts with other signs.

This is where binaries come in, and I introduce students, often in a very overview way, to Derrida's argument that such systems or relationships have an implied center, so that within these systems, one part is more important than another (good/evil, male/female). This, Derrida suggests, is problematic, hence the relevancy of the phrase "violent hierarchy" in considering binary oppositional pairs. Deconstruction, I explain, seeks to undermine such opposition within texts, and I ask students: Does *The Princess and the Frog* present, reverse, complicate, or reinforce binaries more or less than its earlier predecessor and/or other adaptations of the tale? To encourage students to explore this question, I pose several others:

- What are the binaries in the story?
- How are binaries related to one another or overlapping?
- What are the potential problematics of these binaries?
- What binaries from other/earlier variants shift in *Princess and the Frog*?
- Does the film seem to reverse the violent hierarchy Derrida describes?

What amazes me the most is that after only a fifteen-minute introduction to the concept of binaries, students can identify key examples in this Disney film, including rich/poor, male/female, human/nonhuman, good/evil, white/black, and urban/rural. Moreover, this foundation gives students a framework to critique the text and explore the ideologies within it.

For example, students discuss the friendship between Charlotte and Tiana in the film, commenting on the power dynamics between these two women, who become friends because Tiana's mother, a black seamstress, works for Charlotte's overindulgent father, who acquiesces to Charlotte's every whim (as evident by her many, many pink dresses, making her Tiana's mother's best customer). The sharp contrast between Charlotte's massive plantation home and the poor neighborhood where Tiana and her mother return provides additional context to their binary-based friendship. Tiana, who has had to slave at two jobs for years to gather pennies toward her dream of owning a restaurant, is presented in sharp contrast to her white friend, especially when Charlotte easily drops a huge sum of money in her lap, hiring Tiana to make her famous beignets as part of Charlotte's scheme to win the heart of a prince.

Close reading of the scenes featuring both Charlotte and Tiana indicates that while Disney may seem to critique the power differential between these two women, they could be more effective in doing so. In addition to offering a polarized binary that associates rich/poor with white/black, the film suggests this hierarchical binary as normal or acceptable; Charlotte and Tiana's relationship is not critiqued, but celebrated. Moreover, the institutions of the film that create this system of oppression are also left unexamined. Tiana, after all, is able to overcome the hardship and racism that stands in the way of her dream through hard work and a little magic, presenting an ideology that problematically ignores the institutions and systems that perpetuate racial inequality.

The film presents several polarized binaries, all of which are far more subdued in earlier and even other contemporary adaptations. For example, a discussion of the gender roles and romantic relationship between Tiana and Naveen never fails to elicit passionate responses from my students, who often come ready and willing to tear down the hegemonic ideologies of such Disney films as *Cinderella* or *Sleeping Beauty*, and are thus frustrated by the good girl/bad boy paradigm of this more contemporary romantic relationship. Tiana essentially reforms the lazy and philandering Naveen into the prince Charlotte has been dreaming about, reinforcing Charlotte's absurd fixation with marrying royalty by suggesting that such a prince can exist, but only needs the right woman to inspire him to such greatness. Students express anger that Tiana's dedication to hard work is not only set in stark contrast to Naveen, but that the film also criticizes this commitment to her dream, as if what she really needs to do is loosen up a bit and fall in love. Helping my students understand the terminology of binaries gives them a language to express these concerns and a critique of the film, similar to the kinds of work scholars of Disney have done for decades.

Students also discuss the choice to set the film in 1920s New Orleans, which differentiates it from most Disney princess films that do not have such a firm or tangible setting (except, interestingly, those with nonwhite princesses, like *Pocahontas* or *Mulan*). New Orleans is a place where cultures meld in remarkable ways, but the film does not highlight this, instead presenting binaries that exasperate stereotypes related to urban/rural spaces and religion. Good/evil is rooted to practices of voodoo, with Mama Odie seeming a failed attempt to balance Dr. Facilier's villainy, and the animal characters of the bayou draw on a long history of vocal inflection being problematically used in animated film. Again, these elements of the movie can all be considered in terms of binary polarization, and students quickly seem to realize that this is perhaps the defining characteristic of the changes and additions made to the story.

This rich discussion fosters the second key objective in my pedagogy: practicing ideologically based interrogation of texts. Students describe what they believe filmmakers were likely trying to achieve in the film, and then analyze whether they were successful or unsuccessful, and I ask students to brainstorm what positive ideological messages Disney could foster and what negative ideologies we would like to see avoided. By considering how many of the negative ideologies of the film are rooted in polarized binaries, students build from a critically informed and theoretically based foundation to engage critical thinking skills.

As a companion to this discussion in my introductory children's literature and literary foundations courses, one assignment I find useful is the creation of a review blog, either individually or as a class collaboration. After explicating and exploring *The Princess and the Frog*, students can tackle additional Disney-adapted fairy tales, then work in groups to discuss and map connections. I first group students with colleagues who have watched the same film, prompting them to describe ideologies and draw connections to *The Princess and the Frog*, and then break these groups apart so that each student acts as a representative for their film in a discussion with a group of students who have studied other movies, thus able to even more fully consider trends across texts. Then, students collaborate to create a review blog, using webpage software available online to post their observations in a shared space, often after studying examples of other similar blogs and discussing the conventions of reviews as a form of analytical writing. Such an activity allows students to apply their consideration of theory, critical perspectives, and close reading of *The Princess and the Frog* in new settings, extending and articulating their growing analytical abilities through writing.

Adolescence and Power in *Maleficent*: Exploring "So What"

Disney's development of more and more live-action reworkings of its animated "classics" opens unique opportunities to study adaptations geared toward older audiences. While *Cinderella* (2015) and *Beauty and Beast* (2017) would offer worthy studies in this capacity, I find Disney's 2014 *Maleficent* an especially productive film to teach in my adolescent literature courses. *Maleficent* demonstrates significant divergence from its earlier animated predecessor, but also polarizes binaries and shifts ideologies present in early variants in ways that facilitate robust discussion about an element of analysis and written discourse with which students often struggle: articulating the "so what" of their argument or interpretation, or what weight, meaning, and exigency their analysis has when placed in a wider critical context.

Toward this end, *Maleficent* offers the opportunity to study adaptation, but also works well to explore the nature of adolescent literature. As part of my first pedagogical objective, exploring critical context and theoretical perspectives, I use *Maleficent* to encourage a consideration of power dynamics in adolescent texts, building from Trites's description that young adult novels "self-consciously explore the individual's power in relation to the institutions that comprise her or his existence" (*Disturbing* 18). Using Trites's premise that "the YA novel teaches adolescents how to exist within the (capitalistically bound) institutions that necessarily define teenagers' resistance," I use *Maleficent* to help students explore the role binaries play in the power dynamics Trites suggests are key in literature for teens.

Combining my theory of binary polarization in YA film to study of power through Trites's lens, I ask students to not only identify sites of power and binaries within *Maleficent*, but also consider how these dynamics have changed from earlier versions of "Sleeping Beauty." My goal is, in part, to help students develop the ability to take an ideological approach to textual analysis, which Trites models in her reading of YA literature. Trites claims that power defines adolescence, that teens are "repressed and liberated" by their own power, and that "external and internal forces . . . compete to empower and repress individual power" (6). In light of these ideas, I prompt students to think about three questions:

- Who holds power in the story, and when is this person/being most powerful?
- Where does power come from in the story, and how is it reinforced?
- How are these power dynamics different in *Maleficent* as compared to the Perrault variant of "Sleeping Beauty," as well as the Disney animated version of the film?

These questions draw particular attention to Maleficent's backstory as a young fairy who falls in love with a human, and students identify that in her youth Maleficent appears powerful and wise. This continues as she grows up, but her paramour, Stephan, more and more actively seeks power as he matures, his ambition described clearly by the narrator. The binary of the human/fairy worlds is gendered, and although Maleficent is immediately established as knowing, wise, and kind, Stephan clearly has much to learn. Furthermore, the male/female binary is strengthened as these individuals move into adulthood, and Maleficent grows to be the "protector" while Stephan's maturity is defined by his ambition. As such, the film demonstrates binary polarization, but also the concept of the female savior I suggest is an ideological result of this greater conceptual divide between male/female.

In the film, Maleficent and Stephan are separated in adolescence, coming together again when the king creates competition among potential male heirs, and Stephan believes that by conquering the fairy world, he can win the kingdom. This paradigm illustrates institutionally reinforced power structures, and students also point out that technology presents a source of power in story, as Stephan wields iron toward his task because the metal has the ability to wound Maleficent and the other mystical creates.

When Stephan returns to Maleficent, seemingly contrite, the narrator announces that she "forgave Stephan—his folly and his ambition." Analyzing the scene that follows, students look closely at Stephan's use of violence to maim Maleficent in order to gain power; after cutting Maleficent's wings from her body with an iron knife, Stephan presents this trophy to his father and seizes the throne. Students focus on the key details of this moment in the film, including the darkness of this scene, Stephan's drugging Maleficent without her knowledge, his physical position above her, his use of chains, and her waking up not realizing at first what has happened but then screaming in agony once she comes to understand that she has been violated. All of these details work together to display physical violation wrapped in a moment of romance that draws a clear rape connection.

In this way, power within the text seems exceptionally gendered, a notion reinforced in the scenes following Maleficent's violation. Maleficent responds to her agony and betrayal by almost immediately transforming into someone to be feared, and the physical manifestation of her anger is formidable and destructive. In the scenes in which Maleficent reworks the beautiful fairyland into a dark, twisted space filled with thorns, viewers see how good and evil in the story are intertwined with representations of male and female, again grounding the movie in consideration of binaries. In fact, the premise of *Maleficent* is a binary distinction between two worlds, a concept described in the opening lines, which suggest "so vast was the discord between them that it was said only a great hero or a terrible villain might bring them together." Maleficent is originally seen as such a "great hero," but then transforms, at least momentarily, into a terrible villain because she is violated by the true villain of the story.

Stephan and Maleficent's initial romance suggests it might be possible for "true love" to break down the binary between the fairies (who are mostly portrayed as female) and humans (who are almost exclusively male), with Maleficent initially positioned to save Stephan as is common in the YA films I discuss in chapter 3. Stephan's violence upsets this dynamic. When Maleficent shifts in her role from savior to victim, she becomes the villain of the story, a concept only overturned in her return to a nurturing role as she attempts to save not Stephan, but his daughter, Aurora. This, my students contend, is the result of her having reached adulthood. While in adolescence she sought to save the man in her life (as is so commonly the result of widened binaries in YA films), her arrival at Aurora's christening harkens a shift into adulthood and, as such, a move from romantic heroine to mother. Maleficent may not be able to save Stephan, but she is redeemed from her villainy when she attempts to save both Aurora and the society more broadly.

Additionally, students considering the binaries of the text question whether Maleficent is both hero and villain as the final line of the film suggests. In some ways, Maleficent gives into villainy, but perhaps the true failing of the film is that this "fall" is not interrogated further. Her anger, even her villainy, is exceedingly understandable, and she is also far more hero than villain throughout the entirety of the film, even in her darkest moments. Students interrogate this consistent portrayal of good and evil as wholly separate, noting that they never really see Maleficent as anything but the hero, while Stephan is a truly abhorrent villain. Through the lens of a good/evil and male/female binary, viewers see a binary reversal, rather than a complication, and as such, the "violent hierarchy" seems only switched, rather than dismantled. While Maleficent is presented with more nuance than in the 1959 animated film, Stephan's portrayal suffers for it; he is pure ambition and evil. Men must become evil or powerless for an empowered female character to take center stage, my students often decide, and that is the problem.

To extend this discussion, I ask students to map how these binaries—good/evil and male/female—work in other fairy tales as well. Working in pairs or groups and contributing their ideas to the building of a visual map that often spans several dry erase boards, student compare the ideologies of *Maleficent* with their other favorite Disney films, an exercise that allows for a tracking of trends. I ask students to write, either formally or informally, about their perceptions about *Maleficent* and fairy tales more broadly, questioning the ways in which *Maleficent* differs in how it presents ideologies related to good versus evil, romantic relationships, and who needs saving/does the saving? This acts as an assessment for our discussion, and I prompt students to work toward several key objectives. They show whether they are able to 1) take an ideological approach using Trites and Derrida, and 2) interrogate the positive, progressive, and potentially problematic elements of the text by thinking about the ideological ramifications of the ways binaries are presented. In showing me their progress on these two learning outcomes, students demonstrate how far they have come in meeting my first main objective, a developing understanding of critical context and theoretical perspectives.

My second main objective in teaching film adaptations for young viewers focuses on practicing an ideology-based critique of texts, and *Maleficent* can be used to emphasize two analytical skills that are important parts of this goal: close reading and exploring the "so what" of an argument, including its weight and exigency within contemporary social and critical discourse. To do this, I ask students to conduct a scene analysis, first picking apart sections of early variants of "Sleeping Beauty" they feel correspond with the scene in *Maleficent* they are evaluating. I provide a handout that summarizes a few film techniques students might consider, including mise-en-scène and key elements of cinematography, such as lighting techniques and ways filmmakers frame a shot with certain camera angles and movements.

While students often elect to study the scenes surrounding Stephan's abuse of Maleficent and her subsequent rise to power, they also often choose sections of the film that surround Stephan's dissolving into madness and Maleficent's bonding with Aurora. These scenes alternate between shots of Stephan falling more and more deeply into villainy, and Maleficent reestablishing herself as the hero. Students point out the gendered nature of this growing polarization and explain how lighting, costuming, prop choice, and dialogue skew Stephan in traditionally masculine ways, while associations with nature, playfulness of dialogue, color, lighting, and even Maleficent's positioning within the frame present her as nurturing and kind.

Additionally, in contrast to the 1959 Disney *Sleeping Beauty*, Maleficent is far more endearing in 2014, and a substantial portion of the film is devoted to establishing this image. Why, I ask students, do filmmakers find it necessary to redeem Maleficent so completely? She was violated in an unspeakable way by someone she loved, and yet the film focuses on her healing almost immediately, attempting to make it clear that Maleficent is both recovering and not permanently marred by the violence and anger she first exhibits. This, I suggest, not only puts forth a strong and potentially problematic statement about women and trauma, but it also creates a binary, for she and Stephan are portrayed as diametrically opposed.

Throughout the film, this binary widens. For example, as Maleficent playfully harasses the fairies and cares for Aurora, Stephan "darkens," becoming entirely consumed with anger, hatred, violence, and malice, even at the expense of his men. Furthermore, as Stephan's evil grows, it is also accompanied by madness. In a scene in which he is told his wife is dying and may not survive the night, an array of camera angles emphasize his face and hide it, and lighting and sound choices create a sense of dread far more malicious and malevolent than those associated with Maleficent. As Stephan sits conversing with Maleficent's wings, a canted frame highlights the disturbing nature of the scene, which is then contrasted with Maleficent playing with Aurora in the mud—her heart is melting even as Stephan's hardens.

Part of the ideological ramifications of this polarized binary is also a commentary on motherhood. Maleficent may first appear at least somewhat frightening as she watches Aurora, and she contends "I don't like children," but the film establishes this as a façade. Close reading of scenes featuring Maleficent and Aurora prove that deep down, she is nurturing and caring, and she cannot escape this part of herself, no matter how hard she resists. A special child opens Maleficent's heart and makes her a better person. I ask students to consider how this brings new binaries into the mix, for while women often save or attempt to save men (male/female), in many cases, children also seem to save women, speaking to an adult/child binary as well.

Once students have listed, discussed, written about, or mapped their observations about such key scenes in the film, I ask why these filmic choices matter. What, for example, does a widened binary between good/evil associated with male/female suggest about the roles that men and women play in society? Why is it important that Maleficent's redemption is associated with her taking on a mothering role? What are the implications of associating evil with madness? Why do filmmakers shy away from scenes that show Maleficent's working through the negative emotions associated with her trauma, including anger, but perhaps also depression? What do these choices suggest about sexual violence? Would the film be stronger if Stephan's character was more complex and less polarizing? What message does it send that he is simply male and ambitious, which leads him to horrendous acts of violence? These are just some of the questions students might explore in their quest to consider "so what"—why the details they uncover matter in terms of the binaries they represent and the ideologies they establish.

Students might expand this discussion by subsequently studying other fairy-tale and fantasy films for adolescents, such as teen adaptations of Cinderella (*Ella Enchanted*, Disney's 2015 live-action *Cinderella*, *A Cinderella Story*, *Ever After*), Snow White (*Mirror Mirror*, *Snow White and the Huntsman*, *Sydney White*), Beauty and the Beast (Disney's 2017 live-action *Beauty and the Beast*, *Beastly*), or even multi-fairy-tale films like *Into the Woods*, *Enchanted*, or *Shrek*. In fact, students might also choose from a wider range of fantasy film adaptations for teens, such as *Stardust, The Princess Bride, Eragon*, or *Percy Jackson*. By drawing connections between Maleficent and these other movies, students further explore binaries and ideology, but also demonstrate critical thinking by tracking trends.

I ask students to share their research into these films and their findings by placing them in "panels" based on their film selection, and just as in an academic conference, each student from the panel shares their analysis, followed by five to ten minutes for questions and discussion. Depending on the number of students in the class (I have done variations on this assignment in small classes of fifteen students, medium classes with around thirty, and even a lecture class of fifty students), panel presentations can usually be completed in a single week of classes, and allow me to assess students' continued work on the kinds of ideological approaches we have discussed and practiced. Students apply their understanding of theory in a way that mimics the actual kind of academic discourse that scholars use to share their ideas, and I find this creates rich discussion while also fostering an atmosphere of professionalism and collegiality.

Discussion building from such "mini" academic conferences is especially rich, as students are not only invested in their own work, but also wish to support their colleagues, and they find it meaningful to consider how their presentations overlap. In this way, such work engages exactly the kind of meaning-making that academics find beneficial in larger academic circles and discourse. Moreover, students are able to begin tracking trends and drawing conclusions about their own work because they have a common language to use for their analysis, focusing on binaries like we discuss with regards to *Maleficent*, but applying this idea to films for teens more broadly. Just as I have found it productive to think about adaptation in terms of trends in order to make a broader claim about how adaptation for young viewers works, my students also do this kind of work to trace patterns, presenting evidence of their own unique claims about adaptation, adolescence, and fairy tales.

Complicating Ideas about a "Good Adaptation" with *The Jungle Book*

While *Maleficent* allows for a strong discussion of power dynamics and male/female binaries in adolescent fiction, Jon Favreau's 2016 remake of *The Jungle Book* fits especially well in a course that includes children's classics, opening the opportunity to consider contemporary adaptation from a lens that highlights cultural and historical context. The 2016 adaptation of Rudyard

Kipling's Mowgli stories is also part of Disney's trend to create contemporary live-action remakes of films in its corpus of "classic" adaptations, evidenced in *Cinderella* (2015), *Pete's Dragon* (2016), *Beauty and the Beast* (2017), *Dumbo* (2019), *Aladdin* (2019), *The Lion King* (2019), and upcoming remakes of *Mulan*, *Lady and the Tramp*, and *The Little Mermaid*. What makes *The Jungle Book* a particular distinctive example of Disney's work to remake its own corpus, however, is the way it subtly reworks the 1967 animated movie by choosing additional elements from Kipling's text to explore themes of community and power, while also addressing some of the criticism of the 1967 version related to race and representation. As such, it makes for a strong choice in order to teach even those new to the study of literature about how texts exist in context.

Unlike *The Princess and the Frog* and *Maleficent*, *The Jungle Book* live-action adaptation follows many of the key plot details from Kipling's source text. As a result, students can especially engage in comparative analysis that focuses on ideology, unpacking the kinds of messages that filmmakers present in the adaptation as compared to the source text or earlier adaptations. Again, I often ground this in power, asking students to answer some of the same questions I teach in *Maleficent*, but gearing these ideas toward new binaries, including adulthood versus childhood, self versus other, and community versus individuality or individual power.

What I find especially interesting about teaching *The Jungle Book* (2016) is that students are often drawn to the binaries of this text without even having the language to describe this theoretical approach. In one discussion, for example, a student remarked that Mowgli seems to become more and more innocent over time, while Shere Khan and the other animals in the text become both physically larger and increasingly terrifying. Without even realizing it, this student was describing polarized binaries, noting that with each new adaptation, there existed a greater conceptual distinction between what it means to be child versus an adult, a concept that is also linked with a stronger divide between good and evil.

The 2016 live-action *The Jungle Book* film also offers a strong premise to consider amplification of theme. For example, the film focalizes much of its narrative around Kipling's Law of the Jungle. In Kipling's story, Baloo tutors Mowgli in these guiding principles, a shift from both Disney versions, wherein a laid-back and comical Baloo espouses the ideology of caring primarily for his ability to procure the "Bare Necessities." The 2016 film maintains this element of Baloo's character, but utilizes the first several lines from Kipling's poem, emphasizing: "For the strength of the Pack is the Wolf, and the strength of the Wolf is the Pack." In many ways, this concept becomes a cornerstone for the new film, an amplification of theme that foregrounds ideologies surrounding community as a crucial element, further underscored by portrayal of the peace rock and water truce, another element from Kipling's *The Second Jungle Book* that does not appear in the 1967 movie. In both Kipling's story, "How Fear Came," and in the 2016 film, when draught causes the water to recede enough to reveal a rock in the center of the stream, a water truce is called, and all animals can gather without fear.

In addition to amplifying a theme from the source text, the water truce scene in the 2016 film also begins to establish key differences between Shere Khan's portrayals in Kipling's work and the Disney adaptations, a shift which especially emphasizes a polarization of binaries. In Kipling's story, Khan angrily questions whether he will someday have to ask Mowgli for permission to drink, a point that Bagheera concedes as possible. Yet Khan is chastised by the animals for dirtying the water with remnants of his latest hunt, which he admits he killed by choice, not out of need. Hathi, the great elephant, then tells a story of how the First Tiger lost power over the jungle because he brought Death, eventually replaced by Man, who brings Fear. The film eliminates this fable, and instead, Khan casts a tone of intimidation at the truce as Mowgli hides behind Akela (his wolf father). Khan attempts to frighten the other animals and assert power, but Mowgli's wolf mother, Raksha, rebukes him. After a standoff moment between Khan and the wolves, Khan ends by threatening violence when the truce ends, asking, "How many lives is a man cub worth?" Overall, Khan is a far more fearsome and malevolent force in the 2016 film than Kipling's lame tiger, a move that not only creates greater conflict, but also sets up human/animal, adult/child, and good/evil as diametrically opposed.

This threat inspires Mowgli to volunteer to leave the jungle in the 2016 version, an act of self-sacrifice meant to protect his pack. This differs from Kipling's version, wherein Mowgli is overly confident, physically grabbing Khan and using the Red Flower (fire) to frighten him away, consequently also frightening his wolf family and thus deciding to leave. Conversely, in the 2016 film, Khan consistently and purposefully perpetuates a system of terror through threats, violence, and a general tone of intense fear. In Kipling's version and both Disney adaptations, Khan has been literally burned by man's fire, and the 2016 version follows Kipling in that this occurred when Khan attacked Mowgli's family, leaving the boy orphaned. In the 1967 version, this detail is not included; Khan simply "hates man." In Kipling's version, this hatred is at least partially grounded in the fable backstory of the First Tiger, but in the 2016 film, Khan's anger and manipulation is a clear attempt to reassert power within the jungle community. He does this through terrorism, perhaps most exemplified when he kills Akela in order to manipulate Mowgli into returning to face him, an event absent from either the 1967 Disney version or Kipling's text. As such, not only are good/evil and human/animal polarized, but the film seems to set up Khan's fear tactics as set in opposition to the strength of the pack, perhaps even suggesting a dichotomy between power associated with individualism against that gleaned through community.

To explore this, I ask students to study a scene wherein the 2016 adaptation refigures a detail from Kipling: when Khan sits "teaching" Raksha's pups. While textually founded, the film adaptation sets this scene in the location of their father's murder, but also casts a far more frightening tone, using lighting and Idris Elba's incredibly effective tenor to strike dread in viewers. In this way, the film draws from Kipling to amplify theme, but also polarizes another binary of the film—individual versus community—in ways that have important ideological implications. Khan's characterization speaks to ideologies related to terrorism, power, and fear that might find particular weight to a contemporary audience. He is a lone villain, attempting to pit the community against Mowgli to garner power.

Ultimately, community wins out, but the final scenes of the 2016 film shed further light on this terror versus community ideology. I ask students to unpack the details of this scene, in which Mowgli proclaims to Khan, "I'm not afraid of you. No one has to be afraid of you anymore." Khan has planned this moment, however, and turns Mowgli's words against him, telling the animals that Mowgli, as he predicted, is the one to be feared, a notion that resonates because Mowgli has unknowingly released sparks that have set the jungle ablaze. In Kipling's work, Mowgli asserts himself in this scene (he only later kills Khan through expert manipulation of a herd of buffalo), but the 2016 film shifts the dynamic to highlight Khan attempting to instill fear in the community. The other animals back away from Mowgli, showing that Khan's efforts to sow terror are working, but unlike the Kipling tale, Mowgli reverses the dynamic, throwing the fire into the stream and claiming the jungle his home. Khan recognizes the turning point, approaching Mowgli and saying he has nothing, including no friends, until Baloo begins to recite the Law of the Jungle and others join in. They face Khan as a community, and while Mowgli is the one to defeat the tiger, this scene suggests that community trumps terror.

In drawing conclusions about this scene, students identify that while Mowgli can contribute meaningfully to the jungle community through his human ingenuity, which he proves when he saves a young elephant caught in a pit, if he embraces the world of men too much, he is also a danger to his home. In the end, however, and once he defeats Khan, Mowgli bows to show respect to the elephant leaders, the third time he has done so in the 2016 film. The elephants (who are far more aligned to Kipling's portrayal than the humorous satire of British military in the 1967 animated version) then save the jungle, using their tusks to reroute the river and extinguish the fire. Thus, while the 2016 film engages ideologies related to power and terrorism, it simultaneously comments on community to suggest that while individuality is powerful, perhaps more important is "staying together," which Mowgli describes as he trains the next generation of wolf pups in the final scene.

As they work to interpret the end of the film, I ask students whether they see a reversal of power dynamics from Kipling's text, to which they respond that such a reading is complicated when Bagheera's voice-over redirects focus to Mowgli's role in bringing the community together: "That night, I saw something I'll never forget. I saw a little boy, without a people, bring all the jungle together for the very first time." The end of the film, they contend in frustration, is fraught with conflicting messages. Mowgli is only able to face Khan because he has the "pack" of other animals behind him, emphasizing the Law of the Jungle. Nevertheless, he ultimately defeats Khan alone—highlighting individual power. Even this is complicated, however, because it is the elephants that really bring resolution in extinguishing the fire, even though Mowgli is again set apart in being positioned as riding one of the lead elephants. Bagheera then suggests that Mowgli has brought people together. Students ponder the conflicting ideologies of this scene: is Mowgli individual, leader, or member of community? They then study the final scene of the film, which they claim leaves little resolution between these binaries. Mowgli again sets himself apart as a human in teaching the new wolf pups, but also stresses that they are one pack and community who must stick together.

Students suggest that while binaries—and especially the community/individuality binary—are more clearly polarized in the film, there is also a lot of messiness. They want the theme or message to be clearer. This opens an excellent opportunity to bring in a discussion of *adaptive dissonance*, and I suggest to students that maybe this messiness comes from the combination of more polarized binaries with the fact that filmmakers are drawing from a lot of previous Jungle Book adaptations, including Kipling and the 1967 version. Will this always happen, I ask, opening a productive opportunity to consider other instances of multiple adaptations and thematic messiness (or, as I describe it, an internal ideological tension, or adaptive dissonance).

In addition to offering an opportunity to discuss this ideologically driven interrogation of the film, the live-action *The Jungle Book* remake also offers a distinctive chance to explore and apply critical context, and especially the progression of adaptation studies criticism away from fidelity studies. In order to prompt discussion that complicates the question of what makes a good adaptation, I share ways scholars have critiqued Disney films in terms of cultural representation. While this background overlaps to some degree with the information I provide students when teaching *The Princess and the Frog*, I also build from a critical race theory approach to ask students to think about the role that casting of voice actors plays in the filmmaking.

In providing an introduction to adaptation studies, I utilize many of the critical foundations I describe it in my first chapter, but highlight several key critics to succinctly provide a sense of the progression of ideas in an accessible way. After talking briefly with students about what words they associate with adaptation (often listing these on the board), I quote Bluestone's contention that "what happens, therefore, when a filmist undertakes the adaptation of a novel, given the inevitable mutation, is that he does not convert the novel at all. What he adapts is a kind of paraphrase of the novel" (62). I then suggest that an attempt to understand such paraphrases has often focused on categorization, laying out Wagner's paradigm of transposition, commentary, and analogy, and asking students to suggest several examples of each. Next, I introduce Sanders's concept of appropriation to describe adaptation as a "wholesale rethinking of the terms of the original" (28), one which allows for new texts to "stand alongside the texts which have inspired them, enriching rather than 'robbing' them" (41). Drawing from Stam's use of Bakhtin, I emphasize that contemporary critics see films as drawing from a complex web of intertextual influences and, as a result, might "selectively take up, amplify, ignore, subvert, or transform" (Introduction 46) their source texts, concluding that most recent scholarship moves away from fidelity to explore the rich complexity of this web by considering cultural and historical contexts.

At this point, I pose three questions to students, which I ask them to consider as we delve more deeply into some specific critical and popular interpretations of *The Jungle Book* adaptations.

- What do you think are filmmakers' objectives when they adapt a book to a film? How do you know these are their objectives?
- What do you think their goals *should* be?
- What do you think would make a good adaptation (or adaptation of an adaptation)?

Before answering these questions, however, I ask students to consider more specific critical readings of Kipling's source text, for although Kipling's work has been interpreted in a variety of ways, it frequently includes readings that point to problematic depictions of colonialism, wherein Mowgli is positioned as the "Master of the Jungle" to result in, as Jopi Nyman describes, "an imagining of Englishness as a site of power and racial superiority" (206). I also introduce students to Sue Walsh's interpretation of the text, which reconsiders the choice

Mowgli must make between the animal and human worlds to suggest that Kipling actually allows for a consideration of multiple simultaneous identities. Walsh claims that rather than "the consolidating and cohering of an identity into something singular and fixed," Mowgli's journey calls into question the "borders between child and adult, human and animal, 'native' and 'white'; troubling any notions of essentiality" (63).

What many of these readings of Kipling's work have in common is that they hint, often without describing it this way, at the idea of binaries, including adult/child, human/animal, self/other, and colonizer/colonized. I suggest the power dynamics that go along with these binaries seem very purposefully reworked in the adaptations. For example, I ask students to examine sections of Kipling's story that focus on Mowgli's stare, and the fact that the animals cannot look him in the eye, no matter their position. This element is overturned in the adaptations, wherein the jungle animals seem to hold far more power over Mowgli than he does over them. In Kipling's stories, Baloo and Bagheera may seek to teach Mowgli the Law of the Jungle and help him find his place within it, but he also holds a position of power, respected and feared by the jungle animals because he is a human.

I continue this discussion by suggesting that power and race are important elements of critical study of the story's adaptations, and especially the 1967 Disney version. Scholars such as Susan Miller and Greg Rode, Greg Metcalf, and Heather Neff especially critique the depiction of King Louie, suggesting him as a highly racist caricature of African Americanism. As Neff describes, "While contemporary audiences surely recognized this image as yet another incarnation of a century-old tradition in which blackface (and Black) entertainers parodied the unschooled Negro's attempts to assimilate white speech and culture, Disney's representation of an African American 'ape'—a veritable icon in the racist imagery of Hollywood—should be completely unacceptable to today's 'culturally sensitive' audiences" (56). If this jazz-singing, jive-talking ape, who does not appear in Kipling's work, is taken as such—a point that most critics agree upon—the musical number "I Wanna Be Like You" sets up a concerning interpretation of his desire to be more like man because he has "reached the top and had to stop." More even than an insulting caricature, this song offers a troubling depiction of power dynamics between African Americans and their white oppressors.

Students are often somewhat stunned by this reading, and even more stunned when I bring voice acting into the mix. In discussing voice acting in the Jungle Book adaptations, I begin by sharing several examples, such as the controversy surrounding the casting of Charlize Theron, Matthew McConaughey, and other white actors in the principle roles of *Kubo and the Two Strings* (2016), a choice which greatly diminishes the otherwise excellent representation of Japanese culture in the film. We talk about the casting of Christian Bale, Joel Edgerton, and Sigourney Weaver in the adult live-action *Exodus: Gods and Kings* (2014) as well as the casting in the earlier animated *Prince of Egypt* (1998), wherein these casting choices participate in Hollywood whitewashing. I show slides that compare the depictions of Aladdin and Jasmine (both voiced by white actors) with those of the far more Middle-Eastern looking villains of the story and share news stories criticizing Disney's Broadway musical version of Aladdin for similar reasons. I ask students to consider these developments and question what Disney has done and is doing to address some of the critiques regarding whitewashing, voice acting, and cultural authenticity in their films.

This, then, leads to our discussion of *The Jungle Book*, which includes marked changes to eliminate racist elements identified in the 1967 version, foremost removing characterization of King Louie that could be construed as caricature. Voiced by Christopher Walken in the 2016 film, King Louie's power seems primarily derived from his enormous size; he is a Gigantopithecus, an extinct genus of giant ape. The 2016 version also includes a far more diverse cast of voice actors, including Idris Elba as Shere Khan, with Lupita Nyong'o and Giancarlo Esposito voicing the two main wolf characters, Raksha and Akela. I tell students that while overall, the film was positively received for this casting and its attempts to eliminate elements of racism from the 1967 version, some critics still point to the very limited number of Southeast Asian actors cast, suggesting that a more diverse ensemble does not truly address contemporary concerns about characters played by individuals who do not share their race or ethnicity. The film only includes three South Asian actors: Ben Kingsley, whose father is of Indian Gujarati descent, and the two human characters (Mowgli, played by Neel Sethi, and his father, voiced by Ritesh Rajan). Moreover, while critics have noted that characters of power in the 1967 film are given British accents and other characters are not, this trend also continues with Elba's voicing of Khan and Kingsley's voicing of Bagheera.

Given this background, I return students to my questions and, in particular, ask them to discuss what they suppose filmmakers' objectives to be in a movie like *The Jungle Book*. I push this further by asking them what they think their goals *should* be, delving into the question of what makes a good adaptation. By asking students to articulate how the 2016 live-action *Jungle Book* both responds to Kipling, but also revises criticized elements of the 1967 film, I pose questions about how adaptation becomes more complicated when filmmakers rework a story that has been adapted many times (as Disney has become especially fond of doing). I ask students to consider how this changes the goals filmmakers might have.

This prompting leads students to wonder whether the reworked King Louie of the 2016 film really serves to eliminate the obvious racially marked caricatures, especially when the power dynamics between the boy and animal still exist, perhaps in an even greater degree. They identify this as similarly problematic to the changes to Kaa's character, who now voiced as a female, takes on a combined motherly and seductive role that troubles students. Voiced by Scarlett Johansson, Kaa is powerful, but her power comes from a combined nurturing and sexuality that does not really seem to fix any of the problems in the original so much as replace them with new concerns.

All of this discussion leads students toward one key conclusion—that filmmakers, and especially Disney filmmakers, do not seem especially interested in gray areas. This seems an important point, for in addition to my discussions with students about how film adaptations amplify themes and polarize binaries, the finality with which they see this as simply a part of "how Disney works" seems to reinforce the notion that these characteristics are a part of how film adaptation for young viewers functions.

To assess their developing ability to engage and articulate these ideas, I end our discussion of *The Jungle Book* (2016) by asking students to take on a bit of a creative role, placing themselves in the position of filmmaker. First, we discuss other similar adaptations, talking about whether Will Smith's role as the genie in the live-action *Aladdin* positively or problematically engages critical race theory and how Jasmine's new power ballad pushes a positive feminist agenda while potentially limiting cultural authenticity. We analyze the removal of racist elements of the animated *Dumbo*, so similar to *Jungle Book* in its use of caricature in the jive-talking crows, and we contemplate what other race and class-based power dynamics were added and potentially left unexamined. If you were the filmmakers in these cases, I ask students, what would you have done differently?

Then, whether in small groups or as a larger more comprehensive assignment, students pitch the "perfect" live-action adaptation of a Disney favorite. Some of their choices are upcoming films, which provides a rich opportunity for students to engage in what feels like weighty predictions about what choices filmmakers will make and where they will go astray. Will the social media controversies surrounding live-action adaptations of *Mulan* come to fruition? How will *Lady and the Tramp* avoid class-based binaries and rework the terribly racist cats, Si and Am? Will *The Little Mermaid* finally get it right?

These are productive questions, but so are the ones that come from films not yet tasked for Disney's upcoming docket. I am particularly interested in the ways students describe a "fix" for the stereotypical portrayals of Hawaii in *Lilo and Stitch*, because they want to keep the messages about the complexity of family and home, but avoid a human/alien binary from becoming too polarized. I love when students consider that *Tangled* needs a reworking that does not require a "spunky" blond princess to reform a roguish, but good-hearted Flynn Rider. I am fascinated when they consider how a culturally authentic and more historically accurate *Pocahontas* might not polarize colonizer/colonized dichotomies, and I smile when they suggest that a live-action *The Princess and the Frog* could perhaps avoid class-based binaries and rework problematics related gender, race, and spirituality.

All great ideas and noble pursuits, I suggest, but as students try to work out the details, they often come to realize how difficult it is to break from polarization of binaries in Disney, especially without creating new problems even as they fix the old. While this activity or assignment is certainly fun, it also makes an important point—no matter how critically we think about children's film or how much research we do to consider it from every angle, making a "good" adaptation simply is not as easy as it seems—and that is why such critically informed and ideologically founded close reading study must continue.

ACKNOWLEDGMENTS

First and foremost, I want to thank the people who have supported my study of children's literature and film for young people. My parents, Barbara and Michael Meeusen, and my sister, Katie Meeusen, have cheered me on and cheered me up in moments when I was discouraged, always eager to listen to me ramble on long car rides about Disney song lyrics or expound over popcorn about the way a female heroine "is fitting a longstanding trope—don't you think!?" My family has supported every aspect of my life with enthusiasm, and I'll never be able to thank them enough.

My academic journey toward bringing this manuscript into the world has been a long one, but it has only been possible because of the encouragement, insights, and generously shared expertise of my mentors. Roberta Seelinger Trites believed in me from the moment I met her and helped me to see myself as a scholar, opening up doors in my life and my imagination that I never thought possible. Gwen Tarbox has been my never-failing academic rock (and rockstar), opening my eyes to the possibilities of studying children's literature nearly a decade and a half ago and standing by me in every step of my journey. I wouldn't be the writer, teacher, or person I am today without her, and I am forever grateful.

There have been many teachers and mentors that have helped me on my journey, and I especially wish to acknowledge Karen Coats for being just the sounding board I needed so many times; she always knows just what to say to make you believe that the next step is achievable. I'm appreciative to have had the chance to learn from Jan Susina as well, whose wisdom and insight is, in so many ways, unparalleled. Joyce Walker helped me grow into my academic self, and she is one of the most inspiring women I've ever known. Yet even in the days before I knew that the study of children's literature was to be my life's work, there were people who encouraged my love of it. Beth Amidon helped me to see the magic and meaning in children's texts in those very early days, and Karen Vocke not only helped start me on my journey, but also continues to walk it with me today. For these teachers, and all the mentors who helped me to do this work, I express my gratitude.

My friends and colleagues have also been profoundly influential in my life, and so much of this book came out of both our discussions and their continual reminders that my work was of value. Perhaps most of all, I thank Hilary Selznick, who has been my dear friend and unfailing support for over a decade. Years and years of monthly phone conversations with Jennifer McConnel have kept me steady and sane, and Kara Branch has been an integral inspiration in my life for as long as I can remember. Elizabeth Bell, Amy Hicks, and Jordana Hall were the very best friends a graduate student could have, and nearly every major argument of this text was unlocked through a conversation with one of these brilliant women. When I moved into a new stage of life, it was Krystal Howard who stepped in to fill this role and so much more; her friendship and wisdom is something I'll always value. Still, so many other amazing friends were behind the pages of this book: in particular, I wish to thank Beth Pearce, Farrah Norris Sands, Niall Nance-Carroll, Abbie Ventura, Karly Grice, and Shelby Ragan for being a part of my academic family. And I'll never forget my first graduate student comrades—my amazing "pod": Katherine Zlabek, Kate Dernocoeur, Kory Shrum, and Melinda Moustakis.

Finally, I wish to thank the editorial staff at University Press of Mississippi for their faith in my work, and I am especially grateful to Katie Keene, who spent over three years helping me to pursue publication and develop these pages. This book wouldn't exist without her and the hardworking editors who helped me take this project past the finish line so that it could see the world.

BIBLIOGRAPHY

Abate, Michelle Ann. "Taking Silliness Seriously: Jim Henson's *The Muppet Show*, the Anglo-American Tradition of Nonsense, and Cultural Critique." *Journal of Popular Culture*, vol. 42, no. 4, 2009, pp. 589–613.

Albrecht-Crane, Christa, and Dennis Cutchins, editors. *Adaptation Studies: New Approaches.* Fairleigh Dickinson UP, 2010.

Althusser, Louis. *Essays on Ideology.* Verso, 1984.

Althusser, Louis. *Lenin and Philosophy and Other Essays.* Translated by Ben Brewster, Monthly Review Press, 2001.

Andrew, Dudley. *Concepts in Film Theory.* Oxford UP, 1984.

Bakhtin, Mikhail. *The Dialogic Imagination: Four Essays.* Translated by Caryl Emerson and Michael Holquist, U of Texas P, 1981.

Baum, L. Frank. *The Annotated Wizard of Oz: The Wonderful Wizard of Oz.* Edited by Michael Hearn, Norton, 2000.

Beauty and the Beast. Directed by Bill Condon, performances by Emma Watson and Dan Stevens, Walt Disney Studios, 2017.

Bell, Elizabeth, Lynda Haas, and Laura Sells, editors. *From Mouse to Mermaid: The Politics of Film, Gender, and Culture.* Indiana UP, 1995.

Belsey, Catherine. *Critical Practice.* Routledge, 2002.

Bluestone, George. *Novels into Film.* U of California P, 1966.

Bracher, Mark. *Radical Pedagogy: Identity, Generativity, and Social Transformation,* Palgrave Macmillan, 2006.

Brock-Servais, Rhonda, and Matthew Prickett. "From *Bildungsroman* to Romance to Saturday Morning: *Anne of Green Gables* and Sullivan Entertainment's Adaptations." *The Lion and the Unicorn,* vol. 34, no. 2, 2010, pp. 214–27.

Brode, Douglas. *Multiculturalism and the Mouse: Race and Sex in Disney Entertainment.* U of Texas P, 2005.

Brown, Emma. "The Lorax Helps Market Mazda SUVs to Elementary School Children Nationwide." *Washington Post,* 29 February 2012.

Buchbinder, David. "From 'Wizard' to 'Wicked': Adaptation Theory and Young Adult Fiction." *Contemporary Children's Literature and Film: Engaging with Theory,* edited by Kerry Mallan and Clare Bradford, Palgrave, 2011, pp. 127–46.

Burger, Alissa. "A Rainbow for the 21st Century: *The Muppets' Wizard of Oz* and the Reimagination of the American Myth." *Kermit Culture: Critical Perspectives on Jim Henson's Muppets,* edited by Jennifer C. Garlen and Anissa Graham, McFarland, 2009, pp. 103–15.

Burger, Alissa. "Wicked and Wonderful Witches: Narrative and Gender Negotiations from *The Wizard of Oz* to *Wicked*." *Beyond Adaptation: Essays on Radical Transformations of Original Works,* edited by Phyllis Frus and Christy Williams, McFarland, 2010, pp. 123–31.

Byrne, Eleanor, and Martin McQuillan. *Deconstructing Disney*. Pluto Press, 1999.

Cadden, Mike. "The Irony of Narration in the Young Adult Novel." *Children's Literature Association Quarterly*, vol. 25, no. 3, pp. 146–54.

Cahir, Linda Costanzo. *Literature into Film: Theory and Practical Approaches*. McFarland, 2006.

Cappiccie, Amy, Janice Chadha, Muh Bi Lin, and Frank Snyder. "Using Critical Race Theory to Analyze How Disney Constructs Diversity." *Journal of Teaching in Social Work*, vol. 32, no. 1, 2012, pp. 46–61.

Cardwell, Sarah. *Adaptation Revisited: Television and the Classic Novel*. Manchester UP, 2002.

Cartmell, Deborah, and Imelda Whelehan, editors. *Adaptations: From Text to Screen, Screen to Text*. Routledge, 1999.

Cartmell, Deborah, and Imelda Whelehan. "Introduction—Literature on Screen: A Synoptic View." *The Cambridge Companion to Literature on Screen*, edited by Deborah Cartmell and Imelda Whelehan. Cambridge UP, 2007.

Chaston, Joel D. "If I Ever Go Looking for My Heart's Desire: 'Home' in Baum's 'Oz' Books." *The Lion and the Unicorn*, vol. 18 no. 2, 1994, pp. 209–19.

Chaston, Joel D. "The 'Ozification' of American Children's Fantasy Films: *The Blue Bird, Alice in Wonderland, and Jumanji*." *Children's Literature Association Quarterly*, vol. 22 no. 1, 1997, pp. 13–20.

Cheu, Johnson, editor. *Diversity in Disney Films: Critical Essays on Race, Ethnicity, Gender, Sexuality and Disability*. McFarland, 2013.

Cinderella. Directed by Kenneth Branagh, performances by Lily James and Cate Blanchett, Walt Disney Studios, 2015.

Clark, Beverly Lyon. *Kiddie Lit: The Cultural Construction of Children's Literature in America*. John Hopkins UP, 2003.

Coats, Karen. "Between Horror, Humour, and Hope: Neil Gaiman and the Psychic World of the Gothic." *The Gothic in Children's Literature: Haunting the Borders*, edited by Anna Jackson, Karen Coats, and Roderick McGillis, Routledge, 2008, pp. 77–92.

Coats, Karen. *Looking Glasses and Neverlands: Lacan, Desire, and Subjectivity in Children's Literature*. U Of Iowa P, 2004.

Collins, Fiona M., and Jeremy Ridgman, editors. *Turning the Page: Children's Literature in Performance and the Media*. Peter Lang, 2006.

Collins, Suzanne. *Catching Fire*. Scholastic, 2009.

Collins, Suzanne. *The Hunger Games*. Scholastic, 2008.

Coraline. Directed by Henry Selick, Focus Features, 2009.

Cornis-Pope, Marcel. "Hypertextual and Networked Communication in Undergraduate Literature Classes." *Learning Literature in an Era of Change: Innovations in Teaching*, edited by Dona J Hickey and Donna Reiss, Stylus, 2000, 152–67.

Cowell, Cressida. *How to Train Your Dragon*. Little Brown, 2003.

Cutchins, Dennis R., Laurence Raw, and James Michael Welsh, editors. *The Pedagogy of Adaptation*. Scarecrow Press, 2010.

Cutchins, Dennis R., Laurence Raw, and James Michael Welsh, editors. *Redefining Adaptation Studies*. Scarecrow, 2010.

Davis, Amy M. *Good Girls and Wicked Witches: Women in Disney's Feature Animation*. John Libbey, 2006.

Derrida, Jacques. *Positions*. Translated by Alan Bass, U of Chicago P, 1981.

Deutsch, Leonard J. "The Named and the Unnamed." *Children's Novels and the Movies*, edited by Douglas Street, F. Ungar, 1983, pp. 214–26.

DiAngelo, Robin. "White Fragility." *International Journal of Critical Pedagogy*, vol. 3, no. 3, 2011, pp. 54–70.

DiCamillo, Kate. *The Tale of Despereaux*. Candlewick, 2003.

Durand, Kevin K. "The Wicked Wizard of Oz." *The Universe of Oz: Essays on Baum's Series and Its Progeny*, edited by Kevin K. Durand and Mary K. Leigh. McFarland, 2010, pp. 172–78.

Dyer, Richard. *Stars*. British Film Institute, 1998.

Earle, Neil. *The Wonderful Wizard of Oz in American Popular Culture: Uneasy in Eden*. Mellen, 1993.

Ebert, Roger. Review of *The Spectacular Now*. RogerEbert.com, 2 August 2013.

Ebert, Roger. Review of *Where the Wild Things Are*. RogerEbert.com, 14 August 2009.

Elliott, Kamilla. *Rethinking the Novel/Film Debate*. Cambridge UP, 2003.

"Female Film Protagonists Reached All-Time High in 2016, Study Shows." *Guardian*, 21 February 2017.

The 5th Wave. Directed by J Blakeson, performances by Chloë Grace Moretz, Nick Robinson, and Alex Roe, Columbia Pictures, 2016.

Fowkes, Katherine A. *The Fantasy Film*. Wiley-Blackwell, 2010.

Gaiman, Neil. *Coraline*. HarperCollins, 2002.

Genette, Gärard. *Palimpsests: Literature in the Second Degree*. U of Nebraska P, 1997.

Gilbert, Sandra M., and Susan Gubar. *The Madwoman in the Attic: The Woman Writer and the Nineteenth-Century Literary Imagination*. 2nd ed., New Yale UP, 2000.

Giroux, Henry A., and Grace Pollock. *The Mouse That Roared: Disney and the End of Innocence*. Rowman & Littlefield Publishers, 2010.

Gooding, Richard. "'Something Very Old and Very Slow': *Coraline*, Uncanniness, and Narrative Form." *Children's Literature Association Quarterly*, vol. 33, no. 4, 2008, pp. 390–407.

Green, John. *Paper Towns*. Dutton, 2008.

Grimm, Jacob, and Wilhelm Grimm. "The Frog King." *Household Tales*. Translated by Margaret Hunt, George Bell, 1884.

The Grinch Who Stole Christmas. Directed by Ron Howard, performances by Jim Carrey, Jeffrey Tambor, Christine Baranski, Bill Irwin, and Molly Shannon, Universal Pictures, 2000.

Gubar, Marah. "Risky Business: Talking about Children in Children's Literature Criticism." *Children's Literature Association Quarterly*, vol. 38, no. 4, 2013, pp. 450–57.

Hastings, A. Waller. "Moral Simplification in Disney's *The Little Mermaid*." *The Lion and the Unicorn*, vol. 17, no. 1, 1993, pp. 83–92.

Hearn, Michael Patrick. Introduction. *The Wizard of Oz: The Screenplay* by Noel Langley, Florence Ryerson, and Edgar Allan Woolf, edited by Michael Patrick Hearn, Dell, 1989.

Hollindale, Peter. *Ideology and the Children's Book*. Thimble Press, 1988.

Horton Hears a Who! Directed by Jimmy Hayward and Steve Martino, performances by Jim Carrey, Steve Carell, and Carol Burnett, 20th Century Fox, 2008.

How to Train Your Dragon. Directed by Chris Sanders and Dean DeBlois. Paramount Pictures, 2010.

The Hunger Games. Directed by Gary Ross, performances by Jennifer Lawrence, Josh Hutcherson, and Liam Hemsworth, Lionsgate, 2012.

The Hunger Games: Catching Fire. Directed by Francis Lawrence, performances by Jennifer Lawrence, Josh Hutcherson, and Liam Hemsworth, Lionsgate, 2013.

The Hunger Games: Mockingjay Part 1. Directed by Francis Lawrence, performances by Jennifer Lawrence, Josh Hutcherson, and Liam Hemsworth, Lionsgate, 2014.

The Hunger Games: Mockingjay Part 2. Directed by Francis Lawrence, performances by Jennifer Lawrence, Josh Hutcherson, and Liam Hemsworth, Lionsgate, 2015.

Hutcheon, Linda. "Harry Potter and the Novice's Confession." *The Lion and the Unicorn*, vol. 32, no. 2, 2008, pp. 169–79.

Hutcheon, Linda. *A Theory of Adaptation*. Routledge, 2006.

The Internet Movie Database. IMDb.com, Inc., 1990, http://www.imdb.com.

Jameson,Fredric. *Postmodernism, or, The Cultural Logic of Late Capitalism*. Duke UP, 1992.

Jumanji. Directed by Joe Johnston, performances by Robin Williams, Bonnie Hunt, Kirsten Dunst, Bradley Pierce, Jonathan Hyde, and David Alan Grier, TriStar Pictures, 1995.

The Jungle Book. Directed by Wolfgang Reitherman, Disney, 1967.

The Jungle Book. Directed by Jon Favreau, performances by Idris Elba, Ben Kingsley, Christopher Walken, Scarlett Johansson, Lupita Nyong'o, Neel Sethi, Giancarlo Esposito, Ritesh Rajan, Disney, 2016.

Kipling, Rudyard. *The Jungle Book*. Dover, 2000.

Klein, Jeanne. "From Children's Perspectives: A Model of Aesthetic Processing in Theatre." *Journal of Aesthetic Education*, vol. 39, no. 4, 2005, pp. 40–57.

Kozloff, Sarah. *Invisible Storytellers: Voice-Over Narration in American Fiction Film*. U of California P, 1989.

Kristeva, Julia. *The Kristeva Reader*. Edited by Toril Moi, Columbia UP, 1986.

Kuhn, Annette. *Women's Pictures: Feminism and Cinema*. Verso, 1994.

Kuhn, Markus, and Johann N. Schmidt. "Narration in Film." *Handbook of Narratology*, edited by Peter Hühn, Jan Christoph Meister, John Pier, and Wolf Schmid, Walter de Gruyter GmbH & Co KG, 2014, pp. 384–405.

Kümmerling-Meibauer, Bettina. "New Perspectives in Children's Film Studies." *Journal of Education, Media, Memory, and Society*, vol. 5, 2013, pp. 39–44.

Lacroix, Celeste. "Images of Animated Others: The Orientalization of Disney's Cartoon Heroines from *The Little Mermaid* to *The Hunchback of Notre Dame*." *Popular Communication*, vol. 2, no. 4, 2004, pp. 213–29

Lang, Andrew, editor. "Sleeping Beauty." *The Blue Fairy Book*. Dover, 1965.

Leal, Andrew. "Muppets and Money." *Kermit Culture: Critical Perspectives on Jim Henson's Muppets*, edited by Jennifer C. Garlen and Anissa Graham, McFarland, 2009, pp. 202–16.

Lefebvre, Benjamin, editor. *Textual Transformations in Children's Literature: Adaptations, Translations, Reconsiderations*. Routledge, 2013.

Leitch, Thomas M. *Film Adaptation and Its Discontents: From* Gone with the Wind *to* The Passion of the Christ. Johns Hopkins UP, 2007.

Leitch, Thomas M. "How to Teach Adaptations and Why." *The Pedagogy of Adaptation*, edited by Dennis R. Cutchins, Laurence Raw, and James Michael Welsh, Scarecrow Press, 2010, pp. 1–20.

Leitch, Thomas M. "Twelve Fallacies in Contemporary Adaptation Theory." *Criticism*, vol. 45, no. 2, 2003, pp. 149–71.

Leszkiewicz, Anna. "Paper Towns and the Myth That Just Won't Die: The Manic Pixie Dream Girl." *NewStatemanAmerican*, 26 August 2015.

The Lorax. Directed by Chris Renaud. Universal Pictures, 2012.

Mackey, Margaret. "Spinning Off: Toys, Television, Tie-Ins, and Technology." *Handbook of Research on Children's and Young Adult Literature*, edited by Shelby Wolf, Karen Coats, Patricia Enciso, and Christine Jenkins, Routledge, 2011, pp. 495–506.

Maguire, Gregory. *Wicked: The Life and Times of the Wicked Witch of the West*. HarperCollins, 1995.

Maleficent. Directed by Robert Stromberg, performances by Angelina Jolie, Elle Fanning, and Sam Riley, Walt Disney Pictures, 2014.

Marion, Isaac. *Warm Bodies*. Atria Books, 2011.

Martin, Michelle H. *Brown Gold: Milestones of African American Children's Picture Books, 1845–2002*. Routledge, 2004.

Martínez, David, Clifford E. Trafzer, and Jeff Berglund. "The Disney Version." *Seeing Red—Hollywood's Pixeled Skins: American Indians and Film*, edited by LeAnne Howe, Harvey Markowitz, Denise K. Cummings, Michigan State UP, 2013, pp. 37–54.

McCallum, Robyn, and John Stephens. "Ideology and Children's Books." *Handbook of Research on Children's and Young Adult Literature*, edited by Shelby Wolf, Karen Coats, Patricia Enciso, and Christine Jenkins, Routledge, 2011, pp. 359–71.

McFarlane, Brian. *Novel to Film: An Introduction to the Theory of Adaptation*. Clarendon, 1996.

McIntosh, Shawn. "The Evolution of the Zombie: The Monster That Keeps Coming Back." *Zombie Culture: Autopsies of the Living Dead*, edited by Shawn McIntosh and Marc Leverette, Scarecrow Press, 2008, pp. 1–18.

Metcalf, Greg. "'It's a Jungle Book Out There, Kid!': The Sixties in Walt Disney's *The Jungle Book*." *Studies in Popular Culture*, vol. 14, no. 1, 1991, pp. 85–97.

Mieder, Wolfgang. "You Have to Kiss a Lot of Frogs (Toads) Before You Meet Your Handsome Prince": From Fairy-Tale Motif to Modern Proverb." *Marvels and Tales*, vol. 28, no. 1, 2014, pp. 104–26.

Miller, Susan, and Greg Rode. "The Movie You See, The Movie You Don't: How Disney Do's That Old Time Derison." *From Mouse to Mermaid: The Politics of Film, Gender, and Culture*, edited by Elizabeth Bell, Lynda Haas, and Laura Sells, Indiana UP, 1995, pp. 86–104.

Mulvey, Laura. *Visual and Other Pleasures*. Indiana UP, 1989.

The Muppets' Wizard of Oz. Directed by Kirk R. Thatcher, performances by Ashanti, David Alan Grier, and Queen Latifah, Fox Television Studios, 2005.

Myers, Lindsay. "Whose Fear Is It Anyway? Moral Panics and 'Stranger Danger' in Henry Selick's *Coraline*." *The Lion and the Unicorn*, vol. 36, no. 3, 2012, pp. 245–57.

Neff, Heather. "Strange Faces in the Mirror: The Ethics of Diversity in Children's Films." *The Lion and the Unicorn*, vol. 20, no. 1, 1996, pp. 50–65.

Nel, Philip. *Dr. Seuss: American Icon*. Continuum, 2004.

Newell, Kate. "'We're Off to See the Wizard' (Again): Oz Adaptations and the Matter of Fidelity." *Adaptation Studies: New Approaches*, edited by Christa Albrecht-Crane and Dennis Cutchins, Fairleigh Dickinson UP, 2010, pp. 78–96.

Nikolajeva, Maria. *Power, Voice and Subjectivity in Literature for Young Readers*. Routledge, 2010.

Nodelman, Perry. "Interpretation and the Apparent Samenesss of Children's Novels." *Studies in the Literary Imagination*, vol. 18, no. 2, 1985, pp. 5–20.

Nodelman, Perry. *The Hidden Adult: Defining Children's Literature*. Johns Hopkins UP, 2008.

Nodelman, Perry. "Searching for Treasure Island." *Children's Novels and the Movies*, edited by Douglas Street, F. Ungar, 1983, pp. 58–68.

Nodelman, Perry, and Mavis Reimer. *The Pleasures of Children's Literature*. Langara College, 2018.

Nyman, Jopi. "Re-Reading Rudyard Kipling's 'English' Heroism: Narrating Nation in *The Jungle Book*." *Orbis Litterarum*, vol. 56, 2001, pp. 205–20.

Op de Beeck, Nathalie. "Speaking for the Trees: Environmental Ethics in the Rhetoric and Production of Picture Books." *Children's Literature Association Quarterly,* vol. 30, no. 3, 2005, pp. 265–87.

Oz the Great and Powerful. Directed by Sam Raimi, performances by James Franco, Zach Braff, and Michelle Williams, Walt Disney Studios Home Entertainment, 2013.

Paper Towns. Directed by Jake Schreier, performances by Nat Wolff, Cara Delevingne, and Austin Abrams, Fox 2000, 2015.

Parsons, Elizabeth. "Ideology." *Keywords for Children's Literature,* edited by Philip Nel and Lissa Paul, New York UP, 2011, pp. 113–16.

Parsons, Elizabeth, Naarah Sawers, and Kate McInally. "The Other Mother: Neil Gaiman's Postfeminist Fairytales." *Children's Literature Association Quarterly,* vol. 33, no. 4, 2008, pp. 371–89.

Popp, Emily. "Jennifer Lawrence Talks Being Confident, A Powerful Woman." *E! News,* 16 September 2014.

The Princess and the Frog. Directed by Ron Clements and John Musker, Walt Disney Animation Studios, 2009.

Rabin, Nathan. "I'm Sorry for Coining the Phrase 'Manic Pixie Dream Girl.'" *Salon,* 15 July 2014.

Rabin, Nathan. "The Bataan Death March of Whimsy Case File 1: *Elizabethtown.*" *A.V. Club,* 25 January 2007.

Rollin, Lucy, editor. *The Antic Art: Enhancing Children's Literary Experiences through Film and Video.* Highsmith, 1993.

Rose, Jacqueline. *The Case of Peter Pan, or The Impossibility of Children's Fiction.* U of Pennsylvania P, 1993.

Ross, Deborah. "Escape from Wonderland: Disney and the Female Imagination." *Marvels and Tales,* vol. 18, no. 1, 2004, pp. 53–66.

Rudd, D. "Beatrix Potter and Jacques Derrida—Problematic Bedfellows in the Teaching of Children's Literature?" *English in Education,* vol. 30, 1996, pp. 9–17.

Rushdie, Salman. *The Wizard of Oz.* BFI, 1992.

Sanders, Joseph Sutliff. "Chaperoning Words: Meaning-Making in Comics and Picture Books." *Children's Literature,* vol. 41, 2013, pp. 57–90.

Sanders, Julie. *Adaptation and Appropriation.* Routledge, 2006.

Schuhmann, Elizabeth C. "Shift Out of First: Third-Person Narration Has Advantages." *Two Decades of the ALAN Review,* edited by Patricia P. Kelly and Robert C. Small Jr., National Council of Teachers of English, 1999, pp. 314–19.

Sendak, Maurice. *Where the Wild Things Are.* Harper, 1963.

Seuss, Dr. *Horton Hears A Who!* Random House, 1982.

Seuss, Dr. *How the Grinch Stole Christmas!* Random House, 1957.

Seuss, Dr. *The Lorax.* Random House, 1971.

Seymour, Lee. "*The Wiz Live!* Beats *Peter Pan* but Garners Racist Social Media Backlash." *Forbes,* 4 December 2015.

Shepard, Iris, and Ian Wojcik-Andrews. "Are the -Isms Ever in Your Favor? Children's Film Theory and *The Hunger Games.*" *The Politics of Panem: Critical Perspectives on the Hunger Games,* edited by Sean Connor, Sense, 2014, pp. 189–202.

Showalter, Elaine. *Teaching Literature.* Blackwell, 2003.

Sleeping Beauty. Directed by Clyde Geronimi, Walt Disney Productions, 1959.

Smith, Katharine Capshaw. "Middle Age." *Children's Literature Association Quarterly,* vol. 38, no. 2, 2013, pp. 133–36.

The Spectacular Now. Directed by James Ponsoldt, performances by Miles Teller, Shailene Woodley, and Kyle Chandler, Andrew Lauren Productions, 2013.

Stahl, J. D. "Media Adaptation of Children's Literature: The Brave New Genre." *Children's Literature Association Quarterly*, vol. 7, no. 3, 1982, pp. 5–9.

Stam, Robert. "Beyond Fidelity: The Dialogics of Adaptation." *Film Adaptations*, edited by James Naremore, Rutgers UP, 2000, pp. 54–76.

Stam, Robert. Introduction. *Literature and Film: A Guide to the Theory and Practice of Film Adaptation*, edited by Robert Stam and Alessandra Raengo, Blackwell, 2005, pp. 1–52.

Stam, Robert, and Alessandra Raengo, editors. *Literature and Film: A Guide to the Theory and Practice of Film Adaptation.* Blackwell, 2005.

Stephens, John. *Language and Ideology in Children's Fiction*, Longma, 2008.

Street, Douglas, editor. *Children's Novels and the Movies.* F. Ungar, 1983.

Swartz, Mark Evan. *Oz before the Rainbow: L. Frank Baum's* The Wonderful Wizard of Oz *on Stage and Screen to 1939.* Johns Hopkins UP, 2000.

The Tale of Despereaux. Directed by Sam Fell and Robert Stevenhagen, Universal Pictures, 2008.

Tharp, Tim. *The Spectacular Now.* Ember, 2013.

Thomas, Ebony Elizabeth. *Race and the Imagination from Harry Potter to the Hunger Games.* NYU Press, 2019.

Trites, Roberta Seelinger. *Disturbing the Universe: Power and Repression in Adolescent Literature.* U of Iowa P, 2000.

Trites, Roberta Seelinger. *Literary Conceptualizations of Growth: Metaphor and Cognition in Adolescent Literature.* Benjamins, 2014.

Turner, Sarah E. "Blackness, Bayous, and Gumbo: Encoding and Decoding Race in a Color-blind World." *Diversity in Disney Films: Critical Essays on Race, Ethnicity, Gender, Sexuality and Disability*, edited by Johnson Cheu, McFarland, 2015, pp. 83–97.

Van Allsburg, Chris. *Jumanji.* Scholastic, 1981.

Wagner, Geoffrey Atheling. *The Novel and the Cinema.* Fairleigh Dickinson UP, 1975.

Walsh, Sue. *Kipling's Children's Literature: Language, Identity, and Constructions of Childhood.* Ashgate, 2010.

Ward, Annalee R. *Mouse Morality: The Rhetoric of Disney Animated Film.* U of Texas P, 2002.

Warm Bodies. Directed by Jonathan Levine, performances by Nicholas Hoult, Teresa Palmer, and Dave Franco, Mandeville Films, 2013.

Whelehan, Imelda. "Adaptations: The Contemporary Dilemmas." *Adaptations: From Text to Screen, Screen to Text*, edited by Deborah Cartmell and Imelda Whelehan. Routledge, 1999, pp. 3–19.

Where the Wild Things Are. Directed by Spike Jonze, Warner Brothers, 2009.

Wicked: The Untold Story of the Witches of Oz. Music and lyrics by Stephen Schwartz, book by Winnie Holzman, 2003.

Willetts, Kheli R. "Cannibals and Coons: Blackness in the Early Days of Walt Disney." *Diversity in Disney Films: Critical Essays on Race, Ethnicity, Gender, Sexuality and Disability*, edited by Johnson Cheu, McFarland, 2012, pp. 9–22.

Williams, Rhonda. "*The Wiz*: American Culture at Its Best." *The Universe of Oz: Essays on Baum's Series and Its Progeny*, edited by Kevin K. Durand, and Mary K. Leigh, McFarland, 2010.

The Wiz (30th Anniversary Edition). Directed by Sydney Lumet, performances by Diana Ross, Michael Jackson, Richard Pryor, and Lena Horne, Universal Pictures and Motown Productions, 2008.

The Wiz Live! Directed by Kenny Leon and Matthew Diamond, performances by Shanice Williams, and Queen Latifah, Universal Studios Home Entertainment, 2015.

The Wizard of Oz (75th Anniversary Edition). Directed by Victor Fleming, performance by Judy Garland, Metro-Goldwyn-Mayer, 2013.

Wojcik-Andrews, Ian. *Children's Films: History, Ideology, Pedagogy, Theory.* Garland, 2000.

Wood, Naomi. "Domesticating Dreams in Walt Disney's Cinderella." *The Lion and the Unicorn,* vol. 20, no.1, 1996, pp. 25–49.

Yancey, Rick. *The 5th Wave.* Putnam, 2013.

Zipes, Jack David. "What Makes a Repulsive Frog So Appealing: Memetics and Fairy Tales." *Journal of Folklore Research,* vol. 45, no. 2, 2008, pp. 109–43.

INDEX

ABOUT THE AUTHOR

Meghann Meeusen teaches children's and adolescent literature at Western Michigan University, where she works to develop innovative pedagogy approaches centering around the contextual nature of literature and ways individuals can become stronger critical thinkers through reading and research. In addition to teaching, Meghann acts as a liaison to the College of Education and Human Development at WMU, working to create opportunities that help students successfully navigate the evolving challenges they will face when working with young people, and beginning in fall 2020, she will also serve as the English Department's Director of Graduate Studies, similarly supporting advanced literature, education, and creative writing students in their academic and creative pursuits. Meghann earned her PhD from Illinois State University, and her evolving research interests include children's visual culture, diversity and inclusion in films for young viewers, representation in YA fantasy, and film pedagogy.

Lightning Source UK Ltd.
Milton Keynes UK
UKHW040624060721
386705UK00001B/62